Doing Good   *Levy*

Wishing you a healthy happy and successful new year!

SUPPORT OUR CAUSE HELPING CHILDREN, WOMEN, & ORPHANS IN NEED WORLDWIDE :

Send your tax deductible contribution to 81-3549201 via PayPal by scanning the QR code or by going to dg2a.org/help

ArtScroll Judaica Classics®

Rabbi Nosson Scherman / Rabbi Meir Zlotowitz
General Editors

ORCHOS CHAIM

compiled by
R' Alexander Sternbuch

translated by
Yaakov Petroff

edited by
Shlomo Fox Ashrei

אָרְחוֹת חַיִּים לְהָרֹא"שׁ

OF THE ROSH

Rabbeinu Asher's Classic "Paths of Life"
with an Anthology of
Contemporary Expositions

Published by

Mesorah Publications, ltd

FIRST EDITION
First Impression . . . August 1992
Second Impression . . . August 2009

Published and Distributed by
MESORAH PUBLICATIONS, Ltd.
4401 Second Avenue
Brooklyn, New York 11232

Distributed in Europe by
LEHMANNS
Unit E, Viking Business Park
Rolling Mill Road
Jarrow, Tyne & Wear NE32 3DP
England

Distributed in Australia & New Zealand by
GOLDS WORLD OF JUDAICA
3-13 William Street
Balaclava, Melbourne 3183
Victoria Australia

Distributed in Israel by
SIFRIATI / A. GITLER — BOOKS
6 Hayarkon Street
Bnei Brak 51127

Distributed in South Africa by
KOLLEL BOOKSHOP
Ivy Common 105 William Road
Norwood 2192, Johannesburg, South Africa

ARTSCROLL JUDAICA CLASSICS ®
ORCHOS CHAIM — PATHS OF LIFE
© Copyright 1992, by MESORAH PUBLICATIONS, Ltd.
4401 Second Avenue / Brooklyn, N.Y. 11232 / (718) 921-9000

ISBN 10: 0-89906-548-1
ISBN 13: 978-0-89906-548-1

Typography by CompuScribe at ArtScroll Studios, Ltd.
4401 Second Avenue / Brooklyn, N.Y. 11232 / (718) 921-9000

Printed in the United States of America by Noble Book Press Corp.
Bound by Sefercraft Inc., Quality Bookbinders, Brooklyn, N.Y.

בס"ד

י' סיון תשנ"ב

בא לפני הרב ר' אלכסנדר ז. שטרנבוך שליט"א וספרו בידו תירגום ,,אורחות
חיים להרא"ש המבואר" לאנגלית, שהוא בנוסף לתירגום האורחות חיים לרבנו
הרא"ש, גם תירגם קובץ דברים יקרים ופנינים שהם פירושים על הספר או"ח
מדברי רבותינו נ"ע ובמיוחד מגדולי המוסר. וכבר איתמחי גברא בהו"ל חיבורו
,,אורחות חיים להרא"ש המבואר" בלשה"ק שכבר איתפשט בבי מדרשא בכל
אתר.

רואה אני בתרגום זו משום קידוש שם שמים, להציע בשפה השגורה
האורחות חיים עם ביאורים כי כמה מהצמאים לדבר ה' בדורנו לדאבוננו
רחוקים הם מהשפה לשון הקודש ואשר על כן גם מאור המוסר ומזה הטעם
רואה אני ברכה בתרגום ובטחוני שיהיה בס"ד לתועלת גדול.

יהא ה' עמו ועם כל המסייעים על ידו, להגביר חילו ויזכה להו"ל עוד חיבורים
יקרים ומועילים,

וע"ז באעה"ח

בעזהי״ת

מוש״ק בהעלותך את הנרות, גייטסהד

באשר הספר ,,אורחות חיים להרא״ש ז״ל״ נתחבב מאד על בני התורה
ושוחרי היראה, ושמש כמורה דרך ומקור התעוררות במשך כל הדורות
להמשכילים המבקשים לדרוך על אורח חיים ההולכת למעלה ומסירו מן שאול
מטה, וכבר לגודל התועלת היוצאת מלמוד דבריו הק׳ תקן התוס׳ יו״ט ז״ל
שיקראו בו בצבור בכל יום קודם ברוך שאמר כשהצבור מעוטפים בטלית
ותפילין, וגם הטריח עצמו לתרגמו ללשון אשכנז למען יבינו בו גם פשוטי העם,
ובדורות האחרונות התקינו בה,,תלמוד תורה״ הנשגב בקלם ללמוד בו ולהתבונן
היטב בדבריו לכל יום, וכן החזיקו בזה בהרבה ישיבות בחודש אלול, וגילו
אורות נפלאות גנוזות בדקדוק דברי הרא״ש ז״ל וכבר נתעוררו כמה מנכדי
התוס׳ יו״ט ז״ל, הראויים אליו, להמשיך בדרכו למען זכות הרבים בדברי
הרא״ש ז״ל וצרפו יחד הרבה מהדברים שנלמדים מדברי הרא״ש ז״ל וסדרם
בטוב טעם ודעת על גליון הספר, ורבים נאותו לאורם.

וכעת אשר רחש לבו דבר טוב אחד מהמיוחדים מאותם נכדי התוס׳ יו״ט ז״ל
הרב הגדול בתורתו מוהר״ר אלכסנדר שטרנבוך שליט״א מבני ברק לפתוח
שערי אורה, האורות הגדולות של האורחות חיים עם הביאורים היקרים
שנלמדו מדבריו, לפני הצבור הרחב שואפי תורה ויראה ששליטתם בלשון
הקודש הוא מוגבלת, ולהתעסק בתרגום הספר לאנגלית למען הרבות דעת
ויראת השם. וראיתי פרי מלאכתו והוטבו בעיני מאד, הנני לעודדו ולחזקו
להוציא מחשבתו לפועל וזכות הרבים תלוי״ בו.

אברהם במוהר״ר ארי׳ זאב זצוקללה״ה גורביץ

✑§ Introduction

Orchos Chaim was compiled by Rabbeinu Asher ben Yechiel, better known as the *Rosh*. The *Rosh* was born in Germany, in approximately 5010 / 1250. Subsequently, he migrated to Spain, where he lived, taught, and wrote until his death in 5088 / 1327.

His best known work is *Piskei HaRosh*, which has gained such universal acceptance that it is published in virtually all editions of the Talmud. In *Piskei HaRosh*, he condensed the Talmud as it relates to the Halachah, quoting its essential passages, the rulings of the *Rif*, the halachic discussions of the *Tosafists* and others, among them his father-in-law, Rabbi Meir of Rothenberg, and Rabbeinu Yeshayah.

The *Rosh's* son, Rabbeinu Yaakov (known as the *Tur*), composed the halachic compendium, *Arba'ah Turim*, which relies in very great measure on *Piskei HaRosh*. In turn, Rabbi Yosef Karo wrote an extensive commentary on the *Arba'ah Turim*, and this commentary, *Bais Yosef*, and the *Arba'ah Turim* itself became the bases of his *Shulchan Aruch*. Hence, much of the Jewish people's basic code of law can be traced to the *Rosh*. His other well known works were *Tosafos HaRosh*, his collection of the novellae of the Tosafists, and *Pi Sh'nayim*, an abridgment of the commentary of the *Rash* to the Order of *Zeraim*.

Rabbi Yom Tov Lipmann Heller, a disciple of the *Maharal* of Prague, lived in Vienna and Prague some two hundred years after the *Rosh*. He is best known for his monumental commentary *Tosafos Yom Tov* on the Mishnah, in which he bases himself on the shorter, commentary of the *Rav*, Rabbi Ovadiah of Bartenura. The commentary of the *Rav* may be likened to that of *Rashi* and that of the *Tosafos Yom Tov* to that of *Tosafos*. He was also the author of the *Ma'adanei Yom Tov* and *Divrei Chamudos* commentaries on the *Piskei HaRosh*.

After he and his family were miraculously saved from death in a virulent epidemic, he decided to follow in the footsteps of the Patriarch Jacob and the author of the *Zohar*, Rabbi Shimon bar Yochai. They had responded to miraculous interventions by making vows to show their gratitude to God. The *Tosafos Yom Tov* wished to devise a means that would help people avoid inclusion in the four categories that forfeit the privilege of receiving the Divine Presence: insincere flatterers, liars, scoffers, and those who speak *lashon hara* — categories of behavior that are all too enticing for anyone who does not exert himself to avoid them. He also sought to devise a method that would be all-encompassing in raising the level of ethical and religious conduct.

He found his goal in *Orchos Chaim*, which the *Rosh* had composed as a means of elevating people. The *Tosafos Yom Tov* divided *Orchos Chaim* into seven chapters, one for each day of the week, and ordained that a chapter be recited every day before *Baruch She'amar*, while men are wearing their *tallis* and tefillin. He also translated it into the Judaic-German of the time, so that it could be understood and recited by women and children, as well. His translation often elaborates upon and explains the meaning of the *Rosh*, and therefore we have added those enhancements to our English translation.

Although *Orchos Chaim* is uniquely concise, it includes Halachah, Mussar, and even proper modes of everyday behavior. Typical of the genius of the *Rishonim*, it is so rich in its brevity that it can be understood superficially by the unlearned while serving as a treasure trove of ideas for the most accomplished scholars. As noted in the Prologue, it was a basic text in great academies and of historic *gedolim*. So widely studied was it that in the famous academy of Kelm, if a student had to be rebuked for unseemly haste and lack of attention in the performance of a *mitzvah*, it was sufficient to tell him merely, "*Kuf, kuf*," a reference to paragraph 100 [*kuf*] of *Orchos Chaim*, which cautions that one should not act hastily. No elaboration was necessary.

It is noteworthy that the Mussar masters did not write comments on the section of *Orchos Chaim* that is recited on the Sabbath. This is because the Sabbath section begins with the number 1, rather than continuing the numbers of the previous days, leading people to suspect that the *Rosh* was not the author of that section — and that, some conjectured, it might have been written by the *Tosafos Yom Tov*. Accordingly, the Kelm edition of the work (which is also the edition found in *Siddur Ishei Yisrael*) omits the Sabbath section.

However, we have examined a number of manuscripts pre-dating the *Tosafos Yom Tov*, all of which include the Sabbath section. In addition, the *Shach* (*Yoreh De'ah* 249:4) quotes from it and refers to it as *Orchos Chaim* of the *Rosh*. This leads us to conclude that the *Rosh* was the author of the entire work, although it is possible, as *Shevet Mussar* concludes, that the Sabbath section was from a different edition of the work.

In our translation, we have included a small selection of commentaries to *Orchos Chaim*. It should be noted that these comments were not said as abstract, intellectual notes, but were meant to convey to an audience the need to correct a specific behavioral shortcoming, or effect improvement in the observance of a *mitzvah*.

It is our humble hope that this translation will provide the English-speaking public with the opportunity to join those who were privileged to be guided by such luminaries as Rabbi Yerucham Levovitz of Mir, Rabbi Yechezkel Levenstein of Mir and Ponevezh, and Rabbi Yosef Shlomo Kahaneman, *Rav* of Ponevezh.

We must emphasize that this work is not meant to be easy, casual reading, but a manual on the service of God and the performance of *mitzvos*, and we hope and pray that it will assist many in achieving that vital goal.

◈§ Acknowledgments

I take this opportunity to express my deepest appreciation to my dear parents — whose legendary pure love of Torah was a wellspring of inspiration from infancy — who spared no effort to be *mechanech* their children בְּדֶרֶךְ הַתּוֹרָה וְהַיִּרְאָה. May they be privileged to see true Torah *nachas* from their offspring for many, many years עמו"ש.

It is with a very heavy heart that I pay tribute to my dear father-in-law מוהר"ר בנימין בה"ר מאיר וואלף זצ"ל. He was an extraordinary pillar of *chesed*, and his love of Torah knew no bounds. A man who loved Torah, honored those who studied it and gave generously to those who taught it; he labored all his life to attain his sole goal in life — that he should live to see all his children become *gedolei Torah*. May his exemplary life of devotion to Torah continue to be a source of inspiration to his children, grandchildren and great-grandchildren. I take this opportunity to express my deep feelings of gratitude to his lifelong partner in his pursuit of Torah and *mitzvos*, תבלחטו"א מרת אסתר וואלף תחי׳. May she be *zocheh* to see many years of true *Yiddishe nachas* in the best of health from all of her offspring.

Many of the commentaries were originally collected and edited in Hebrew by a noteworthy *talmid chacham* who insists on remaining anonymous. His wish to remain anonymous does not excuse me from expressing my feelings of gratitude. I have been privileged to have been guided by Rabbi Avrohom Gurowicz *shlita*, *Rosh Yeshivah* of Gateshead, from whom I drew guidance and inspiration, among all else, in the learning of *Orchos Chaim*.

I also owe gratitude to the entire Mesorah staff for publishing this translation and in particular Shmuel Blitz, who guided and in fact undertook the entire publication of this work on his shoulders.

Also I offer my thanks to Rabbi Yaakov Petroff who translated this work, R' Shlomo Fox who edited, and R' Shalom Kaplan and R' Asher Margoliot who also helped in the editing.

Last, but definitely not least, may I express my deepest appreciation to my *eishes chayil*, whose enthusiasm for this project, among all else, is a continuous source of inspiration. May she be granted her constant fervent wish: that our children grow up to be true *gedolei Yisrael*, and a source of *nachas* to Hashem Yisbarach.

Alexander Sternbuch

אייר תשנ"ב

אָרְחוֹת חַיִּים לְהָרֹא''שׁ

ORCHOS CHAIM
OF THE ROSH

৵§ Prologue

Few *sefarim* have enjoyed the popularity equal to that of the *Orchos Chaim*. Close to four hundred years ago, the *Tosafos Yom-Tov* noted that many *siddurim* and *machzorim* contained this work. The *Tosafos Yom-Tov* added much to the popularity of the *Orchos Chaim*, foremost, by translating it into the-then spoken Yiddish. His avowed purpose was to make the work understood by women and children. Moreover, the *Tosafos Yom-Tov* divided the *sefer* into seven portions, corresponding to the seven days of the week, and decreed that a portion should be read every day of the week before reciting the prayer *Baruch She'amar*, while wearing one's *tallis* and *tefillin*.

In the Yeshivah of Kelm, the *Orchos Chaim* became one of its fundamental teachings, with much time and thought given to the in-depth learning of this *sefer*. Every day, after the morning prayers, the *chazzan* would slowly chant the daily portion followed thoughtfully by all the students of the *yeshivah*. This custom still exists today in several *yeshivos*, in particular during the month of *Elul*. Many graduates of Lakewood, Telz, and Gateshead recall many years later the *Orchos Chaim* they heard during the *Elul z'man*.

It is therefore not surprising that numerous editions of the *Orchos Chaim* have been printed and the text has inspired many commentaries. The *sefer's* unique character is a blend of *halachah* and *mussar* which advises a person how to behave on a day-to-day level.

It should be borne in mind that the *Orchos Chaim* was used by leading Torah personalities, and in particular by the followers of the *Beis HaMussar* in Kelm, as the cornerstone of their work and as a means to fulfill their aspirations of attaining perfection in their service to Hashem.

R' Yechezkel Levenstein zt"l expounded on the *Orchos Chaim* to an inner circle of students during the golden years of the Mirrer Yeshivah in Shanghai. R' Yechezkel would explain a *takanah* as he folded his *tallis* and put away his *tefillin* after the morning service, and these words became the guiding force for his *talmidim* on that particular day.

The Rav of Ponevezh zt"l devoted much of his time in the post-war years to the *Orchos Chaim*. The selection of his quotations included here is but a minute part of the hundreds of lectures he gave on the *Orchos*

Chaim each day, after *Shacharis*. On many occasions he spent a whole lesson expounding on a single *takanah*.

The purpose of this edition is not merely to provide a collection of commentaries on the *Orchos Chaim*, but also to provide insight, in the English language, into the spiritual heights attained by these Torah giants, and to portray how *gedolim* achieved such perfection in *middos*. Hopefully this will guide us, in some small way, to follow in their footsteps and emulate their way in achieving such lofty spiritual heights.

⊷§ Selected Commentaries by the Gedolim on the Orchos Chaim

⊷§ I have learned from my elders and, hence, wish to convey precepts for the enjoyment of all, which deal with man's behavior when he sits in his home, when he walks on his way, when he retires and when he rises. This has already been written and introduced by our master and teacher who enlightened the whole of the Exile through his works, Rabbeinu Asher, the father of Rabbeinu Yaakov, who compiled the *Turim*. It is called *Orchos Chaim* and consists wholly of ethical prescriptions and has been printed in some editions of the *siddur*. In order to lighten the load, I have divided it into seven parts, one for each of the seven days of the week. I have introduced the custom that each day a part be recited before *Baruch She'amar*, after those assembled for prayer are wrapped in their *talleisim* and have put on their *tefillin*.

His words are so dear to me that I hardly found it a task to translate them into Yiddish in order to allow the women who are without knowledge of the Holy Tongue [access to the work]. For it is expressed in abbreviated form, and at times uses difficult words and a shorthand notation of the statements of the Sages. Certainly the righteous women, who wish and desire to hear works of ethics, will find a Yiddish edition very useful. And it will also serve the youth and those who are unlearned. I have done this so that both great and small may receive moral instruction. They will listen to it, that is, to this work. [The practice of reading it before the prayers] will go into effect tomorrow, the coming first day of the week, "and it shall not be removed from their mouths."   (*Tosafos Yom-Tov* — from the introduction to his translation of the *Orchos Chaim*)

✑ This is an old and ancient work, and like well-aged wine... It was first printed long ago and is still a joy to behold, and will give law and judgment to Israel ... It serves as a general reminder of morality; it stands as a fence which turns them from the crooked path.

(*Sha'agas Aryeh* — in his writ of approval to the
Tosafos Yom-Tov's translation of the *Orchos Chaim*, 5527)

✑ If one missed learning [the *Orchos Chaim*] at the fixed time, he should make it up during that day, and inform the *mechazeik*, the person in charge of strengthening the studies.

(Institutions and Resolutions of the *Beis HaTalmud* of Kelm)

✑ It is a fine idea to institute the study of the *Orchos Chaim* of the *Rosh* in these days. It is found in prayerbooks. We could divide it into days, just as the *Tosafos Yom-Tov* did. He had them read it in Vienna at the time of prayer. It contains matters of great note and feeling about the fear of Heaven and ethical behavior. It would be excellent to have it studied on a daily basis or on certain days of the week. It should be an immutable practice which should not be transgressed, and if someone should fail to study [it], he should be fined.   (R' Simchah Zissel of
Kelm, *Pinkas HaKabalos*)

✑ The *Orchos Chaim* of the *Rosh* contains rules of behavior which encompass all of life's issues and man's deeds. They direct man to ascend the route of the upward path of intelligence. The *Tosafos Yom-Tov* divided it into seven parts to fit the days of the week, and while in Vienna introduced the practice of studying the work before recital of prayers throughout the year. In the *yeshivos* they studied it in the days of *Elul*, which should bring man to repent and place him on the paths of the intellect. In the Yeshivah of Kelm it was studied throughout the year.

It is a work of *halachah*, and each word should be carefully examined, for it is a work of one of the giants amongst the early commentators.

He begins the work by indicating what should be avoided at all costs. These are the stumbling blocks which lie constantly at our feet throughout life. They are the "snares of death." Man's task is to see that his actions be in the "light of life." He must, therefore, remove himself as far as he can from these primal vices which are arrogance, anger and the sins involving speech. The *Rosh* repeats his admonitions against these vices in the course of the work, for they are very basic to man.

(R' Yosef Shlomo Kahaneman, Rav of Ponevezh)

These are the matters that a man should beware of, so that he may veer away from the snares of death and be illuminated with the light of life.

≼ Sunday ≽

1. To remove oneself as far as possible from pride.

2. And so, too, from flattery.

3. And so, too, from falsehood and deceit.

4. And so, too, from scoffing.

5. And so, too, from talebearing.

6. And so, too, from anger.

7-8. One should take care to avoid the trap of vows the deception of others, whether with money or words. And one should take care to avoid their envy and their hatred.

9. Do not dub someone with a nickname, nor call someone by the nickname that others have given, unless he is known and honored by that name.

10. One should not engage in harmful gossip nor accept it from others.

11. One should not keep company with idlers, nor sit in the gatherings of the ignorant.

12. One should not gaze at a woman who is forbidden to him.

וְאֵלֶּה הַדְּבָרִים שֶׁיִּזָּהֵר בָּהֶם
לָסוּר מִמּוֹקְשֵׁי מָוֶת
וְלֵאוֹר בְּאוֹר הַחַיִּים

❧ ליום ראשון ❧

א. לְהִתְרַחֵק מִן הַגַּאֲוָה בְּתַכְלִית הָרִיחוּק.

ב. וְכֵן מִן הַחֲנִיפוּת.

ג. וְכֵן מִן הַשֶּׁקֶר וְהַכָּזָב.

ד. וְכֵן מִן הַלֵּיצָנוּת.

ה. וְכֵן מִן הָרְכִילוּת.

ו. וְכֵן מִן הַכַּעַס.

ז־ח. שֶׁיִּזָּהֵר מִמִּכְשׁוֹל הַנְּדָרִים, וּמֵאוֹנָאוֹת הַבְּרִיּוֹת, הֵן בְּמָמוֹן הֵן בִּדְבָרִים. וּמִקִּנְאָתָם וּמִשִּׂנְאָתָם.

ט. שֶׁלֹּא יְכַנֶּה שֵׁם לַחֲבֵרוֹ, שֶׁלֹּא יִקְרָאֵנוּ בְּכִנּוּי שֶׁכִּנּוּהוּ אֲחֵרִים, אִם לֹא יִהְיֶה נִזְכָּר וְנִכְבָּד בִּשְׁמוֹ.

י. שֶׁלֹּא יְסַפֵּר לְשׁוֹן הָרַע וְשֶׁלֹּא יְקַבְּלוֹ.

יא. שֶׁלֹּא יֵשֵׁב עִם יוֹשְׁבֵי קְרָנוֹת, וְלֹא בִּישִׁיבַת בָּתֵּי כְּנֵסִיּוֹת שֶׁל עַמֵּי הָאָרֶץ.

יב. שֶׁלֹּא יִסְתַּכֵּל בְּאִשָּׁה שֶׁהִיא אֲסוּרָה לוֹ.

13. One should not speak over the "cup of blessing."

14. One should not speak from when he begins *Baruch She'amar* until after he has finished the silent *Shemoneh Esrei*, nor while the *shaliach tzibbur* (prayer-leader) is repeating the *Shemoneh Esrei* aloud, unless he must [do one of the following:] speak words of Torah; perform a *mitzvah;* or greet someone or return someone's greeting.

15. One should not speak during the recitation of *Hallel*, nor while the reader is reciting the public Torah-reading.

16. One should not eat bread that was baked by non-Jewish homemakers or commercial bakeries, unless bread baked by Jews is not available to him.

17. One should not partake of an optional meal.

18. One should not engage in idle conversation. Take care to study Torah at night until one falls asleep during words of Torah, not idle conversation.

19. One should not put himself in the position of doubt as to whether Friday night has arrived. And he should caution his family concerning Shabbos observance. He should recite the Friday *Minchah* prayer early, in order to accept the Shabbos [upon himself] while it is still day.

20. When the appointed time for any of the three daily prayers arrives, one should put aside all his concerns and pray. Above all else, one should prevent his eyes from looking at whatever is not his.

21. One should not speak between the washing of hands [for a meal] and the blessing of *hamotzi* [over bread]. And one should be the first to greet whomever he meets.

יג. שֶׁלֹּא יָסִיחַ עַל כּוֹס שֶׁל בְּרָכָה.

יד. שֶׁלֹּא יְסַפֵּר מִשֶּׁיַּתְחִיל בָּרוּךְ שֶׁאָמַר עַד שֶׁיְּסַיֵּים תְּפִלּוֹת לַחַשׁ, וְלֹא בְּעוֹד שֶׁשְּׁלִיחַ צִבּוּר חוֹזֵר וּמִתְפַּלֵּל הַתְּפִלָּה, אֶלָּא אִם כֵּן בְּדִבְרֵי תּוֹרָה, אוֹ בִּדְבַר מִצְוָה אוֹ לָתֵת שָׁלוֹם וּלְהַחֲזִיר שָׁלוֹם.

טו. שֶׁלֹּא יְדַבֵּר בִּקְרִיאַת הַהַלֵּל, וְלֹא בְּעוֹד שֶׁשְּׁלִיחַ צִבּוּר קוֹרֵא בַּתּוֹרָה.

טז. שֶׁלֹּא יֹאכַל פַּת בַּעֲלֵי בָתִּים שֶׁל כּוּתִים וְלֹא שֶׁל פַּלְטָר, אֶלָּא אִם כֵּן לֹא יִזְדַּמֵּן לוֹ שֶׁל יִשְׂרָאֵל.

יז. שֶׁלֹּא יִסְעוֹד בִּסְעוּדַת הָרְשׁוּת.

יח. שֶׁלֹּא יָשִׂיחַ שִׂיחָה בְּטֵלָה. וְיִזָּהֵר לִלְמוֹד בַּלַּיְלָה עַד שֶׁיִּישַׁן מִתּוֹךְ דִּבְרֵי תוֹרָה, וְלֹא מִתּוֹךְ שִׂיחָה בְּטֵלָה.

יט. שֶׁלֹּא יַכְנִיס עַצְמוֹ בִּסְפֵק חֲשֵׁכָה. וְיִזָּהֵר בְּנֵי בֵיתוֹ עַל שְׁמִירַת שַׁבָּת, וְיַקְדִּים לְהִתְפַּלֵּל עֶרֶב שַׁבָּת תְּפִלַּת מִנְחָה כְּדֵי שֶׁיְּקַבֵּל עָלָיו הַשַּׁבָּת מִבְּעוֹד יוֹם.

כ. כְּשֶׁיַּגִּיעַ עֵת תְּפִילָה מִשָּׁלֹשׁ תְּפִלוֹת שֶׁבַּיּוֹם, יַנִּיחַ כָּל עֲסָקָיו וְיִתְפַּלֵּל. וְרֹאשׁ כָּל הַדְּבָרִים שֶׁיִּשְׁמוֹר אֶת עֵינָיו מִכָּל דָּבָר שֶׁאֵינוֹ שֶׁלּוֹ.

כא. אַל יְדַבֵּר בֵּין נְטִילַת יָדַיִם לְבִרְכַּת הַמּוֹצִיא. וְיַקְדִּים שָׁלוֹם לְכָל אָדָם.

22. One should bless his Creator, Who has satisfied his craving soul. And should others curse or vilify him, he should not answer them at all, but should be among those who are insulted [but do not insult others].

23. And one should not be quick to get involved in a quarrel. And he should distance himself from oaths and vows — for children pass away because of the sin of [their parents'] unfulfilled vows.

24. And one should distance himself from frivolity and from anger, for it confuses a person's spirit and mind. One should constantly serve his Maker with love. And one should not fail to carry out a single detail of this regime of conduct.

25. Love Hashem with all your heart and all your soul and all your possessions. And whenever you say [in the *Shema,*] "Love Hashem your God with all your heart...," be determined to sacrifice your body and your possessions for His sanctification. In this way you yourself will fulfill the words of the Psalmist: "For Your sake we are slaughtered all day long" (*Tehillim* 44:23).

26. Trust in Hashem with all your heart, and believe in His Providence upon every detail [of the world.] In this way you will fulfill in your heart the perfect Unity of Hashem, by believing that His eyes roam over the entire world, and His eyes are upon all the ways of men, testing the heart and analyzing feelings [i.e. for "Unity of Hashem" implies not merely that God exists and is the Creator, but His total awareness and guidance of all events, without exception]. For whoever does not believe the verse, "...Who took you out of the land of Egypt" [*Shemos* 20:2 which teaches Hashem's control of

כב. לְבָרֵךְ אֶת בּוֹרְאוֹ שֶׁהִשְׂבִּיעַ נֶפֶשׁ שׁוֹקֵקָה. וְאִם
יְקַלְלוּהוּ בְּנֵי אָדָם אוֹ יְחָרְפוּהוּ, אַל יָשִׁיב לָהֶם
דָּבָר אֶלָּא יְהֵא מִן הַנֶּעֱלָבִים.

כג. וְאַל יֵצֵא לָרִיב מַהֵר, וְיִתְרַחֵק מִן הַשְּׁבוּעוֹת.
וּמִן הַנְּדָרִים, כִּי בַּעֲוֹן הַנְּדָרִים בָּנִים מֵתִים.

כד. וְיִתְרַחֵק מִן הַשְּׂחוֹק, וּמִן הַכַּעַס, כִּי מְבַלְבֵּל
רוּחוֹ וְדַעְתּוֹ שֶׁל אָדָם. וְשֶׁיַּעֲבוֹד תָּמִיד לְיוֹצְרוֹ
בְּאַהֲבָה. וְשֶׁלֹּא יַנִּיחַ דָּבָר לַעֲשׂוֹת מֵעִנְיַן זֹאת
הַתַּקָּנָה.

כה. לֶאֱהוֹב אֶת ה׳ בְּכָל לְבָבְךָ וּבְכָל נַפְשְׁךָ וּבְכָל
מְאֹדֶךָ. וְהַסְכֵּם בְּאָמְרְךָ אֶת ה׳ אֱלֹקֶיךָ בְּכָל
לְבָבְךָ וְגוֹ׳ לִמְסוֹר גּוּפְךָ וּמָמוֹנְךָ עַל קְדוּשָׁתוֹ.
וּבָזֶה תְּקַיֵּם בְּעַצְמְךָ דִּבְרֵי הַמְשׁוֹרֵר כִּי עָלֶיךָ
הוֹרַגְנוּ כָּל הַיּוֹם.

כו. לִבְטוֹחַ בַּה׳ בְּכָל לְבָבְךָ וּלְהַאֲמִין בְּהַשְׁגָּחָתוֹ
הַפְּרָטִית.
וּבָזֶה תְּקַיֵּם בִּלְבָבְךָ הַיִּחוּד הַשָּׁלֵם בְּהַאֲמִין
בּוֹ כִּי עֵינָיו מְשׁוֹטְטוֹת בְּכָל הָאָרֶץ וְעֵינָיו עַל
כָּל דַּרְכֵי אִישׁ וּבוֹחֵן לֵב וְחוֹקֵר כְּלָיוֹת, כִּי מִי
שֶׁאֵינוֹ מַאֲמִין "אֲשֶׁר הוֹצֵאתִיךָ מֵאֶרֶץ מִצְרַיִם"
אַף "בְּאָנֹכִי ה׳ אֱלֹקֶיךָ" אֵינוֹ מַאֲמִין. וְאֵין זֶה

nature], also does not believe [the beginning of that verse]: "I am Hashem your God" and [such a flawed belief] is not the perfect Unity. This [complete faith] was Israel's unique treasure above all the nations, and this [true] belief is the foundation of the entire Torah.

❧ Monday ❧

27. Stay far from pride and anger. Oppose the evil inclination (*yetzer hara*) that entices you to follow the ways of your heart. Do not deviate, for His ways are pure and upright. [variant: Do not deviate into his — the yetzer hara's — ways, for your own ways are pure and upright.]

28. Distance yourself from falsehood. Do not pronounce the Holy One's Name in vain or in an unclean place.

29. Remove yourself from reliance on human beings [variant: reliance on a broken, weak reed i.e. human beings], and walk modestly with your Creator. And do not make gold your infatuation, for that is the beginning of idol worship. Instead, distribute your money in accordance with Hashem's Will, for He has the power to supply what you lack and give sustenance to your household.

30. Know the God of your father. Weigh your words on the scales of justice and use an honest measure. The expenditure of money should be easier for you than the expenditure of words. Your mouth should not rush to utter a bad word, until you have weighed it on the scales of your intelligence.

יִחוּד שָׁלֵם. כִּי זֶה הָיָה [נ״א הוּא] סְגֻלַּת
יִשְׂרָאֵל עַל כָּל הָעַמִּים וְזֶה יְסוֹד כָּל הַתּוֹרָה
כֻּלָּהּ.

❧ ליום שני ❧

כז. לְהַרְחִיק גַּאֲוָה וָכַעַס, וְגָעַר בְּיֵצֶר הָרָע
הַמַּשִּׁיאֲךָ לָלֶכֶת בְּדַרְכֵי לִבָּךְ. וְאַל יֵשְׁט, כִּי
דְרָכָיו [נ״א וְאַל תֵּשְׁט אֶל דְּרָכָיו כִּי דְרָכֶיךָ] זַךְ וְיָשָׁר.

כח. מִדְּבַר שֶׁקֶר תִּרְחָק. וְאַל תּוֹצִיא שֵׁם שָׁמַיִם
לְבַטָּלָה וְלֹא בְּמָקוֹם מְטוּנָּף.

כט. הָסֵר מִמְּךָ [נ״א מִשְׁעֶנֶת הַקָּנֶה הָרָצוּץ] מִשְׁעֶנֶת בְּנֵי
אָדָם וְהַצְנֵעַ לֶכֶת עִם בּוֹרַאֲךָ. וְאַל תָּשִׂים זָהָב
כִּסְלֶךָ, כִּי זֹאת תְּחִלַּת עֲבוֹדַת עַכּוּ״ם, וּפַזֵּר
מָמוֹנְךָ כַּאֲשֶׁר הוּא רְצוֹנוֹ. כִּי בְּיָדוֹ לְמַלְּאוֹת
חֶסְרוֹנְךָ וְלָתֵת טֶרֶף בְּנֵי בֵיתֶךָ.

ל. דַּע אֶת אֱלֹקֵי אָבִיךָ. וּדְבָרֶיךָ בְּמֹאזְנֵי צֶדֶק
תִּשְׁקֹל וְהִין צֶדֶק יִהְיֶה לָךְ. וְיֵקַל בְּעֵינֶיךָ,
הוֹצָאַת מָמוֹנְךָ מֵהוֹצָאַת דְּבָרֶיךָ. וּפִיךָ אַל
יְמַהֵר לְהוֹצִיא דָבָר רַע עַד אֲשֶׁר תִּשְׁקְלֵהוּ
בְּמֹאזְנֵי שִׂכְלֶךָ.

31. Don't neglect the confession of your sins evening and morning, nor the remembrance of Zion and Jerusalem with a broken heart, with concern, sighing and tears.

32. Constantly remember the day of death, and prepare provisions for the journey. Place these two things [the remembrance and the preparation] constantly between your eyes, and they [your provisions] will be ready for you on the day of departure. Soak your bed with weeping [over your sins]. Let your thoughts be disturbed when you remember the trembling fear of Rabban Yochanan [ben Zakkai], of blessed memory [on his deathbed; see *Berachos* 28b].

33. Be a good friend of those who fear Hashem. Keep their company, and stay away from the company of those who act unjustly. And love those who admonish [you].

34. It is good and proper for you to denigrate your good deeds in your own eyes and to emphasize your sins [variant: and emphasize your sins in your eyes], and to magnify the kindnesses of your Creator, Who formed you from the time you were in the womb and Who gives you your food in its proper time. And when you perform His *mitzvos*, do not serve in order to receive a reward.

35. Day or night, mention of Him shall not depart from your mouth. When you lie down to sleep, be infatuated with love for Him, and when you rise up and walk about, you should find Him. In your waking hours you should find delight in Him, and He will straighten your paths.

36. Have proper intention (כַּוָּנָה) in your prayer, for prayer is the service of the heart.

לא. וִידּוּי עַל עֲוֹנוֹתֶיךָ עֶרֶב וָבֹקֶר אַל יֶחְסַר. וְזִכְרוֹן צִיּוֹן וִירוּשָׁלַיִם בְּשִׁבְרוֹן לֵב וּבְדְאָגָה וּבַאֲנָחָה וּבְדִמְעָה.

לב. זְכֹר יוֹם הַמָּוֶת תָּמִיד. וְצֵידָה לַדֶּרֶךְ הָכֵן. וְשִׂים בֵּין עֵינֶיךָ שְׁנֵי אֵלֶּה תָּמִיד וְיִהְיוּ מְזֻמָּנִים לְךָ לְיוֹם הַפֵּירוּד וּמִטָּתְךָ בְּדִמְעָה תַמְסֶה. וְיִבָּהֲלוּךָ רַעְיוֹנֶךָ מִדֵּי זִכְרְךָ חֶרְדַּת רַבָּן יוֹחָנָן זִכְרוֹנוֹ לִבְרָכָה.

לג. חָבֵר טוֹב הֱיֵה לְיִרְאֵי ה׳. הִתְחַבֵּר בְּחֶבְרָתָם. וּמֵחֶבְרַת פּוֹעֲלֵי אָוֶן הַרְחֵק, וֶאֱהוֹב הַמּוֹכִיחִים.

לד. טוֹב וְיָשָׁר לְךָ לְהַמְעִיט בְּעֵינֶיךָ פְּעֻלּוֹתֶיךָ הַטּוֹבִים וְהַגְדִּיל פְּשָׁעֶיךָ. [נ״א ולהגדיל בעיניך פשעיך] וּלְהַרְבּוֹת חַסְדֵי בּוֹרְאָךְ, וְיוֹצֶרְךָ מִבֶּטֶן, וְנוֹתֵן אָכְלְךָ בְּעִתּוֹ. וְלֹא תִהְיֶה מְשַׁמֵּשׁ עַל מְנַת לְקַבֵּל פְּרָס בַּעֲשׂוֹתְךָ מִצְוֹתָיו.

לה. יוֹמָם וָלַיְלָה זִכְרוֹ מִפִּיךָ אַל יָמוּשׁ. בְּשָׁכְבְּךָ תְּשַׂגֶּה בְּאַהֲבָתוֹ, וּבְקוּמֶךָ, וּבְהִילוּכְךָ תִּמְצָאֶנּוּ, וַהֲקִיצוֹת בּוֹ תְּשַׁעֲשַׁע, וְהוּא יְיַשֵּׁר אוֹרְחוֹתֶיךָ.

לו. כַּוֵּן בִּתְפִלָּתְךָ כִּי הַתְּפִלָּה הִיא עֲבוֹדַת הַלֵּב.

If your son were to speak to you, but not from his heart, would it not anger you? How, then, can a putrid drop [a human being] act this way before the King of the universe?

Do not be like a servant who has been given an honorable task for his own benefit, and then spoils it. How, then, can he stand before the King?

How good it is to seek forgiveness for the fact that you say, "Forgive us!" [in the *Shemoneh Esrei*] without proper intention. And if it is impossible [to have proper intention] throughout all the prayers, [then have it] during the first blessing of the *Shemoneh Esrei*. Do not omit [proper intention in] the first verse of the *Shema*. For he who does not have proper intention when saying these does not fulfill the obligation of prayer.

37. Study your [weekly Torah] portions along with the community [by reading] the text of the Torah twice and the translation [of *Onkelos*] once, and the commentary of *Rashi z"l*. Study it carefully as best as you can and so shall you do with *Gemara;* for to occupy oneself with *Gemara* is a good trait, and reward is given for it. There is no better trait than this, as the *Mishnah* says: "The study of Torah is equal to all [the good deeds] combined" [*Peah* 1:1].

❧ Tuesday ❧

38. Any food that may be eaten or drink that may be imbibed should not be [ingested] without a blessing before and after. Concentrate on it as best as you can. Cover your head when you mention His Name, and close your

וְאִם בִּנְךָ יְדַבֵּר לְךָ וְלֹא מִלְבּוֹ, הֲלֹא יִחַר לְךָ, וּמַה תַּעֲשֶׂה טִפָּה סְרוּחָה לִפְנֵי מַלְכּוֹ שֶׁל עוֹלָם.

וְלֹא תִהְיֶה כְּעֶבֶד שֶׁמָּסְרוּ לוֹ מְלָאכָה נִכְבֶּדֶת לְטוֹבָתוֹ, וְחִבְּלָה. וְאֵיךְ יַעֲמֹד לִפְנֵי הַמֶּלֶךְ.

וּמַה טּוֹב לְבַקֵּשׁ סְלִיחָה, עַל אָמְרְךָ סְלַח לָנוּ, בְּלֹא כַוָּנָה.

וְאִם אִי אֶפְשָׁר בְּכָל הַתְּפִלּוֹת, בְּרָכָה רִאשׁוֹנָה שֶׁל שְׁמוֹנָה עֶשְׂרֵה. וּפָסוּק רִאשׁוֹן שֶׁל קְרִיאַת שְׁמַע אַל יֶחְסַר. כִּי לֹא יָצָא חוֹבַת הַתְּפִלָּה מִי שֶׁלֹּא כִוֵּן בָּהֶם.

לז. לִמֹד פַּרְשִׁיּוֹתֶיךָ עִם הַצִּבּוּר, שְׁנַיִם מִקְרָא וְאֶחָד תַּרְגּוּם וּפֵרוּשׁ רַשִׁ"י ז"ל, וּתְדַקְדֵּק בּוֹ כַּאֲשֶׁר תּוּכַל וְכֵן יִהְיֶה לְךָ בַּגְּמָרָא, כִּי הָעוֹסֵק בַּגְּמָרָא מִדָּה טוֹבָה וְנוֹתְנִין עָלֶיהָ שָׂכָר. וְאֵין לְךָ מִדָּה טוֹבָה הֵימֶנָּה וּתְנַן תַּלְמוּד תּוֹרָה כְּנֶגֶד כֻּלָּם.

❊ לְיוֹם שְׁלִישִׁי ❊

לח. מִכָּל מַאֲכָל אֲשֶׁר יֵאָכֵל וּמִכָּל מַשְׁקֶה אֲשֶׁר יִשָּׁתֶה, אַל תִּהְיֶה בְּלֹא בְּרָכָה תְּחִלָּה וָסוֹף. וְכַוֵּן בָּהּ כַּאֲשֶׁר תּוּכַל. וְכַסֵּה רֹאשְׁךָ כְּשֶׁתַּזְכִּיר אֶת ה', וְיַזְמוּ

eyes. For when one speaks of Him [during prayers or blessings], it should not be like the verse (*Yeshayahu* 29:13), "With one's mouth and one's lips they honored Me, but one distanced his heart from Me [i.e. their prayers were insincere].

39. Wash your hands for prayer and for eating [bread]. When you have fulfilled your bodily functions recite the *Asher Yatzar* blessing ["...Who created man with wisdom..."], but do not recite the blessing for washing hands, unless you have wiped yourself or rinsed yourself and wish to pray immediately – then you should recite *Asher Yatzar* and the blessing for washing hands.

40. Put *tzitzis* on the four corners of your garment so that you may remember [all the *mitzvos*] and sanctify yourself in all your activities.

Be modest in the bathroom and in your home, for a man will have to account for even a light-hearted conversation between himself and his wife. Do not act in a lightheaded manner; and the fear of Heaven should be upon you. Take care not to gaze at a woman, even an unmarried one.

Mezuzos should not be missing on the doorways of your home.

41. Do not reveal someone else's secret. Even what was not told to you in a secretive manner, you should conceal within the walls of your heart. Even if you hear it from another, do not say, "I have already heard that." Guard the openings of your mouth from the one who lies in your bosom.

42. Evening, morning and afternoon, keep the times assigned to prayer. And open your heart for a period of time before prayer. Take care to be one of the first ten [arriving at the synagogue for prayer].

[נ"א ותסגור] עֵינֶיךָ. כִּי מִדֵּי דַבְּרוֹ בּוֹ, אַל תְּהִי כְּאָמוּר: "בְּפִיו וּבִשְׂפָתָיו כִּבְּדוּנִי, וְלִבּוֹ רִחַק מִמֶּנִּי."

לט. נְטוֹל יָדֶיךָ לַתְּפִלָּה וְלַאֲכִילָה, וּבְעֵת צֵאתְךָ מִצְּרָכֶיךָ בָּרֵךְ אֲשֶׁר יָצַר, וְעַל נְטִילַת יָדַיִם לֹא תְבָרֵךְ. אִם לֹא קִנַּחְתָּ אוֹ שִׁפְשַׁפְתָּ וְתִרְצֶה לְהִתְפַּלֵּל מִיָּד אָז תִּתְפַּלֵּל [נ"א תברך] אֲשֶׁר יָצַר וְעַל נְטִילַת יָדַיִם.

מ. גְּדִילִים תַּעֲשֶׂה לָךְ, עַל אַרְבַּע כַּנְפוֹת כְּסוּתְךָ. לְמַעַן תִּזְכּוֹר וְקַדֵּשׁ עַצְמְךָ בְּכָל דְּבָרֶיךָ. וֶהֱוֵי צָנוּעַ בְּבֵית הַכִּסֵּא. וְעִם בֵּיתְךָ, כִּי אֲפִילוּ שִׂיחָה קַלָּה שֶׁבֵּין אִישׁ לְאִשְׁתּוֹ, עָתִיד לִתֵּן עָלֶיהָ אֶת הַדִּין, וְאַל תִּנְהַג עַצְמְךָ בְּקַלּוּת רֹאשׁ. וִיהִי מוֹרָא שָׁמַיִם עָלֶיךָ, וְהִשָּׁמֵר מִלְהִסְתַּכֵּל בְּאִשָּׁה וַאֲפִילוּ פְּנוּיָה. וּמְזוּזוֹת עַל פִּתְחֵי בֵּיתְךָ אַל יֶחְסְרוּ.

מא. סוֹד אַחֵר, אַל תְּגַל. גַּם אֶל הַדְּבָרִים אֲשֶׁר יְדַבְּרוּ לְפָנֶיךָ שֶׁלֹּא עַל דֶּרֶךְ סוֹד, טוֹמְנֵהוּ בְּקִירוֹת לִבֶּךָ. [נ"א טמנם בקרב לבך] גַּם אִם תִּשְׁמְעֶנּוּ מֵאַחֵר אַל תֹּאמַר כְּבָר שְׁמַעְתִּי זֶה וּמְשׁוֹכֶבֶת חֵקֶךָ שְׁמוֹר פִּתְחֵי פִיךָ.

מב. עֶרֶב וָבֹקֶר וְצָהֳרַיִם שְׁמוֹר הָעִתִּים הַקְּבוּעִים לַתְּפִלָּה, וּפְתַח לִבְּךָ שָׁעָה אַחַת קוֹדֶם תְּפִלָּה.

Do not engage in idle talk in the synagogue. And *tefillin* should not be lacking from your head and arm.

43. "Steer your course to be level" (*Mishlei* 4:26), by regulating yourself on the path of moderation when eating, drinking and in all your traits. Do not veer to the right or to the left. So, too, in your speech and demeanor towards others, be honest, and pursue peace.

44. Establish set times for Torah study, before eating and retiring. Discuss Torah at your table.

   In accordance with them [i.e. the words of Torah], alert the members of your household to direct them in accordance with the Torah in all matters that require caution, so that they guard their lips from boasting [variant: desecrating themselves] — for the first issue in a man's [final] judgment is, "Did you establish set times for studying Torah?"

45. Rejoice when you hear reproof, as if you have found a great treasure. Reprimand the wise man and he will love you. For open rebuke is better than hidden love, and it will be pleasant for those who reprimand.

46. At the outset of your actions, look at their outcome, and calculate the loss caused by doing a *mitzvah* against its reward, and the gain from a transgression against its loss. For "the wise man has his eyes in his head" (*Koheles* 2:14).

47. Take care not to rely on your heart. Listen to advice and accept guidance. Be diligent in the performance of whatever you are obligated to do. Beyond every charge, safeguard your heart.

וֶהֱוֵי זָהִיר שֶׁתִּהְיֶה מֵעֲשָׂרָה הָרִאשׁוֹנִים. וְאַל תְּדַבֵּר שִׂיחָה בְּטֵלָה בְּבֵית הַכְּנֶסֶת. וּתְפִילִין עַל רֹאשְׁךָ וְעַל זְרוֹעֲךָ אַל יֶחְסָרוּ.

מג. פַּלֵּס מַעְגַּל רַגְלֶיךָ, לְיַשֵּׁר עַצְמְךָ בְּדֶרֶךְ בֵּינוֹנִי בְּמַאֲכָל וּבְמִשְׁתֶּה, וּבְכָל מִדּוֹתֶיךָ. וְאַל תֵּט יָמִין וּשְׂמֹאל. וּבְדִיבּוּרֶיךָ וּבְהַסְבָּרַת פָּנִים, עִם הָאֱמוּנָה. וּרְדוֹף אַחַר הַשָּׁלוֹם.

מד. קְבַע עִיתִּים לַתּוֹרָה, קוֹדֶם אֲכִילָה, וּשְׁכִיבָה וְדִבַּרְתָּ בָּם עַל שֻׁלְחָנֶךָ.
וְהִזְהַרְתָּ בָּם אַנְשֵׁי בֵיתְךָ לְהַדְרִיכָם עַל פִּי הַתּוֹרָה, בְּכָל הַדְּבָרִים הַצְּרִיכִים אַזְהָרָה. לִשְׁמוֹר פִּיהֶם מִלְהִתְהַלֵּל, [נ"א מלהתחלל] כִּי תְּחִלַּת דִּינוֹ שֶׁל אָדָם קָבַעְתָּ עִתִּים לַתּוֹרָה.

מה. שְׂמַח בְּשָׁמְעֲךָ תוֹכַחַת, כְּמוֹצֵא שָׁלָל רָב. וְהוֹכַח לֶחָכָם וְיֶאֱהָבֶךָ. כִּי טוֹבָה תוֹכַחַת מְגוּלָּה מֵאַהֲבָה מְסוּתֶּרֶת וְלַמּוֹכִיחִים יִנְעָם.

מו. תְּחִלַּת מַעֲשֶׂיךָ הַבֵּט סוֹפָם, וֶהֱוֵי מְחַשֵּׁב הֶפְסֵד מִצְוָה כְּנֶגֶד שְׂכָרָהּ, וּשְׂכַר עֲבֵרָה כְּנֶגֶד הֶפְסֵידָהּ. כִּי הֶחָכָם עֵינָיו בְּרֹאשׁוֹ.

מז. הִזָּהֵר שֶׁלֹּא תִסְמוֹךְ בִּלְבָבְךָ וּשְׁמַע עֵצָה וְקַבֵּל מוּסָר וְתִהְיֶה זָרִיז לַעֲשׂוֹת כָּל מַה שֶׁמּוּטָל עָלֶיךָ לַעֲשׂוֹת, וּמִכָּל מִשְׁמָר נְצוֹר לִבֶּךָ.

48. Do not rise from your bed like a lazy person, but with alacrity, in order to serve your Creator.

49. Do not delay to run to the house of prayer. Protect your feet lest they become filthy. Do not turn your heart [to look] behind [you, so to speak,] during prayer, and concentrate on blessing your Creator.

50. Do not speak [even] in an abbreviated speech or in a different tongue [i.e. in code words] as long as the *chazzan* is praying. And answer: "Amen."

51. Do not forget the stroke of death, which will come suddenly. And bear in mind that one will stand in judgment.

52. Do not engage in a *mitzvah* to get a reward, and do not avoid transgressions because of the punishment, but serve only because of love.

❈{ Wednesday }❈

53. Do not be negligent about [performing] a *mitzvah* if it comes to hand. Perform it for the sake of Heaven without delay.

54. Do not be indolent regarding the Blessing of the Moon, for if Israel had gained nothing more than the privilege of receiving the Divine Presence (*Shechinah*) each month, that would have been sufficient for them.

55. Do not do that which people will ridicule, for it is their nature to ignore the good and expose the bad.

מח. אַל תָּקוּם מִמִּטָּתְךָ כְּאִישׁ עָצֵל כִּי אִם בִּזְרִיזוּת כְּדֵי לַעֲבוֹד לְיוֹצְרֶךָ.

מט. אַל תְּאַחֵר לָרוּץ אֶל בֵּית הַתְּפִלָּה. וְשָׁמַרְתָּ רַגְלֶיךָ פֶּן יִהְיוּ מְטוּנָפוֹת אַל תָּשִׂים לִבְּךָ אֲחוֹרַנִּית בִּשְׁעַת הַתְּפִלָּה, וְהִתְכַּוֵּן לְבָרֵךְ לְיוֹצְרֶךָ.

נ. אַל תְּדַבֵּר בְּלַעֲגֵי שָׂפָה וּבְלָשׁוֹן אַחֶרֶת כָּל עֵת שֶׁהַחַזָּן מִתְפַּלֵּל, וְתַעֲנֶה אָמֵן.

נא. אַל תְּנַשֶּׁה פְּגִיעַת הַמָּוֶת שֶׁתָּבוֹא פִּתְאוֹם, וְתִזְכּוֹר מַעֲמַד הַדִּין.

נב. אַל תִּתְעַסֵּק בְּמִצְוָה כְּדֵי לְקַבֵּל פְּרָס וְאַל תִּרְחַק מִן הָעֲבֵרוֹת מִפְּנֵי הָעוֹנֶשׁ, רַק עֲבוֹד מֵאַהֲבָה.

﷽ לְיוֹם רְבִיעִי ﷽

נג. אַל תִּתְרַשֵּׁל בְּמִצְוָה אִם בָּאָה לְיָדְךָ וְתַעֲשֶׂנָּה לְשֵׁם שָׁמַיִם בְּלֹא אִיחוּר.

נד. אַל תִּתְעַצֵּל בְּבִרְכַּת הַלְּבָנָה שֶׁאִם לֹא זָכוּ יִשְׂרָאֵל אֶלָּא לְהַקְבִּיל פְּנֵי שְׁכִינָה בְּכָל חוֹדֶשׁ דַּיָּם.

נה. אַל תַּעֲשֶׂה דָבָר שֶׁיַּלְעִיגוּ הַבְּרִיוֹת, שֶׁדַּרְכָּם לְהַעֲלִים הַטּוֹבוֹת וּלְגַלּוֹת הָרָעוֹת.

56. Do not hold your father and mother in light esteem, and do not cause them pain. Honor them to the best of your ability all their days.

57. Let your face not be angry toward wayfarers. Receive them with a radiant countenance.

58. Do not forget to give them food, provide them with an escort, and soothe them with words.

59. Do not fix your gaze on one who has become wealthier than you, but on the one who is below you.

60. Do not be provoked to anger about anything. Be slow to anger, lest you lose your wisdom.

61. Do not let crooked speech nor obscene language come forth from your lips, for you shall face judgment for all your words.

62. Do not maintain your anger against your comrade for [even] a single day. Rather be submissive before him to beg his forgiveness first [before he apologizes to you] .

63. Do not speak with insolence and do not be brazenfaced, by not accepting the fear of Heaven upon yourself.

64. Do not reply to those who shame you and to those who call you a liar [variant: humiliate you]; rather, put your hand on your mouth and be silent, lest your heart become inflamed.

65. Do not take sides in a quarrel that is not yours, for in the end they will make peace between themselves and you will be left with anger.

66. Do not be arrogant towards people; be humble and like the dust upon which everyone treads.

נו. אַל תַּקְלֶה אָבִיךָ וְאִמֶּךָ, וְאַל תְּצַעֵר אוֹתָם, וְכַבְּדֵם כְּפִי יְכָלְתְּךָ כָּל יְמֵיהֶם.

נז. אַל יִהְיוּ פָּנֶיךָ זוֹעֲמוֹת נֶגֶד עוֹבְרִים וְשָׁבִים, וְקַבֵּל אוֹתָם בְּפָנִים מְאִירִים.

נח. אַל תִּשְׁכַּח לְהַעֲנִיק לָהֶם צֵדָה וְלַעֲשׂוֹת לֵוָיָה לָהֶם וּתְנַחֲמֵם בִּדְבָרִים.

נט. אַל תָּשִׂים עֵינְךָ לְמִי שֶׁעָלָה לְעוֹשֶׁר יוֹתֵר מִמְּךָ, אֶלָּא לְמִי שֶׁהוּא תַּחְתֶּיךָ.

ס. אַל תְּבַהֵל לִקְצוֹף מִשּׁוּם דָּבָר. וְהַאֲרֵךְ אַפֶּךָ, פֶּן תְּאַבֵּד אֶת חָכְמָתֶךָ.

סא. אַל תּוֹצֵא מִמְּךָ עַקְשׁוּת פֶּה וְנִיבוּל פֶּה כִּי עַל כָּל דְּבָרֶיךָ תָּבֹא בְמִשְׁפָּט.

סב. אַל תַּחֲזִיק כַּעַסְךָ עִם חֲבֵירְךָ יוֹם אֶחָד, וְתִכָּנַע לְפָנָיו לְבַקֵּשׁ מִמֶּנּוּ מְחִילָה קוֹדֶם.

סג. אַל תְּדַבֵּר בְּצַוָּאר עָתָק וְאַל תָּעִיז מֵצַח שֶׁלֹּא לְקַבֵּל עָלֶיךָ יִרְאַת שָׁמַיִם.

סד. אַל תָּשִׁיב לִמְחָרְפֶיךָ וְלִמְכַזְּבֶיךָ, [נ"א ולמבזיך] וְתָשִׂים יָד לַפֶּה וּשְׁתוֹק, פֶּן יֵחַם לְבָבְךָ.

סה. אַל תִּתְעַבֵּר עַל רִיב לֹא לָךְ, כִּי לְסוֹף הֵם יַשְׁלִימוּ בֵּינֵיהֶם וְאַתָּה תִשָּׁאֵר בְּכַעַס.

סו. אַל תִּתְגָּאֶה עַל הַבְּרִיּוֹת, וְתִהְיֶה שְׁפַל רוּחַ וְכֶעָפָר שֶׁהַכֹּל דָּשִׁין בּוֹ.

67. Do not despise anyone or anything, for there is no man who does not have his time, and nothing that does not have its place.

68. Always pursue charity, for he who pursues charity and kindness will find life, righteousness, and honor. Do not fail to give a half-shekel once each year — and each month and each week, whatever you can afford. Every day do not fail to give some small gift, at least before prayer. If you have income to tithe, give it. See to it that there are provisions in your home at all times, so that you may benefit the living and the dead, the poor and the rich.

69. Desire what your Creator desires. Rejoice with your lot, whether small or great, and entreat Him constantly to turn your heart to His testimonies.

In all your other ways cast your burden on Hashem. Do not consider it difficult to spend [money] for any necessities of the Sabbath and festivals.

Make an effort to honor them and accept them [i.e. those days] upon yourself while it is still day. Enjoy them with food and drink, and spend half the time in the house of study.

Honor [Shabbos] when it enters, and when it departs by setting a table in the evening, after Shabbos is over.

70. Do not sleep a long sleep like a sluggard, but accustom yourself to wake at sunrise. Rise from your bed upon the song of the bird.

סז. אַל תְּהִי בָז לְכָל אָדָם וּלְכָל דָּבָר, שֶׁאֵין לְךָ אָדָם שֶׁאֵין לוֹ שָׁעָה וְאֵין לְךָ דָּבָר שֶׁאֵין לוֹ מָקוֹם.

סח. צֶדֶק צֶדֶק תִּרְדּוֹף, כִּי רוֹדֵף צְדָקָה וָחֶסֶד יִמְצָא חַיִּים צְדָקָה וְכָבוֹד. וְאַל יֶחְסַר מִמַּחֲצִית הַשֶּׁקֶל בְּכָל שָׁנָה בְּפַעַם אֶחָד, וּבְכָל חֹדֶשׁ וּבְכָל שָׁבוּעַ כְּפִי מִסַּת יָדֶךָ. וּבְכָל יוֹם לֹא תֶחְסַר מַתָּנָה מוּעֶטֶת לְכָל הַפָּחוֹת קוֹדֶם תְּפִלָּה. וְאִם הִגִּיעַ לְמַעֲשֵׂר תִּתֵּן. וִיהִי טֶרֶף בְּבֵיתֶךָ. בְּכָל אֲשֶׁר תִּמְצָא יָדֶךָ לִגְמוֹל, הֵן לַחַיִּים הֵן לַמֵּתִים הֵן לָעֲנִיִּים הֵן לָעֲשִׁירִים.

סט. רְצֵה בַּאֲשֶׁר יִרְצֶה יוֹצְרֶךָ, שְׂמַח בְּחֶלְקְךָ אִם מְעַט וְאִם הַרְבֵּה. וְהִתְחַנֵּן לְפָנָיו תָּמִיד לְהַטּוֹת לְבָבְךָ לְעֵדוֹתָיו.

וּבִשְׁאָר דְּרָכֶיךָ הַשְׁלֵךְ עַל ה׳ יְהָבְךָ וְאַל יִקְשֶׁה בְּעֵינֶיךָ לְהוֹצִיא לִכְבוֹד הַשַּׁבָּת וְיוֹם טוֹב בְּכָל הַצָּרִיךְ.

וְהִשְׁתַּדֵּל לְכַבְּדָם, וּלְקַבְּלָם מִבְּעוֹד יוֹם. וּלְהִתְעַנֵּג בָּהֶם בַּאֲכִילָה וּשְׁתִיָּה וְחֶצְיוֹ לְבֵית הַמִּדְרָשׁ.
וְכַבְּדֵהוּ בִּכְנִיסָתוֹ וּבִיצִיאָתוֹ, לַעֲרוֹךְ שֻׁלְחָן בְּמוֹצָאֵי שַׁבָּת.

ע. אַל תִּישַׁן כְּעַצֵּל שֵׁינָה רַבָּה, וְתַרְגִּיל אֶת עַצְמְךָ לְהָקִיץ בְּהָנֵץ הַחַמָּה, וּלְקוֹל הַצִּפּוֹר קוּם מִמִּטָּתֶךָ.

71. Do not pray without clean hands and without purity, for your prayer will not be heard.

72. Do not pray except with the proper intention in your heart and with calm, so that your ear will hear that which you utter.

73. Do not forget the Rock Who gave you birth and formed you. In all your ways, know Him and place Him constantly before you.

❧ Thursday ❧

74. Do not be overly happy. Remember that your life is [mere] wind. You were created from dust and your end will be rot.

75. Do not say of any *mitzvah*, "I will do it tomorrow." For perhaps you will not be free to do it.

76. Do not separate yourself from thinking about wisdom and moral instruction (*mussar*). Sit in the dust of the Sages' feet, and become wise.

77. Do not lay aside the way of piety, even though people ridicule you, and do not feel ashamed regarding a *mitzvah*.

78. Do not close your hand from giving constantly to the poor and the destitute, and do not ignore your flesh and blood [relatives].

79. Do not delay to run and to hurry to set a table and food before them, for perhaps they are famished.

80. Do not be indolent in bringing tithes to the treasury, for secretly given [charity] suppresses [Hashem's] wrath.

עא. אַל תִּתְפַּלֵּל בְּלֹא נְקִיּוּת כַּפַּיִם וּבְלֹא טָהֳרָה, כִּי תְּפִלָּתְךָ לֹא תְּהֵא נִשְׁמַעַת.

עב. אַל תִּתְפַּלֵּל כִּי אִם בְּכַוָּנַת הַלֵּב וּבְנַחַת, כְּדֵי שֶׁיִּשְׁמַע הָאֹזֶן.

עג. אַל תִּשְׁכַּח צוּר יְלָדְךָ וּמְחוֹלְלֶךָ וּבְכָל דְּרָכֶיךָ דָעֵהוּ וּתְבִיאֵהוּ [נ״א ותשווהו] לְנֶגְדְּךָ תָמִיד.

⛭ לְיוֹם חֲמִישִׁי ⛭

עד. אַל תַּרְבֶּה לִשְׂמוֹחַ. וּזְכוֹר, כִּי ״רוּחַ חַיֶּיךָ״. אַתָּה נוֹצַר מֵעָפָר, וְאַחֲרִיתְךָ רִמָּה.

עה. אַל תֹּאמַר עַל שׁוּם מִצְוָה אֲעֶשֶׂה אוֹתָהּ לְמָחָר, שֶׁמָּא לֹא תִפָּנֶה לַעֲשׂוֹת.

עו. אַל תִּפָּרֵד מֵהֲגַיִּת [נ״א מהגיון] חָכְמָה וּמוּסָר, וְתִתְאַבֵּק בַּעֲפַר רַגְלֵי חֲכָמִים וְהִתְחַכֵּם.

עז. אַל תַּנִּיחַ דֶּרֶךְ חֲסִידוּת אַף עַל פִּי שֶׁמַּלְעִיגִין עָלֶיךָ, וְאַל תֵּיבוֹשׁ לִדְבַר מִצְוָה.

עח. אַל תִּקְפֹּץ יָדֶיךָ מִלִּתֵּן תָּמִיד אֶל הָעֲנִיִּים וְלָאֶבְיוֹנִים, וּמִבְּשָׂרְךָ אַל תִּתְעַלֵּם.

עט. אַל תְּאַחֵר לָרוּץ וּלְמַהֵר וּלְהָכִין לִפְנֵיהֶם שֻׁלְחָן לֶחֶם, כִּי שֶׁמָּא הֵם רְעֵבִים.

פ. אַל תִּתְעַצֵּל לְהָבִיא מַעֲשֵׂר אֶל בֵּית הָאוֹצָר, כִּי מַתָּן בַּסֵּתֶר יִכְפֶּה אָף.

81. Do not look at one who is inferior to you in service and fear [of the Creator], but [look] to one who is superior to you.

82. Do not lift your hand against your comrade, even if he curses your father and mother to your face.

83. Do not speak slander or malicious gossip of anyone, nor be a participant in quarrel-mongering or talebearing.

84. Do not hurry to respond brazenly, [even] to one who has said that which is not good.

85. Do not make your voice heard outside. Do not screech like an animal. Let your words be [spoken] calmly.

86. Do not shame another in public, for one who does so has no portion in the World to Come.

87. Do not show your power before any man, though your arm is strong, for you do not know when you will be the weaker.

88. Do not pursue honor, and do not ascend to a height that is not fit for you.

89. Do not let people honor you, lest someone rebel and humble you.

90. Do not slacken your hand from seeking friends and those who love you. And do not underestimate even a single enemy.

91. Do not deprecate another's purchase and do not cause him uncertainty, for that is the way of those who lack sense.

פא. אַל תַּבִּיט לְמִי שֶׁהוּא קָטָן מִמְּךָ בַּעֲבוֹדָה וּבְיִרְאָה, כִּי אִם לְגָדוֹל מִמְּךָ.

פב. אַל תָּרִים יָדֶיךָ עַל חֲבֵירְךָ, וְאַף אִם הוּא מְקַלֵּל אֶת אָבִיךָ וְאֶת אִמְּךָ בְּפָנֶיךָ.

פג. אַל תּוֹצִיא דִבָּה וּלְשׁוֹן הָרָע עַל שׁוּם בְּרִיָּה. וְלֹא לֵזוּת וּרְכִילוּת.

פד. אַל תְּהִי נִבְהָל לְהָשִׁיב בְּעַזּוּת לְמִי שֶׁאָמַר דְּבָרִים אֲשֶׁר לֹא טוֹבִים.

פה. אַל תַּשְׁמִיעַ בַּחוּץ קוֹלֶךָ, וְאַל תִּהְיֶה צֹוֵחַ כַּבְּהֵמָה. וּדְבָרֶיךָ יִהְיוּ בְנַחַת.

פו. אַל תַּלְבִּין פְּנֵי חֲבֵרְךָ בָּרַבִּים, כִּי הָעוֹשֶׂה כֵן אֵין לוֹ חֵלֶק לָעוֹלָם הַבָּא.

פז. אַל תַּרְאֶה יְכוֹלֶת נֶגֶד שׁוּם אָדָם אִם יָדְךָ גָּבְרָה, כִּי לֹא תֵדַע אִם תֶּחֱלוֹשׁ.

פח. אַל תִּרְדּוֹף אַחַר הַכָּבוֹד, וְלֹא תַעֲלֶה בְּמַעֲלָה שֶׁאֵינָה רְאוּיָה לָךְ.

פט. אַל יְכַבְּדוּךָ בְּנֵי אָדָם פֶּן יָבַעַט וְיַשְׁפִּילֶךָ.

צ. אַל תֶּרֶף יָדְךָ מִלְּבַקֵּשׁ רֵעִים וְאוֹהֲבִים. וְאַל יִמְעַט לְפָנֶיךָ שׂוֹנֵא אֶחָד.

צא. אַל תִּגְנָה מֶקַח חֲבֵירְךָ, וְאַל תַּחֲלִישׁ דַּעְתּוֹ כִּי זֶה מִנְהָג לַחֲסִירֵי דַעַת.

92. [When Hashem grants you benefits] do not say, "It is because of my righteousness [variant: because of my righteousness, have I become wealthy]." Be fearful that you should not receive your reward in this world.

93. Do not lead your comrade from a path of goodness to a path of evil, such as the one who entices and drives a person [toward idolatry], and the like.

94. Do not gorge yourself with food, to the point that you fill your stomach, for many illnesses result from overeating.

95. Do not be one of those who swill wine and gorge themselves on meat, lest you forget your Creator, and become ill [variant: and sin].

96. Do not cast excessive fear on your household, for much harm comes from great fear.

97. Do not be secluded with any woman other than your wife, mother, or daughter; not even with two women.

98. Do not praise a woman for her beauty, nor for her good deeds, lest those who hear also praise her.

99. Do not give yourself [airs of] grandeur and do not hold yourself in high esteem; make yourself small.

100. Do not be hasty in your actions.

101. Do not speak too much [even] about matters that are useful and not harmful, but speak briefly.

102. Do not slacken your hand from acquiring a loyal friend. Guard him and do not lose him, for it is good.

צב. אַל תֹּאמַר בְּצִדְקָתִי [נ״א בצדקתי העשרתי] וְתִירָא
שֶׁלֹּא תְּקַבֵּל שְׂכָרְךָ בָּעוֹלָם הַזֶּה.

צג. אַל תַּטֶּה אֶת חֲבֵירְךָ מִדֶּרֶךְ טוֹבָה אֶל דֶּרֶךְ
רָעָה, כְּגוֹן מֵסִית וּמַדִּיחַ וְכַיּוֹצֵא בָּזֶה.

צד. אַל תֹּאכַל אֲכִילָה גַסָּה עַד שֶׁתִּמָּלֵא כְּרֵיסְךָ,
כִּי הַרְבֵּה חֳלָאִים בָּאִים עַל רוֹב אֲכִילָה.

צה. אַל תְּהִי בְּסוֹבְאֵי יַיִן בְּזוֹלְלֵי בָשָׂר, פֶּן תִּשְׁכַּח
אֶת בּוֹרְאֶךָ וְתַחְלִיא. [נ״א ותחטא]

צו. אַל תַּטִּיל אֵימָה יְתֵירָה בְּתוֹךְ בֵּיתְךָ כִּי הַרְבֵּה
קִלְקוּלִים בָּאִים עַל רוֹב מוֹרָא.

צז. אַל תִּתְיַיחֵד עִם שׁוּם אִשָּׁה חוּץ מֵאִשְׁתְּךָ וְאִמְּךָ
וּבִתְּךָ, וַאֲפִילוּ עִם שְׁתֵּי נָשִׁים.

צח. אַל תְּשַׁבַּח אִשָּׁה בְּיָפְיָהּ. וּבְטוּב מַעֲשֶׂיהָ,
יְאַשְּׁרוּהָ הַשּׁוֹמְעִים.

צט. עַל תִּתֵּן תִּפְאֶרֶת לְעַצְמְךָ וְאַל תְּיַקֵּר גּוּפְךָ
בְּעֵינֶיךָ, וְתַקְטִין אֶת עַצְמְךָ.

ק. אַל תְּבַהֵל מַעֲשֶׂיךָ.

קא. אַל תַּרְבֶּה לְדַבֵּר בִּדְבָרִים הַמּוֹעִילִים, וּבְלֹא
נֶזֶק, כִּי אִם בְּקוֹצֶר לָשׁוֹן.

קב. אַל תֶּרֶף יָדְךָ לִקְנוֹת לְךָ חָבֵר נֶאֱמָן וּשְׁמוֹר
אוֹתוֹ וְאַל תְּאַבְּדֵהוּ כִּי טוֹב.

⊰ Friday ⊱

103. Do not entice another with a smooth tongue and flattery, and do not speak with a contradictory heart.

104. Do not anger [variant: cheat] any non-Jew, for there is no non-Jew who does not have his time [when he can retaliate], and their anger is harbored permanently.

105. Do not be friendly with an evil man, a sinner, an angry man, or a fool, lest you bring humiliation upon yourself.

106. Do not contemplate triumph over a wise man [to make yourself seem wiser than he], for doing so will not increase your own wisdom.

107. Do not become angry at any sort of person over a minor issue lest you accumulate enemies needlessly.

108. Do not be overanxious to know secrets between one man and another, nor that which is hidden from you.

109. Do not do privately that which you would be ashamed to do publicly, and do not say, "Who sees me?"

110. Do not impugn a person who comes before you to apologize whether it is the truth or a lie.

111. Do not rely on the gifts of human beings, but work to seek your sustenance.

112. Let not your money be dearer to you than your body, for example by violating customs regulations or traveling alone.

✣ ליום הששי ✣

קג. אַל תִּפְתֶּה אֶת חֲבֵירְךָ בְּשִׂפְתֵי חֲלָקוֹת וּבַחֲנִיפוּת, וְאַל תְּדַבֵּר בְּלֵב וָלֵב.

קד. אַל תַּכְעִיס [נ"א תונה] לְשׁוּם נָכְרִי כִּי אֵין עַכּוּ"ם שֶׁאֵין לוֹ שָׁעָה וְעֲבַרְתָּם שְׁמוּרָה נֶצַח.

קה. אַל תִּתְחַבֵּר לְאָדָם רָע וְחוֹטֵא וְכַעֲסָן וּכְסִיל פֶּן תָּבִיא כְּלִימוֹת עָלֶיךָ.

קו. אַל תַּעֲלֶה בְּדַעְתְּךָ לְנַצֵּחַ אֶת הֶחָכָם כִּי לֹא תַרְבֶּה עַל חָכְמָתְךָ חָכְמָה.

קז. אַל תְּהִי קַפְּדָן לִדָבָר מוּעָט נֶגֶד שׁוּם אָדָם פֶּן תְּלַקֵּט שׂוֹנְאִים עַל חִנָּם.

קח. אַל תְּהִי לָהוּט לָדַעַת הַסְּתָרִים שֶׁבֵּין אָדָם לַחֲבֵרוֹ וְדָבָר הַמְכוּסֶה מִמְּךָ.

קט. אַל תַּעַשׂ בַּסֵּתֶר מַה שֶׁתִּתְבַּיֵּיש בְּגָלוּי וְאַל תֹּאמַר מִי רוֹאֵנִי.

קי. אַל תַּחְשׁוֹב עָוֹן לְמִי שֶׁיָּבוֹא לְהִתְנַצֵּל לְפָנֶיךָ אִם אֱמֶת וְאִם שֶׁקֶר.

קיא. אַל תִּסְמוֹךְ לְיַד מַתְּנַת בָּשָׂר וָדָם וְתַעֲבוֹד לְבַקֵּשׁ מְזוֹנוֹתֶיךָ.

קיב. אַל יְהִי מָמוֹן שֶׁלְּךָ חָבִיב עָלֶיךָ יוֹתֵר מִגּוּפָךְ, כְּמוֹ לַעֲבוֹר עַל הַמֶּכֶס וְלָלֶכֶת יְחִידִי.

113. Do not put envy into your heart; for it is a serious illness that has no cure.

114. Do not be accustomed to take oaths or make vows, for children perish because of [their parents'] transgressions regarding vows.

115. Do not accustom yourself to swear by your body [i.e. by accepting bodily harm if you violate the oath], even on matters that are true.

116. Do not delay to repent fully and to seek a cure for your soul's sickness.

117. Do not labor for [that which blows away with] the wind [i.e. for matters of no value], and do not listen to idle words.

118. Do not call another by a derisive nickname [variant: for your comrade], for one who calls another by a [variant adds: bad] nickname has no portion in the World to Come.

119. Do not rely on your wealth, for one who relies on his wealth accumulates enemies, and will stumble beneath his enemies.

120. Do not be stubborn towards your townsmen; submit your will to the will of others.

121. Do not accustom yourself to eat outside of your home, in a large gathering, when it is not a meal for a *mitzvah*.

122. Do not break your body [variant: intoxicate your body] by becoming drunk from wine, lest you be disgusting, speak foully, and regret it.

123. Do not be angry at your wife. If you have pushed her away with your left hand, bring her close with your right hand without delay.

קיג. אַל תִּתֵּן בִּלְבָבְךָ קִנְאָה שֶׁזּוֹ הִיא חוֹלָה רָעָה שֶׁאֵין לָהּ רְפוּאָה.

קיד. אַל תְּהִי רָגִיל לֹא בִּשְׁבוּעָה וְלֹא בִּנְדָרִים כִּי בַּעֲוֹן נְדָרִים בָּנִים מֵתִים.

קטו. אַל תַּרְגִּיל לִישָׁבַע עַל גּוּפְךָ וַאֲפִילוּ עַל דְּבַר אֱמֶת.

קטז. אַל תְּאַחֵר לַעֲשׂוֹת תְּשׁוּבָה שְׁלֵמָה, וּלְבַקֵּשׁ רְפוּאָה לְחוֹלִי נַפְשֶׁךָ.

קיז. אַל תַּעֲמוֹל לָרוּחַ, וְאַל תִּשְׁמַע דְּבָרִים בְּטֵלִים.

קיח. אַל תְּכַנֶּה שֵׁם רַע [נ״א לחברך] כִּי הַמְכַנֶּה שֵׁם [נ״א רע] לַחֲבֵרוֹ אֵין לוֹ חֵלֶק לָעוֹלָם הַבָּא.

קיט. אַל תִּבְטַח בְּעָשְׁרְךָ כִּי הַבּוֹטֵחַ בְּעָשְׁרוֹ מְלַקֵּט שׂוֹנְאִים, וְיִכָּשֵׁל תַּחַת שׂוֹנְאָיו.

קכ. אַל תְּהִי סַרְבָן אֶל אַנְשֵׁי עִירְךָ, לְבַטֵּל רְצוֹנְךָ מִפְּנֵי רְצוֹן אֲחֵרִים.

קכא. אַל תַּרְגִּיל עַצְמְךָ לֶאֱכוֹל חוּץ מִבֵּיתְךָ, עִם קִיבּוּץ הַרְבֵּה שֶׁלֹּא לִסְעוּדַת מִצְוָה.

קכב. אַל תְּשַׁבֵּר [נ״א תשכר] גּוּפְךָ לְהִשְׁתַּכֵּר מִיַּיִן, פֶּן תִּהְיֶה מְגוּנֶּה וּתְנַבֵּל אֶת פִּיךָ וְתִתְחָרֵט.

קכג. אַל תִּכְעַס בְּאִשְׁתְּךָ, וְאִם רִחַקְתָּ אוֹתָהּ בִּשְׂמֹאל קָרֵב אוֹתָהּ בְּיָמִין בְּלֹא אִיחוּר.

124. Do not degrade your wife. Honor her and thereby remove her from sin.

125. Do not accustom yourself to sit among the scorners and lowlifes, lest they cause you to sin.

126. Do not be indolent in seeking wisdom, nor in rebuking another privately and respectfully.

127. Do not speak at an inappropriate time, or on a useless matter. And safeguard the openings of your mouth.

128. Do not speak with someone who is mad or mentally incompetent, for he will not accept your words, but will hold them in contempt.

129. Do not be an ingrate. Honor anyone who has opened a door to help you seek your needs.

130. Do not utter a false or unreliable word. Prove trustworthy to every man, even a non-Jew.

131. Do not be indolent in being the first to extend a greeting to everyone, even if he is a non-Jew, in order to preserve the ways of peace.

132. Do not accustom yourself to stand anywhere but near a wise man. Listen and pay attention to his words.

This concludes the code of conduct
arranged by the Rosh z"l

קכד. אַל תְּבַזֶּה אֶת אִשְׁתְּךָ וְכַבֵּד אוֹתָהּ, וּתְסִירֶנָּה מִן הַחֵטְא.

קכה. אַל תְּהִי רָגִיל לֵישֵׁב עִם הַלֵּצִים פְּחִיתֵי הַנֶּפֶשׁ פֶּן יַחֲטִיאוּךָ.

קכו. אַל תִּתְעַצֵּל לְבַקֵּשׁ חָכְמָה, וּלְיַסֵּר אֶת חֲבֵירְךָ בְּסֵתֶר וְדֶרֶךְ כָּבוֹד.

קכז. אַל תְּדַבֵּר בְּלֹא עִתּוֹ וּבְדָבָר שֶׁאֵין בּוֹ תּוֹעֶלֶת, וּשְׁמוֹר פְּתָחֵי פִיךָ.

קכח. אַל תְּדַבֵּר עִם מְהוֹלָל וּמְשׁוּגָּע שֶׁלֹּא יְקַבֵּל דְּבָרֶיךָ וִיבַזֶּה אוֹתָם.

קכט. אַל תְּהִי כְּפוּי טוֹבָה, וְכַבֵּד כָּל מִי שֶׁפָּתַח לְךָ פֶּתַח לְבַקֵּשׁ דֵּי סִיפּוּקֶךָ.

קל. אַל תּוֹצִיא מִפִּיךָ דְּבַר שֶׁקֶר וְכָזָב, וְנֶאֱמָן לְכָל אָדָם וַאֲפִילוּ לְנָכְרִי.

קלא. אַל תִּתְעַצֵּל לְהַקְדִּים שָׁלוֹם לְכָל אָדָם, וַאֲפִילוּ לְנָכְרִי מִפְּנֵי דַּרְכֵי שָׁלוֹם.

קלב. אַל תַּרְגִּיל עַצְמְךָ לַעֲמוֹד, כִּי אִם אֵצֶל חָכָם, וּשְׁמַע וְהַאֲזִין דְּבָרָיו.

סליק הנהגה אשר תיקן הרב רבנו אשר זצ"ל

⚜ The Sabbath ⚜

This is the way of life
to ascend for the wise man,
in order that he turn away from the abyss below.

1. One should set aside a tenth of all profit that Hashem, Exalted be He, brings to his hand, [and spend the tenth for charity and other *mitzvos*].

2. One should give what he can to charity immediately; and at the end of each month and each year, one-and-a-half gold coins.

3. One should pray with the community every day, evening and morning.

4. One should put on *tefillin* each day.

5. One should place a *mezuzah* on all the gateways of his home that require a *mezuzah*.

6. One should establish fixed times for Torah study.

7. One should be trustworthy in his business dealings and in his speech.

8. One should honor those who study Torah as much as he can.

9. One should reprove his fellow, but not bear a sin on his account [by embarrassing him].

10. One should judge his fellow with a presumption of merit.

11. Every night before retiring, one should forgive everyone who has sinned against him in word.

‏﷽ ליום השבת ﷽

אֹרַח חַיִּים לְמַעְלָה לְמַשְׂכִּיל
לְמַעַן סוּר מִשְּׁאוֹל מָטָּה

א. שֶׁיַּפְרִישׁ מַעֲשֵׂר מִכָּל רֶיוַח שֶׁיָּבִיא ה' יִתְעַלֶּה לְיָדוֹ.

ב. שֶׁיִּתֵּן מִיָּד לִצְדָקָה אֲשֶׁר תַּשִּׂיג יָדוֹ, וְלִבְסוֹף כָּל חֹדֶשׁ וְלִסוֹף כָּל שָׁנָה זָהָב וָחֵצִי.

ג. שֶׁיִּתְפַּלֵּל עֶרֶב וָבוֹקֶר בְּכָל יוֹם עִם הַצִּיבּוּר.

ד. שֶׁיָּנִיחַ תְּפִילִין בְּכָל יוֹם.

ה. שֶׁיִּקְבַּע מְזוּזָה בְּכָל שַׁעֲרֵי בֵּיתוֹ הַמְחוּיָּבִים בִּמְזוּזָה.

ו. שֶׁיִּקְבַּע עִתִּים לַתּוֹרָה.

ז. שֶׁיִּהְיֶה נֶאֱמָן בְּמַשָּׂאוֹ וּבְמַתָּנוֹ וּבְדִבּוּרוֹ.

ח. שֶׁיְּכַבֵּד לוֹמְדֵי תוֹרָה בְּכָל יְכָלְתּוֹ.

ט. שֶׁיּוֹכִיחַ אֶת עֲמִיתוֹ וְלֹא יִשָּׂא עָלָיו חֵטְא.

י. שֶׁיָּדִין אֶת חֲבֵירוֹ לְכַף זְכוּת.

יא. שֶׁיִּמְחוֹל בְּכָל לַיְלָה קוֹדֶם שֶׁיִּלִין לְכָל מִי שֶׁחָטָא לוֹ בִּדְבָרִים.

12. One should try to bring peace between a man and his wife, and between a man and his fellow man.

13. One should alert the members of his household about prayer, washing of the hands, and the blessings over enjoyment (food, drink and aromas).

14. One should make up for the Continual Offering (*Tamid*) each Friday.

15. One should study the weekly Torah portion each week, twice in the Hebrew, once in the Aramaic translation, and with the commentary of *Rashi, z"l.*

16. One should read the "Letter on *Teshuvah*" by Rabbeinu Yonah, during the week in which Rosh Hashanah falls.

17. One should have a third meal every Shabbos after the *Minchah* prayer.

18. One should honor Shabbos, according to the means with which Hashem his God has blessed him.

19. One should set his table every *Motzaei Shabbos* (the evening after Shabbos has departed) and eat, even if only a small amount.

20. One should help his fellow man in every way he may require, whether physically or by speaking with him.

21. One should confess his sins each night before going to sleep, except for the nights when it is forbidden to eulogize or to fast, and one should grieve over his sins, the length of our exile, and the destruction of our sacred and glorious Temple, may it be built quickly in our days.

יב. שֶׁיִּשְׁתַּדֵּל לְהַכְנִיס שָׁלוֹם בֵּין אִישׁ לְאִשְׁתּוֹ וּבֵין אָדָם לַחֲבֵירוֹ.

יג. שֶׁיַּזְהִיר אֶת בְּנֵי בֵּיתוֹ עַל הַתְּפִילָה וְעַל נְטִילַת יָדַיִם וְעַל בִּרְכַּת הַנֶּהֱנִין.

יד. שֶׁיִּפְרַע הַתָּמִיד בְּכָל שִׁשִּׁי.

טו. שֶׁיִּלְמוֹד הַפָּרָשָׁה בְּכָל שָׁבוּעַ שְׁנַיִם מִקְרָא וְאֶחָד תַּרְגּוּם, וּפֵירַשׁ"י ז"ל.

טז. שֶׁיִּקְרָא אִגֶּרֶת הַתְּשׁוּבָה שֶׁחִיבֵּר רַבֵּינוּ יוֹנָה ז"ל בַּשָּׁבוּעַ שֶׁיָּחוּל רֹאשׁ הַשָּׁנָה לִהְיוֹת בְּתוֹכָהּ.

יז. שֶׁיִּקְבַּע סְעוּדָה שְׁלִישִׁית בְּכָל שַׁבָּת אַחַר מִנְחָה.

יח. שֶׁיְּכַבֵּד אֶת הַשַּׁבָּת כְּבִרְכַּת ה' אֱלֹקָיו אֲשֶׁר נָתַן לוֹ.

יט. שֶׁיַּעֲרוֹךְ שֻׁלְחָן בְּכָל מוֹצָאֵי שַׁבָּת וְיֹאכַל אֲפִילוּ דָּבָר מוּעַט.

כ. שֶׁיְּסַיֵּיעַ לַחֲבֵירוֹ בְּכָל מַה שֶּׁיִּצְטָרֵךְ בְּגוּפוֹ וּבִדְבָרָיו.

כא. שֶׁיִּתְוַדֶּה בְּכָל לַיְלָה קוֹדֶם שֶׁיִּישָׁן מִלְבַד הַלֵּילוֹת שֶׁהֵן אֲסוּרוֹת בְּהֶסְפֵּד וּבְתַעֲנִית וְיִתְאַבֵּל עַל עֲווֹנוֹתָיו וְעַל אוֹרֶךְ גָּלוּתֵנוּ וְעַל חוּרְבַּן בֵּית מִקְדָּשֵׁנוּ וְתִפְאַרְתֵּנוּ שֶׁיִּבָּנֶה בִּמְהֵרָה בְּיָמֵנוּ.

22. One should fast one day each month, on a day when the Torah is read; and if he cannot fast, he should give two coins to charity.

23. One should act modestly [away from the public eye], in perfecting his good deeds, for that is the service of Hashem that is most desirable and acceptable before Him.

Conclusion

כב. שֶׁיַּעֲשֶׂה יוֹם אֶחָד תַּעֲנִית בְּכָל חֹדֶשׁ בְּיוֹם שֶׁקּוֹרִין בַּתּוֹרָה וְאִם לֹא יָכוֹל לְהִתְעַנּוֹת שֶׁיִּתֵּן שְׁנֵי פְּשִׁיטִין לִצְדָקָה.

כג. שֶׁיְּקַיֵּים בְּהַצְנֵעַ לְכַלְכֵּל מַעֲשָׂיו הַטּוֹבִים כִּי הוּא עֲבוֹדַת ה׳ יִתְבָּרַךְ הַנִּבְחֶרֶת וְהָרְצוּיָה לְפָנָיו.

סְלִיק סְלִיק סְלִיק

וְאֵלֶּה הַדְּבָרִים שֶׁיִּזָּהֵר בָּהֶם
לָסוּר מִמּוֹקְשֵׁי מָוֶת
וְלֵאוֹר בְּאוֹר הַחַיִּים

These are the matters
that a man should beware of,
so that he may veer away
from the snares of death
and be illuminated
with the light of life.

❧ Sunday ❧

1

לְהִתְרַחֵק מִן הַגַּאֲוָה בְּתַכְלִית הָרִיחוּק.
To remove oneself as far as possible from pride.

◦§ If the *Beis HaTalmud* [our *yeshivah*] had been established solely to study the *Orchos Chaim* in depth, that would have been enough of a reason.

On the first day of each week we say the first paragraph: "To remove oneself as far as possible from pride." Let me give an illustration which can show us how great man's obligation is to accustom himself to putting distance between himself and pride. In the blessing following the *Shema* we find: "He casts down the haughty and raises the lowly (מַשְׁפִּיל גֵּאִים וּמַגְבִּיהַּ שְׁפָלִים)." Let us picture the speed of electricity through which the telegraph system operates. It races thousands of miles in an instant. That is its normal speed. Who knows its rate if its power were to be increased?

In a similar fashion, so to speak, the Blessed One casts down the haughty with a powerful thrust.. How far, then, will the proud person fall in a single instant — and that, for but a single moment of pride! That should tell us something about the depth of the fall of one who feels pride for an entire day, let alone for several days. Let that teach us to stay away from honor, too, which is a branch of pride.

From the above example, one can see the force of an illustration. Using a metaphorical illustration, one can more clearly visualize the depth of the concept of eternity.

You, too, will learn how to value the study of *Orchos Chaim*, and great benefit will come to you from that.

(*Orach Yesharim*: R' Simchah Zissel of Kelm, *HaSefer HaKatan*)

◄§ The *Rosh* opened his prescriptions with the need "to remove oneself as far as possible from pride," because pride is the root and basis for all the evil ethical values. By negating feelings of pride, one gains all virtues. Pride, which is the great source of all that is impure, contains all the corrupting qualities of evil. That is why we should avoid it as much as we can.

R' Simchah Zissel of Kelm would say that just as the student who studies the laws of *treifos* (the defects in animals that make meat non-kosher) will not benefit from his learning, if he doesn't get to see the lungs and the other (animal) organs; similarly, one who learns about "the *treifos* (non-kosher defects) of the human heart" — about pride — and becomes more and more aware of the shame involved in being haughty will not gain anything from all this, if he does not know what pride is, or its extent and true reality. It is quite possible that he is haughty and thinks he is humble. In that case, what benefit does he have from learning that pride is shameful?

(Or Yechezkel: Reshimos Talmidim)

◄§ The Torah, when speaking about the Jewish king, teaches, "so that his heart not be lifted up above his brothers" *(Devarim* 17:20). According to Rabbeinu Yonah, this verse tells us to remove feelings of pride from our souls, and the greater man should not be arrogant towards the lesser *(Sha'arei Teshuvah* III, 34). That is the first prescription of the *Rosh*: "to remove oneself as far as possible from pride." Even a great man should not feel that he is any more than a lesser man. He should have no feeling of superiority at all. And if one knows that he has not labored to uproot pride, he can be certain that it increases within him. The prescription is "to remove (it) from our souls," and if we do not feel the presence of pride, that is one of the sure signs that it is on the increase within us.

(Or Yechezkel: Kovetz Inyanim, Elul 5727)

◄§ We find the topic of pride many times in the *Orchos Chaim* of the *Rosh*. He admonishes us about it and opens the work with: "to remove oneself as far as possible from pride."

According to the division made by the *Tosafos Yom-Tov* (who divided *Orchos Chaim* into seven parts, each to be read one day of the week), we find the issue of pride and honor discussed almost every day of the week. In the section of the second day: "Stay far from pride and anger" (paragraph 27); of the third day: "Take care not to rely on your heart" (paragraph 47); of the fourth day: "Do not be arrogant towards people" (paragraph 66); of the fifth day: "Do not pursue honor" (paragraph 88); "Do not let people honor you" (paragraph 89); "Do not give yourself [airs of] grandeur" (paragraph 99); of the sixth day: "Do not think to triumph over a wise man" (paragraph 106).

For it is a fundamental principle that the matters which are of chief interest to a man are pride and honor, as opposed to humility and modesty. These are the two concerns which direct a man to good or bad. They are the foundation of man and his greatest impediment.

The prophet has said: "Thus says Hashem, 'The heavens are My seat and the earth My footstool. What house can you build for Me and where can My resting place be? — And to this I will look [this means an in-depth look, to contemplate the fulfillment of the purpose of Creation]: to the poor man, the lowly, and to him who is concerned about My Word'" (Yeshayahu 66:1-2). "The poor man" refers to modesty; "the lowly" refers to humility. They are the keys and basis for being "concerned about My Word."

Chazal have said that the statement in our verse, "who is concerned about My Word," refers to the Torah scholars, who are engaged in learning. It is only through the study of Torah that a man is cured of the vice of pride. As long as a man feels the "I," he is unable to reach the level of being "concerned about My Word." Thus, the Rosh teaches us, "The path of life leads upwards for the wise" (Mishlei 15:24): first, "to remove oneself as far as possible from pride." Throughout the Orchos Chaim he teaches us the principles of man's life in his world — virtues, clinging to Hashem, prayer, etc. But first and foremost is the need to stay extremely far from pride, for when a man is haughty he cannot attain anything. The first blossoming and ascent, "life leads upwards for the wise," is modesty and humility. That is why he directs us to them so often.

This fits with Chazal's comment on the verse: "Because of modesty there is fear of Hashem" (Mishlei 22:4). The word for "because of" is עֵקֶב (ekev), which also means "heel." Chazal connect this with another verse: "The beginning of wisdom is fear of Hashem" (Tehillim 111:10) (see Tanchuma Bereishis 1). Here, the word for "beginning" (רֵאשִׁית, reishis) is based on the same root as the word for "head" (רֹאשׁ, rosh). Thus, Chazal comment: "What wisdom has taken as its crown (i.e. fear of Hashem), modesty has taken as the heel of her foot." Indeed, "the beginning of wisdom is fear of Hashem," while modesty is the key to all the ways of life.

(Orach Yesharim: R' Yosef Shlomo Kahaneman, Rav of Ponevezh)

৶ The Rosh begins with pride and mentions anger only in paragraph 6.

So, too, when he speaks of keeping pride and anger at a distance (paragraph 27), he speaks of pride before speaking of anger. Yet, later on (paragraphs 62-65), anger is given precedence to pride. Perhaps one might say that here, in the earlier paragraphs, the *Rosh* speaks of putting distance between oneself and evil. And on this point, one should stay completely away from pride, more so than from anger.

The *Rambam* writes, regarding anger: "one should only become angry for a great matter over which it is fitting to be angry" (*Hilchos De'os* 1:4). But concerning pride [he mentions no circumstances at all in which it is proper to be proud], he writes that one should distance oneself from it to the farthest extreme!

The *Orchos Tzaddikim*, in his preface to his First Gate, writes of pride: "For it is the door to many evils and we have not seen anything like it in any of the moral failings."

[Thus, when he speaks of distancing ourselves from bad traits, the *Rosh* places pride first.]

In the later precepts, perhaps the *Rosh* is instructing us how to correct ourselves, and tells us to correct the tendency towards anger before we eradicate pride. For as the *Orchos Tzaddikim* has written in his Gate of Anger: "Anger is close to pride, and the angry man cannot escape pride." Thus, one must eradicate the tendency towards wrath as a prelude to correcting his fault of pride.

Similarly, my teacher, R' Avrohom Gurowicz, directed me to the comment in the *Letter of the Ramban*: "When you free yourself from anger, then modesty, which is the best of all virtues, will rise in your heart." (See further *Rambam*, beginning of *Hilchos De'os*, and the *Even HaEzel* there.)   (*Orach Yesharim*)

&§ Essentially, removing oneself from pride involves not considering *oneself* important. Even if one knows that he has important attributes (a quick grasp of matters or a good memory, for example), he should see them as gifts from Heaven. He should view himself like a bird who soars above the other birds. There is no reason for the bird to feel arrogant; it is only an element of nature, as the *Mesilas Yesharim* has written. He should be firm in his belief in Divine Providence and know that everything comes from Hashem, and therefore there is no reason to be proud. Furthermore, he should think constantly of his failings and that he has nothing about which to be proud. Basically, when the *Rosh* speaks of removing oneself from pride, he refers to one's thoughts.

(*Orach Yesharim*: Citing an anonymous scholar)

2

וְכֵן מִן הַחֲנִיפוּת.
And so, too, from flattery.

⋆§ The *Rosh* should have continued, it would seem, after speaking of pride, to discuss those things that lead to anger. Why did he choose to write about flattery, which is contrary to pride and anger? Perhaps he wishes to say that even if one avoids pride in the extreme, he should not fall into flattery and falsehood because of that. So, too, scoffing (paragraph 4) and talebearing (paragraph 5) result at times when a man wishes to avoid pride. That is why the *Rosh* immediately admonishes us on flattery, scoffing and talebearing.

But one can also note, to the contrary, a direct tie between pride and flattery. Because a man wants honor, he may indulge in flattery to achieve it. But the modest and humble man who does not seek honor will not be given to flattery. *(Or Yechezkel:* Main Disciples)

3

וְכֵן מִן הַשֶּׁקֶר וְהַכָּזָב.
And so, too, from falsehood and deceit.

⋆§ There are two kinds of lies — falsehood (שֶׁקֶר) and deceit (כָּזָב). Falsehood is that which was a lie from the outset, but deceit means that a person truly intended to do something at first, yet changed his mind.(Gaon of Vilna to *Mishlei* 12:22)

⋆§ Man has a knack for falsehood and a love for it. He does not feel that he is speaking falsely. He takes pleasure from it. The *Mesilas Yesharim* speaks of the sect of liars: "There are men whose trade is really falsehood. They think up total lies" (Chapter 11).

For man is all lies; he speak vanities with his mouth. How frightening, if a man does not think about what he says and does, and never attains the truth as it really is, and never assimilates the truth that: "Hashem is Elokim and there is nothing except Him!" (*Devarim* 4:35).

(*Or Yechezkel, Iggeres* 255)

4

וְכֵן מִן הַלֵּיצָנוּת.
And so, too, from scoffing.

◄§ Scoffing (לֵיצָנוּת) is that which involves not recognizing the truth. We find it spelled out by Rabbeinu Yonah: Scoffers are those who do not recognize the importance of Torah. And R' Yisrael Salanter writes that whoever does not learn *mussar* scoffs at the fear of Hashem, for he does not grant importance to the concept of Fear of Heaven.

(*Or Yechezkel, Iggeres* 255)

5

וְכֵן מִן הָרְכִילוּת.
And so, too, from talebearing.

◄§ The *Tosafos Yom-Tov* indicates that the *Rosh* is concerned here about talebearing (רְכִילוּת, *rechilus*), not harmful gossip (לָשׁוֹן הָרָע, *lashon hara*). For there is a specific paragraph below (10) in which the *Rosh* states that one should not speak or accept harmful gossip. [Malicious talk (*lashon hara*) means relaying harmful information about someone, even if it is true. Talebearing (*rechilus*) means telling someone that someone else spoke badly about him.]

Indeed, there is an implied distinction between talebearing and harmful gossip, for following the reading of the *Tosafos Yom-Tov*, it seems that the phrase "to remove oneself as far as possible" (paragraph 1) refers to all of the faults down to paragraph 7. One is then to avoid talebearing in the extreme but we are not admonished to avoid malicious talk in the same measure.

To the *Rambam*, harmful gossip (*lashon hara*) is a worse transgression than is talebearing (*rechilus*), but the *Raavad* disagrees and views talebearing as being worse. That, says the *Raavad*, is why talebearing is said to "slay three," but malicious talk slays only the speaker himself (see *Rambam, Hilchos De'os* 7:2 and the *Raavad* there).

Perhaps when the *Rosh* says that one should avoid talebearing in the extreme, he means that one should avoid it even when he does not intend that the person hearing the story should feel enmity towards the party about whom they spoke. That, too, is forbidden (see *Chofetz Chaim, Issur Rechilus* 1:3). Yet, why does he not say that harmful gossip (*lashon hara*) should be avoided in the extreme, also? This matter requires more study. (*Orach Yesharim*)

6

וְכֵן מִן הַכַּעַס.
And so, too, from anger.

⇜§ How does one correct moral faults?

Aside from the principal remedy provided by the study of *mussar*, guidance and logical strategies are useful. R' Yisrael Salanter gave, for example, the following as a cure for anger. One should constantly pay attention to being a good individual, to do good to one and all. This will make it easier to refrain from wrath.

(*Orach Yesharim*: R' Naftali of Amsterdam, *Or HaMussar I*, 76)

⇜§ This [paragraph about anger] should have been written, it would seem, immediately after the prescription to remove oneself as far as possible from pride, just as pride and anger are juxtaposed in paragraph 27. But the intention of the *Rosh* is to tell us that in order to avoid anger we must first correct ourselves with regard to flattery, falsehood and so forth. Only then can we speak of being careful about anger.

(*Or Yechezkel*: Main Disciples)

7-8

שֶׁיִּזָּהֵר מִמִּכְשׁוֹל הַנְּדָרִים, וּמֵאוֹנָאוֹת הַבְּרִיּוֹת,
הֵן בְּמָמוֹן הֵן בִּדְבָרִים. וּמִקִּנְאָתָם וּמִשִּׂנְאָתָם.

One should take care to avoid the trap of vows
and the deception of others,whether with money
or words. And one should take care to avoid
their envy and their hatred.

TOSAFOS YOM TOV
One should take care not to fall into the sin of vows; that is, one should
not vow to do something or not to do something. One should also take
care not to cause people to be deceived, either financially or verbally. And
one should be careful that people do not envy him; for one of those [who
envy him] is liable to become his enemy.

◆§ *One should take care to avoid the trap of vows and the deception of
others . . .*

Accepted tradition has it that the paragraph division was made by the
Rosh himself. If this is so, why did he run paragraphs seven and eight
together? Furthermore, since the main topic here [at the beginning of
Orchos Chaim] is matters between man and his fellow-man, why did
he introduce "the trap of vows," which concerns the relationship
between man and God?

The fact that these two paragraphs come together as one comes to
teach us that we are dealing with a single issue in paragraphs 7 and 8.
The *mitzvos* between man and his fellow man are not prescribed just to
promote the harmony of nations and peace among men. We are to
perform them because He in His wisdom has so decreed, and in their
performance we will be drawn closer to Him. Besides, the *mitzvos* which
refer to the dealings of man towards his fellow man are a ladder by
which we reach the *mitzvos* between man and God. *Chazal* have said
this, more or less (*Mishnas R' Eliezer*): "One who denies the good which
another has done for him will tomorrow deny the good his Creator has
granted."

Whoever is correct in his dealings with his fellow man will easily be correct in his God-related concerns; whoever is honest and careful in fulfilling promises to another will easily fulfill his vows or those resolutions which he takes upon himself in his suffering or on Yom Kippur. But he who is a liar in human affairs and cheats others will also act that way towards Heaven, for he has no misgivings about cheating.

(*Orach Yesharim*: R' Simchah Zissel of Kelm)

⋘ R' Simchah Zissel of Kelm asked what connection there is between "the trap of vows" and "deception of others." From the fact that the *Rosh* combined them, it would seem that they share a common force. This force is falsehood. If a man makes vows which he does not fulfill, this stems from the force of falsehood; and if he lies to himself, he will lie to others. R' Simchah Zissel gave the following example: If one who is making a vow declares that his is "like the vows which the wicked make," his vow is valid. Not so if he takes upon himself a vow "like the vows which the righteous make," for righteous persons do not vow, whereas the wicked man does not cease vowing (see *Nedarim* 9). The righteous man is so frightened of sin that he will not sanctify an animal until he has actually brought it to the threshold of the *Beis HaMikdash*. Only then is he certain that he will be able to give it as an offering. That is the force of the attribute of truth.

(*Orach Yesharim*: R' Abba Grossbard)

⋘ Many have noted the break in the flow of the *Orchos Chaim* caused by the introduction of "the trap of vows." These are matters of man-God relations, between prescriptions, both before and after, which concern man's relations to his fellow man. I think that the *Rosh* has indicated an important point by this placement. He wishes to tell us that it is impossible for a person to turn away from the sins that he habitually and thoughtlessly commits unless he puts up barriers to avoid the sin, as *Chazal* have said: "Vows are a safeguard for abstinence (פְּרִישׁוּת)." If this is so, one must, of necessity, implant the fear of "the trap of vows" first, and then, [once he has the proper respect for the seriousness of vows,] he will be able to guard himself against all the faults upon which he has thoughtlessly trodden, as it is written: "I have sworn [i.e. vowed] and I will fulfill it, to keep the laws of Your righteousness" (*Tehillim* 119:106).

(*Orach Yesharim*: R' Avraham Yaffen,
HaMussar V'HaDa'as, Elul p. 45)

⋘ *To avoid the trap of vows . . .*

The *Tosafos Yom-Tov* in his commentary says that one should not vow to do or not do something. He seems to say that one should not make any vows at all. But the *Rosh* writes later that one should not "acquire the habit" of making vows (paragraph 114). The *Shulchan Aruch*, too, opens the section on vows with the injunction, "Do not acquire the habit of making vows" (*Yoreh Deah* 203:1). Yet, in paragraph 4 there, the *Shulchan Aruch* himself writes that one should make no vows at all.

The *Bach* explains that even though the Talmud praises vows as being a safeguard to abstinence, this refers only to vows such as: "I will rise early and learn Torah" (which is a vow for a *mitzvah*). Even with these, the praiseworthy type of vows, one should not be prone to make too many. [But regarding other kinds of vows, one should not make any at all.] (*Tur, Yoreh Deah* 203)

This can also be applied to explain the seeming contradiction in *Orchos Chaim*. (*Orach Yesharim*)

ᴈ§ *To avoid their envy and their hatred.*

He has grouped envy and hatred together, because they are traits which are embedded only in the human soul; they are not to be found in the make-up of other creatures.

Envy is at times proper — envy (zealousness) on behalf of Hashem, or the competitive envy of scholars who spur one another on to greater efforts. So, too, hatred is at times fitting; there is an obligation to hate heretics as well as those who incite and lead one to sin.

These forces have been given to man for good or for evil — and they are advantageous when they are used as they should be. That is why the *Rosh* specifies that what is to be avoided is "envy of *them*" and "hatred of *them*." He wishes to point out that one should not be envious of the essential person himself; that would be improper. However, one may feel envy of someone's wisdom and good deeds. The same distinction holds true for hatred. [Though he should hate the evil deeds of the wicked, for example, he is not permitted to hate their essential selves.]

(*Orach Yesharim*: R' Yosef Shlomo Kahaneman, Rav of Ponevezh)

ᴈ§ The *Tosafos Yom-Tov* says that one should take care that men do not envy him because one of them might become an enemy.

This comment of the *Tosafos Yom-Tov* applies to material goods which a man might acquire through his wealth. Others might envy his possessions and come to hate him. True, such hatred runs contrary to the Torah. After all, he has done nothing to the other man to engender his hatred. Besides, he who envies another is a heretic, for he does not believe fully that all comes from the Creator. Nevertheless, he who is the cause of the envy bears the fault of the sin, too.

We see that Rachel was envious of Leah when she gave birth to Yehudah. Leah called him Yehudah to proclaim to all that she thanked Hashem for receiving more than her portion of sons. Nevertheless, [because she caused Rachel's envy,] there was a halt to her having children (*Bereishis* 29:35-30:1). An even more telling example is that of Peninah, the wife of Elkanah (*I Shmuel* 1:4-9). She angered her rival wife, Chanah, for righteous reasons (*Bava Basra* 16a). But because she aroused Chanah's envy, her children died.

When we speak of the non-material, however, there is no reason for one to be concerned with another's envy. On the contrary, envy among Torah scholars increases wisdom. After all, we all have the obligation to engage in the study of Torah. (*Orach Yesharim*)

9

שֶׁלֹּא יְכַנֶּה שֵׁם לַחֲבֵרוֹ, שֶׁלֹּא יִקְרָאֶנּוּ בְּכִינּוּי
שֶׁכִּינּוּהוּ אֲחֵרִים, אִם לֹא יִהְיֶה נִזְכָּר וְנִכְבָּד בִּשְׁמוֹ.

Do not dub someone with a nickname, nor call someone by the nickname that others have given, unless he is known and honored by that name.

◆§ *Do not dub someone with a nickname . . .*

The Talmud says that all those who descend to *Gehinnom* will ascend [from there] except for three [kinds of individuals], who will descend but not rise — he who commits adultery with the wife of another, he who shames another in public and he who calls another by a derisive nickname. It goes on to ask: Since calling one by a nickname is a matter of shaming him, why is it listed separately? The Talmud answers that this refers to a nickname to which he is accustomed — that is, there is no present shame in calling him by that name. Yet, even so, the one who employed the nickname will not rise from *Gehinnom*! (see *Bava Metzia* 58b).

To understand the issue, we should note that the Creator gave a particular name to each thing which He has created, as it is said: "He gives all of them names" (*Tehillim* 147:4). By so doing, He explains the make-up and essence of each thing. He called man Adam (אָדָם) because he was taken from the earth (אֲדָמָה). Each name explains the nature of the existence of the particular thing which bears that name.

∗§ If one calls another by a degrading name, he is imposing on that individual a new definition of his existence. The gravity of the offense lies in removing the image and existential view concerning that man and replacing it with a different one.

He who shames another acts similarly. He removes something from him and blemishes his soul — "for his [normal] color passes and paleness takes its place" (*Bava Metzia* loc. cit.). This is like the nickname, which transforms his previous being and mars the essence of the man. And he who commits adultery with the wife of another does something of the same sort. He compels the Holy One to change the nature of the fetus whose soul the adulterer has marred. Thus, the adulterer has committed a sin worse than that of a murderer, who only blemishes the body.

The common element in all three offenses mentioned by the Talmud is the gravity of the flaw produced on the victim's soul. For this reason, the offenders will not ascend from *Gehinnom*.

With each paragraph, the *Rosh* teaches us the way of life. Here, he tells us not to call another by a nickname which could change the man's state of existence and the true essence by which he is remembered and honored.

(*Orach Yesharim*: R' Yosef Shlomo Kahaneman, Rav of Ponevezh)

∗§ In paragraph 118 the *Rosh* has written: "Do not call another by a derisive nickname. For he who calls another by a [*derisive*] nickname has no portion in the World to Come." Here (in paragraph 9), he has warned against calling another by a nickname. Even if it does not have a negative connotation, one should not give someone any nickname — nor should one make use of a nickname that others are already using (in *Kuntres L'Ma'alah L'Maskil* we conclude that such a practice is even called a death trap).

However, it is only one who calls another by a bad nickname who is punished by not receiving a portion in the World to Come. The phraseology of the Gemara indicates as much: "He who calls another by a derisive nickname" never leaves *Gehinnom* (*Bava Metzia* 58b) — specifically, a derisive name. Nevertheless, a nickname which is not derisive, though it does not cause everlasting descent to *Gehinnom*, is called a death trap. For we find that when his disciples asked R' Yochanan ben Zakkai how he had merited to attain longevity, he replied that he had never called anyone by a nickname (see *Megillah* 27b). This implies that every nickname, even one that is not bad, is a death trap.

(Orach Yesharim)

10

שֶׁלֹּא יְסַפֵּר לְשׁוֹן הָרָע וְשֶׁלֹּא יְקַבְּלוֹ.
One should not engage in harmful gossip nor accept it from others.

TOSAFOS YOM TOV

One should not engage in harmful gossip (*lashon hara*); that is, one should not speak *lashon hara* about anyone. Likewise, one should not accept it; that is, if someone tells us that others have spoken evil about us, we should not accept it as true.

◆§ The Kabbalists have written that each day we should pronounce six statements of remembrance which are the foundation of a Jew. The six statements remind us of the Exodus, of *Shabbos*, etc. Among them is: "Remember what Hashem your God did to Miriam" (*Devarim* 24:9), which is an admonition against engaging in harmful gossip (*lashon hara*). We would, I imagine, have assumed that this involves just one of the 365 [Scriptural] negative prohibitions. Why, then, was it included in the six statements of remembrance, which are basic principles of faith? This shows us that the basis of everything is to imitate Hashem, the source of good and kindness. Harmful gossip, however, is evil; it is the antithesis of the goal of clinging to the good.

(Or Yechezkel: Main Disciples)

11

שֶׁלֹּא יֵשֵׁב עִם יוֹשְׁבֵי קְרָנוֹת,
וְלֹא בִּישִׁיבַת בָּתֵּי כְנֵסִיּוֹת שֶׁל עַמֵּי הָאָרֶץ.

**One should not keep company with idlers,
nor sit in the gatherings of the ignorant.**

TOSAFOS YOM TOV
One should not keep company with those who spend their time idly. And one should not take part in gatherings of the ignorant [those who know nothing of Torah study].

12

שֶׁלֹּא יִסְתַּכֵּל בְּאִשָּׁה שֶׁהִיא אֲסוּרָה לוֹ.

**One should not gaze at a woman
who is forbidden to him.**

◆§ In paragraph 40 the *Rosh* warns further: "Take care not to gaze at a woman, even an unmarried one." He emphasizes the point: "even an unmarried one," whereas here he writes: "at a woman who is forbidden to him."

L'Ma'alah L'Maskil points out that paragraph 40 lists that which one should guard against because of the precept: "You shall be holy to your God" (*Bamidbar* 15:40). Here, however, he admonishes us about those things we should guard against: "to turn away from death traps" (*Mishlei* 13:14). It is only when the woman is "not permitted to marry" that we speak of a death trap. (*Orach Yesharim*)

13

שֶׁלֹּא יָסִיחַ עַל כּוֹס שֶׁל בְּרָכָה.
One should not speak over the "cup of blessing."

> **TOSAFOS YOM TOV**
> Neither the one who leads Birkas HaMazon nor the participants should speak from the beginning of Birkas HaMazon until he has drunk the cup of wine over which he has recited Birkas HaMazon.

◆§ Man is made up of body and soul. The soul is a portion of the supernal God. And in the war between body and soul, man, that creature of flesh and blood, can only be victorious through the study of Torah and the performance of its *mitzvos*, which sanctify him. The purpose of man's eating is to allow him to live and to engage in perfecting his powers of choice for the virtues of Torah and *mitzvos*. That is what is meant by: "to cultivate [the garden] and guard it" (*Bereishis* 2:15).

When a man eats he is partaking, as it were, in the service of the *Beis HaMikdash* as is hinted in the verse: "This is the table which is before Hashem" (*Yechezkel* 41:22), which *Chazal* say alludes to a person's own table (see *Berachos* 55a). Before he eats, he must wash his hands, just as the *Kohen* does before his service. And when he pronounces the Grace after Meals (*Birkas HaMazon*), he is required to have a cup of wine over which he will say a blessing, including the name of Hashem and a reference to His Kingship.

There are ten factors which are optimally present so that this cup be considered a "cup of blessing." Their presence is a sign of respect for the cup. Among them is the condition that the one who holds the cup should be properly dressed. This is comparable to the garments of the *Kohen* which are required for his service in the *Beis HaMikdash*.

When a man eats in a sanctified way, in accordance with the *halachos* mentioned, having properly prepared his body for service to Hashem, it is as if he is bringing a sacrifice before Hashem. That is what is meant by: "the path of life leads upwards for the wise" (*Mishlei* 15:24). He grows and rises in sanctity to the level of the perfect man. This is what the *Rosh* meant in writing: "One should not speak... until he has drunk from the cup." For the cup of blessing is to be seen only as a means to rise and ascend in service of Hashem, on the path of life that "leads upwards for the wise."

(*Orach Yesharim*: R' Yosef Shlomo Kahaneman, Rav of Ponevezh)

14

שֶׁלֹּא יְסַפֵּר מִשֶּׁיַּתְחִיל בָּרוּךְ שֶׁאָמַר עַד שֶׁיְּסַיֵּים תְּפִלּוֹת לַחַשׁ, וְלֹא בְּעוֹד שֶׁשָּׁלִיחַ צִבּוּר חוֹזֵר וּמִתְפַּלֵּל הַתְּפִלָּה, אֶלָּא אִם כֵּן בְּדִבְרֵי תּוֹרָה, אוֹ בִּדְבַר מִצְוָה אוֹ לָתֵת שָׁלוֹם וּלְהַחֲזִיר שָׁלוֹם.

One should not speak from when he begins
***Baruch She'amar* until after he has finished**
the silent *Shemoneh Esrei*, nor while
the *shaliach tzibbur* (prayer-leader)
is repeating the *Shemoneh Esrei* aloud,
unless he must [do one of the following:]
speak words of Torah; perform a *mitzvah;* or
greet someone or return someone's greeting.

TOSAFOS YOM TOV
One should take care not to speak from the time he begins *Baruch She'amar* until after he finishes the *Shemoneh Esrei* including the additional supplications [the ones beginning אֱלֹקַי נְצוֹר לְשׁוֹנִי מֵרָע, "My God, guard my tongue from evil"], nor while the prayer-leader (*shaliach tzibbur*) is repeating the *Shemoneh Esrei* aloud — unless one must [do one of the following:] render a halachic ruling; perform an urgent *mitzvah* that cannot be performed later; greet someone, or return someone's greeting.

⋅§ One should not speak from when he begins Baruch She'amar.
A pious man met Eliyahu. He was loading three hundred camels with punishments. "For whom are these?" he asked. Eliyahu replied: "For the one who talks between *Baruch She'amar* and the end of *Shemoneh Esrei*." (*Orchos Yisrael* citing the *Pesikta*)

◆§ They should not speak from the start of *Baruch She'amar* until after the prayer. Then it will be received [by Heaven]. Otherwise: "Who required this of your hands, to trample My courtyards?" (*Yeshayahu* 1:12).
(*Orach Yesharim*: Responsa of R' Yehudah the son of the *Rosh*, no. 91)

◆§ Do not look outside of the prayerbook from *Baruch She'amar* until after *Shemoneh Esrei*, so that nothing might divert your attention, and so that you gain full and perfect tranquility of soul.
(*Orach Yesharim: Reshimos Talmidim*, from the Regulations Instituted by R' Eliahu Lopian)

◆§ One who gets into the habit of listening attentively and calmly to the prayer-leader's repetition of the *Shemoneh Esrei* acquires thereby, many virtues. Among them is the habit of concentration of the mind, which is altogether impossible to attain except in this way. He also learns to be submissive and not follow his every urge. Moreover, this will teach him to be patient and humble, for pride prevents patience.
(*Or Yechezkel: Reshimos Talmidim*)

◆§ The *Rosh* has placed "not speaking between *Baruch She'amar* and *Shemoneh Esrei*" in the same paragraph as the prescription against speaking during the repetition of the *Shemoneh Esrei*. Indeed, it is not a hardship to be silent during *Pesukei D'zimrah*. Everyone is silent then. But people are not careful about not speaking during the prayer-leader's repetition of the *Shemoneh Esrei*; it seems extremely difficult.
But the truth of the matter is that the difference has arisen only because of habit. We have become accustomed, from childhood on, to remain silent during *Pesukei D'zimrah*; it is a matter of second nature after a while. This should teach us how everything depends on habit.
(*Orach Yesharim*)

15

שֶׁלֹּא יְדַבֵּר בִּקְרִיאַת הַהַלֵּל,
וְלֹא בְּעוֹד שֶׁשְּׁלִיחַ צִבּוּר קוֹרֵא בַּתּוֹרָה.

One should not speak during
the recitation of *Hallel,* nor while the reader
is reciting the public Torah-reading.

16

שֶׁלֹּא יֹאכַל פַּת בַּעֲלֵי בָתִּים שֶׁל כּוּתִים וְלֹא שֶׁל
פַּלְטָר, אֶלָּא אִם כֵּן לֹא יִזְדַּמֵּן לוֹ שֶׁל יִשְׂרָאֵל.

One should not eat bread that was baked by non-
Jewish homemakers or commercial bakeries, unless bread baked by Jews is not available to him.

17

שֶׁלֹּא יִסְעוֹד בִּסְעוּדַת הָרְשׁוּת.

(וּכְפִי מַה שֶּׁכָּתוּב עוֹד לְהַלָּן בְּסִי׳ קכא)

One should not partake of an optional meal
(as described below in paragraph 121).

18

שֶׁלֹּא יָשִׂיחַ שִׂיחָה בְּטֵלָה. וְיִזָּהֵר לִלְמוֹד בַּלַּיְלָה
עַד שֶׁיִּישָׁן מִתּוֹךְ דִּבְרֵי תּוֹרָה,
וְלֹא מִתּוֹךְ שִׂיחָה בְּטֵלָה.

One should not engage in idle conversation.
Take care to study Torah at night
until one falls asleep during words
of Torah, not idle conversation.

TOSAFOS YOM TOV
One should take care not to engage in idle conversation, even on matters
not involving sin. He should also take care to study Torah at night, until the
study causes him to become tired and makes him sleep, so that he goes
to sleep at a time when he is in the midst of speaking Torah, and not idle
conversation.

᪐ *One should not engage in idle conversation . . .*

If one learns Torah just before sleeping, his sleep will be sweet. The words of Torah will flourish and grow throughout the night, for everything depends on what comes just before it (סָמוּךְ), and the success of any act depends on its beginning, its consistency and its closing.

(*Orach Yesharim*: R' Yerucham Levovitz, *Da'as U'Mussar II*, p. 153)

᪐ Idle talk is the most difficult thing to avoid. The Talmud (*Bava Basra* 165a) states that the majority of people steal, a minority indulge in forbidden relations, but everyone violates the Rabbinic laws against malignant gossip (*avak lashon hara*). Even though not everyone is ensnared by malignant gossip itself [i.e. on the spiritual level], all fall into the trap of that which has an air of forbidden talk [i.e. on the Rabbinic level].

The *Rosh* in the *Orchos Chaim* puts much stress on the matter of speech, because speech comes from the power of man's soul, his "speaking spirit" (רוּחַ מְמַלְּלָא).[1]

The *Rosh's* statement that "One should not engage in idle conversation" is based on the Gemara: "And you shall speak of them [Hashem's commandments]" (*Devarim* 6:7). *Chazal* tell us this means that we are permitted to speak "of them," but not of idle matters (*Yoma* 19b). And the Talmud says: "What is man's craft (אוּמָנוּת) in this world? He should conduct himself as if he were mute" (*Chullin* 89a). That is truly a craft, to accustom oneself to be silent, for speech comes very easily.

The deaf-mute is grouped [for certain halachic purposes] with the mentally incompetent and the child, because he lacks the "speaking spirit." Idle talk is a very serious fault because when thus engaged, man employs the highest power within himself in a fruitless fashion, whereas he is obliged to use speech only in matters of Torah and wisdom, as the Gemara says: "Perhaps, we should not speak even in matters of Torah? [There is a position taken at first that silence is preferable even to a discussion involving Torah.] Therefore, Scripture needs to tell us: 'Speak righteously' " (*Tehillim* 58:2) (*Chullin* loc. cit.).

(*Orach Yesharim*: R' Yosef Shlomo Kahaneman, Rav of Ponevezh)

---

1. *Onkelos* translates the verse which speaks of the creation of man as follows: "And He breathed into his nostrils a soul of life and it became in man a speaking spirit (רוּחַ מְמַלְּלָא) — *Bereishis* 2:7.

19

שֶׁלֹּא יַכְנִיס עַצְמוֹ בְּסָפֵק חֲשֵׁכָה. וְיַזְהִיר בְּנֵי בֵּיתוֹ
עַל שְׁמִירַת שַׁבָּת, וְיַקְדִּים לְהִתְפַּלֵּל עֶרֶב שַׁבָּת
תְּפִלַּת מִנְחָה כְּדֵי שֶׁיְּקַבֵּל עָלָיו הַשַּׁבָּת מִבְּעוֹד יוֹם.

One should not put himself in the position of
doubt as to whether Friday night has arrived. And
he should caution his family concerning Shabbos
observance. He should recite the Friday *Minchah*
prayer early, in order to accept the Shabbos
[upon himself] while it is still day.

20

כְּשֶׁיַּגִּיעַ עֵת תְּפִילָה מִשָּׁלֹשׁ תְּפִלּוֹת שֶׁבַּיּוֹם,
יַנִּיחַ כָּל עֲסָקָיו וְיִתְפַּלֵּל. וְרֹאשׁ כָּל הַדְּבָרִים
שֶׁיִּשְׁמֹר אֶת עֵינָיו מִכָּל דָּבָר שֶׁאֵינוֹ שֶׁלּוֹ.

When the appointed time for any of
the three daily prayers arrives,
one should put aside all his concerns and pray.
Above all else, one should prevent his eyes
from looking at whatever is not his.

ـ§ *When the appointed time for any of the three daily prayers arrives,
one should put aside all his concerns and pray.*

Let this moment be the focus of his time and its result. All other inter-
vals of time should be like roads which lead up to it. He should strongly
anticipate this time, for then he is likened to the spiritual forces and puts
himself at a distance from the animal instincts. The consequence of his
day and night should be the three times designated for prayer.

This program is to the soul as eating is to the body; one prays for the soul and eats for the body. The force of the blessings of prayer continues to have effect upon him until the next prayer, just as the daytime meal sustains him until he eats in the evening. The longer the soul is distanced from the moment of prayer by its contact with the ways of the world, the more downcast it becomes. With the moment of prayer, one purifies his soul from all that came before and prepares it for the future, so that not a week of such a program goes by without one improving himself, body and soul. (*Orach Yesharim: Kuzari* 3:5)

◆§ *Above all else, one should prevent his eyes from looking at whatever is not his.*

[Why is this admonition combined with the one about prayer?] I see the association of prescriptions as follows: Prayer is a matter of the internal higher workings of man (פְּנִימִיּוּת). He must free himself, then, of all the outer considerations (חִיצוֹנִיּוּת) and set aside all his occupations. But that is difficult; the desire for wealth and pleasures burns within his heart. Hence, he is enjoined to "guard his eyes from looking at whatever is not his" and thus not foster the desire in his heart.

The source of the *Rosh* seems to be: "Do not allow your eyes [to stare] at money that is not yours, for they cause the gates of Heaven to sink" (*Derech Eretz Zuta* 4). Eyes which look at and desire other people's money cause the gates of Heaven to sink; they do not allow his prayers to be accepted. It is not only the actual bodily pleasure which blocks the rise of prayer; even an attachment to the means of attaining such pleasure — money — obstructs its path.

(*Orach Yesharim: R' Alei Shur, Sha'ar* 3, *Ma'arachah* 2, Chapter 4)

◆§ The *Rosh* has joined the prescription to put aside all our concerns when praying, with the injunction to guard our eyes from looking at whatever is not ours.

When a person is involved in his business affairs and the like, he finds it difficult to forget everything and begin the prayer. The *Ramban* in his *Iggeres* has written, "Purify your thoughts" during prayer. That is, one should try not to think about other matters while praying. It has been suggested that prior to prayer one should sit and learn Torah.

The *Rosh* has further written that one should not look at that which is not his. This also includes schooling himself to feel that he has no rights to that which is not his. He should realize that the time of prayer does not belong to him, and then his mind will not rest on other matters during prayer, for that time is not his. (*Orach Yesharim*)

≈§ It is known that the *Rosh* wrote the *Orchos Chaim* for himself. This shows his great fear of Hashem. He feared looking at an object that was not his, lest it cause him to be envious and this would confuse his prayers. That is why he joined the two topics here.

(*Or Yechezkel: Reshimos Talmidim*)

≈§ The *Rosh* wishes to indicate that even if one sets aside all his thoughts and all that he is doing, nevertheless, when he wishes to pray the silent *Shemoneh Esrei*, it is quite easy to have stray thoughts about what he saw in passing and about things which he generally does not see. Such is the nature of the mind when the body is at rest. Because of this, the *Rosh* admonishes us to guard our eyes completely from looking at whatever is not ours, so that we do not start to think about such things during the silent prayers. (*Orach Yesharim*)

21

אַל יְדַבֵּר בֵּין נְטִילַת יָדַיִם לְבִרְכַּת הַמּוֹצִיא. וְיַקְדִּים שָׁלוֹם לְכָל אָדָם.

One should not speak between the washing of hands [for a meal] and the blessing of *hamotzi* [over bread]. And one should be the first to greet whomever he meets.

≈§ The *Rosh* would seem to imply here that we should not keep silent between the washing of one's hands for a meal and pronouncing the blessing over the bread, if we have occasion to greet someone.

The *M'kor Chaim* notes that the *Rosh* is consistent with his own ruling in this matter. The *Tur*, the *Rosh's* son, in commenting about his father's practice, would seem to imply that the prohibition against talking between the washing of one's hands and reciting the blessing over bread is a matter of voluntary strictness (חוּמְרָא) which is not required by the letter of the law (see *Tur, Orach Chaim* 166). It would then not apply when one is faced with the *mitzvah* of being first to greet someone.[1] (*Orach Yesharim*)

---

1. The *mitzvah* here is that whenever we meet someone (e.g. in passing on the street,) or when one comes to our home, we should greet him even before he greets us (see *Avos* 4:15).

22

לְבָרֵךְ אֶת בּוֹרְאוֹ שֶׁהִשְׂבִּיעַ נֶפֶשׁ שׁוֹקֵקָה.
וְאִם יְקַלְלוּהוּ בְּנֵי אָדָם אוֹ יְחָרְפוּהוּ,
אַל יָשִׁיב לָהֶם דָּבָר אֶלָּא יְהֵא מִן הַנֶּעֱלָבִים.

One should bless his Creator, Who has satisfied
his craving soul. And should others curse
or vilify him, he should not answer them at all,
but should be among those who are insulted
[but do not insult others].

∾ *One should bless his Creator ... And should others curse or vilify him ...*

What does the *Rosh* mean to say by placing "and should others curse or shame him" in the prescription on blessing his Creator?

Just as eating and its blessings involve physical satiety, so too, man's soul craves spiritual satiety. This paragraph has reference also to the satisfaction of the spirit. A person should wish to ascend to the highest rung and fulfill the soul's desire not to be aware of the body. Thus, his trials may increase because of this, as *Chazal* have said (*Succah* 52a), "The greater a man is, the greater is his Evil Inclination" [in other words, the higher a man's strivings, the greater the obstacles, both inner and outer, that are placed in his way]. Nevertheless, if he is cursed and insulted — things that cause him to falter and be held back — he should not reply to his revilers, but should choose instead to be among those who are shamed and pay no attention.

(*Or Yechezkel: Reshimos Talmidim*)

∾ The *Rosh* has joined these two prescriptions to tell us that it is easier for a man to join the company of the shamed who do not reply to their tormentors, if he thinks about the many favors he receives from the Creator and [thus] is full of satisfaction. But if a man assumes that he has received no favors, then each thing, even the most insignificant, will annoy him and he will not control his temper.

There is another possible way to explain the juxtaposition: Included in the blessings for satisfaction caused by the food, there is the blessing for the sense of satisfaction gained from all that is good in this world.

Human nature is such that, because he is envied, the rich man is hated. As the *Chovos HaLevavos* has said, men see whatever good another possesses as if it had been taken from them. King Shlomo, may peace be upon him, has warned against this by stating, "Do not curse the rich man" (*Koheles* 10:20). And *Chazal* have said: "People do things in order not to appear wealthy," because of their fear of others (*Bava Basra* 175a). If a man is prepared to disregard all forms of degradation, he will not find it difficult to acknowledge openly the blessings God has given him. (See, also, our comments to paragraph 89.) (*Or Yechezkel*)

⊷§ The *Tosafos Yom-Tov* has interpreted: "One should be of those who are determined not to be concerned if shamed." R' Yehudah Segal of Manchester reported that a certain great personage of the Torah world, who had seen the *Chofetz Chaim*, had told him that the *Chofetz Chaim* lamented that no one shamed him, and hence he could not be counted among those who "are humiliated but do not humiliate, of whom it is written: 'And those who love Him are like the sun when it emerges in its strength' " (*Yoma* 23a).

23

וְאַל יֵצֵא לָרִיב מַהֵר, וְיִתְרַחֵק מִן הַשְּׁבוּעוֹת. וּמִן הַנְּדָרִים, כִּי בַּעֲוֹן הַנְּדָרִים בָּנִים מֵתִים.

And one should not be quick to get involved in a quarrel. And he should distance himself from oaths and vows — for children pass away because of the sin of [their parents'] unfulfilled vows.

⊷§ *And one should not be quick to get involved in a quarrel.*

The *Rosh* wrote specifically: "One should not be quick to get involved in a quarrel." Often a man thinks that truth and justice are on his side; yet, if he would ponder the issue he would realize that he is not right. That is why the *Rosh* mentions vows and oaths here. As the *Ran* explains, the Gemara compares the person who takes a vow to the person who builds an altar for idol worship. In both instances the individual imagines that he is performing a *mitzvah* whereas, in truth, he is committing a sin.   (*Orach Yesharim*)

•§ By writing "One should not be quick to get involved in a quarrel," the *Rosh* underlines the point that every quarrel and [feeling of] hatred are a result of haste and come from a lack of pondering the issue. As R' Yechezkel Sarna noted, we say in the *Kinos* on Tishah B'Av evening, "Woe! We are closely *pursued*, because we *pursued* baseless hatred." The source of baseless hatred lies in its being pursued. In our hasty pursuit we do not find the time to think about the source of our hatred. The punishment is designed to fit the sin — pursuit for pursuit.

(*Delios Yechezkel III*, p. 268).

24

וְיִתְרַחֵק מִן הַשְּׂחוֹק, וּמִן הַכַּעַס, כִּי מְבַלְבֵּל רוּחוֹ
וְדַעְתּוֹ שֶׁל אָדָם. וְשֶׁיַּעֲבוֹד תָּמִיד לְיוֹצְרוֹ בְּאַהֲבָה.
וְשֶׁלֹּא יַנִּיחַ דָּבָר לַעֲשׂוֹת מֵעִנְיַן זֹאת הַתַּקָּנָה.

And one should distance himself from frivolity
and from anger, for it confuses a person's spirit
and mind. One should constantly serve his Maker
with love. And one should not fail to carry out a
single detail of this regime of conduct.

TOSAFOS YOM TOV
One should draw himself away from frivolity and anger, because anger confuses one's understanding, knowledge and thinking ability. On the contrary, one should hold firmly to always serving his Creator with love. And one should be very careful not to omit a single detail mentioned in this list of practices.

ـﺔ§ *And one should distance himself from frivolity and from anger, for it confuses a person's spirit and mind.*

The *Tosafos Yom Tov* translated: "anger confuses one's understanding, knowledge and thinking ability..."

He did not interpret the word "confuses" as applying to frivolity also, but only to anger. The Paris manuscript supports his view, for the variant reading there is: "for anger confuses one's mind so that he cannot concentrate on loving his Creator." Further support may be drawn from a comment in the *Sefer HaYirah* (Os 170): "Whenever someone becomes angry, he confuses his mind so that he cannot stand firm in the love of his Creator."

(*Orach Yesharim*)

25

לֶאֱהוֹב אֶת ה' בְּכָל לְבָבְךָ וּבְכָל נַפְשְׁךָ
וּבְכָל מְאֹדֶךָ. וְהַסְכֵּם בְּאָמְרְךָ אֶת ה' אֱלֹקֶיךָ
בְּכָל לְבָבְךָ וְגוֹ' לִמְסוֹר גּוּפְךָ וּמָמוֹנְךָ
עַל קְדוּשָׁתוֹ. וּבָזֶה תְּקַיֵּם בְּעַצְמְךָ
דִּבְרֵי הַמְשׁוֹרֵר כִּי עָלֶיךָ הוֹרַגְנוּ כָּל הַיּוֹם.

Love Hashem with all your heart and all your soul
and all your possessions. And whenever you say
[in the *Shema*,] "Love Hashem your God with all
your heart...," be determined to sacrifice your
body and your possessions for His sanctification.
In this way you yourself will fulfill the words
of the Psalmist: "For Your sake we are
slaughtered all day long" (*Tehillim* 44:23).

ـﺔ§ *Love Hashem with all your heart and all your soul and your possessions.*

Many are accustomed to deceive themselves when reciting the *Shema*. They think about the intent to suffer martyrdom for the sanctity of the Name. That is indeed a high purpose. The *Rosh* in the

Orchos Chaim writes that thereby one fulfills the verse: "For Your sake we are slaughtered all day long" (*Tehillim* 44:23). Here there is, indeed, room for self-deceit, for who knows what he would actually do if the opportunity for such martyrdom might, Heaven forbid, arise.

But *Rashi* in his commentary to the first paragraph of the *Shema* on the verse: "And these words which I am commanding you today, shall be on your heart" (*Devarim* 6:6), writes that by fulfilling this verse — i.e. by having these words on your heart [learning and remembering the Torah] — you fulfill the commandment, "You shall love Hashem your God with all your heart. . ." (*Devarim* 6:5). This is something you can test immediately after prayer. Are you placing the words on your heart or not? Why not think of this, too, while reciting the verse: "You shall love Hashem your God. . ."? It is only that man, who is prone to error, deceives himself.　　　　(*Orach Yesharim*: R' Simchah Zissel of Kelm, *Da'as Chochmah U'Mussar I*, p. 14)

◄§ *And whenever you say [in the Shema] "Love Hashem your God with all your heart . . ." be determined to sacrifice . . .*

Speech is close to action. That is why the *Rosh* writes: "Whenever you say . . . be determined." It is amazing how many stages a person passes through before he arrives at speech. The speaking should come only after all thought and contemplation. And from that comes forth the fruit, an utterance: "You shall love Hashem your God with all your heart."　　　　(*Orach Yesharim*: R' Yerucham Levovitz, *Da'as Chochmah U'Mussar III*, p. 29)

◄§ We are obligated to recite the *Shema* twice daily and it is the basic expression of our acceptance of the yoke of Heaven. The *Rosh* thus explains the essence of the *mitzvah*: "Love Hashem. . ." Each one should contemplate his own state to see if he experiences these feelings and if his inner self is at one with the words being expressed by his lips.

Accepting the yoke of Heaven means exactly that — accepting a veritable yoke, like the ox receives its yoke or the donkey its pack, without any sense of self but complete subjection to the kingship of the Holy One. First, one must uproot thoughts of sin and inclinations towards heresy by planting the foundations of faith. He should draw his heart near to that which comes forth from his lips, and then there is hope that he will reach the goal. If it is difficult to demand of men that the sense of the dominion of Heaven be apparent throughout the day, let the heart at least truly feel the uniqueness of Hashem and the sense of Heavenly dominion when the *Shema* is being recited. That can only come through the toil and effort of thought and reflection. And that is difficult, because it is hard to alter an ingrained habit [one's old habit of reciting *Shema* without this conviction].

(*Or Yechezkel: Emunah* p. 166 and *Reshimos Talmidim*)

◦§ *To sacrifice your body and your possessions for His sanctificaiton.*

If one truly feels that the soul is his existential self and the body is but its clothing, he will not find the *mitzvah* of self-sacrifice (מְסִירוּת נֶפֶשׁ) difficult, for he will not feel that he is sacrificing his true self. His soul remains intact and the body which he is offering is not himself but only his clothing.

If one is fortunate to reach the point where he has a taste and a desire for a spiritual life, then it is likely that he can come close to genuine thoughts of self-sacrifice when he recites the *Shema*.

(*Or Yechezkel: Kovetz Inyanim*, 5728, p. 76)

◦§ These are lofty levels, and who can attain them? Yet, this does not exempt us from seeking counsel on how to relate to them in terms of appreciating them, desiring them and contemplating them. Though we be far removed from such a level in practice, we are, nevertheless, not exempt from approaching it in thought. The *Rosh* teaches us how important such thought is, so much so, that he writes: "With this, you fulfill the words of the Psalmist: 'For Your sake we are slaughtered all day long,'" even though nothing has been done in terms of action.

(Ibid.)

26

לִבְטוֹחַ בַּה' בְּכָל לְבָבֶךָ וּלְהַאֲמִין בְּהַשְׁגָּחָתוֹ הַפְּרָטִית. וּבָזֶה תְּקַיֵּים בִּלְבָבֶךָ הַיִּחוּד הַשָּׁלֵם בְּהַאֲמִין בּוֹ כִּי עֵינָיו מְשׁוֹטְטוֹת בְּכָל הָאָרֶץ וְעֵינָיו עַל כָּל דַּרְכֵי אִישׁ וּבוֹחֵן לֵב וְחוֹקֵר כְּלָיוֹת, כִּי מִי שֶׁאֵינוֹ מַאֲמִין "אֲשֶׁר הוֹצֵאתִיךָ מֵאֶרֶץ מִצְרָיִם" אַף "בְּאָנֹכִי ה' אֱלֹקֶיךָ" אֵינוֹ מַאֲמִין. וְאֵין זֶה יִחוּד שָׁלֵם. כִּי זֶה הָיָה [נ"א הוּא] סְגוּלַת יִשְׂרָאֵל עַל כָּל הָעַמִּים וְזֶה יְסוֹד כָּל הַתּוֹרָה כֻּלָּה.

Trust in Hashem with all your heart, and believe
in His Providence upon every detail [of the
world.] In this way you will fulfill in your heart
the perfect Unity of Hashem, by believing
that His eyes roam over the entire world,
and His eyes are upon all the ways of men,
testing the heart and analyzing feelings [i.e. for
"Unity of Hashem" implies not merely that God
exists and is the Creator, but His total awareness
and guidance of all events, without exception].
For whoever does not believe the verse, ". . .Who
took you out of the land of Egypt" [*Shemos* 20:2
which teaches Hashem's control of nature],
also does not believe [the beginning of that
verse]: "I am Hashem your God" and [such a
flawed belief] is not the perfect Unity. This
[complete faith] was Israel's unique treasure
above all the nations, and this [true] belief
is the foundation of the entire Torah.

⊷§ *Trust in Hashem with all your heart, and believe in His Providence
upon every detail [of the world].*

There are two articles of faith being discussed here: "I am Hashem
your God," which is the belief in the constant renewal of the Creation;
and the Exodus of Israel from Egypt, which is the belief in Divine
Providence over every detail of Creation (הַשְׁגָּחָה פְּרָטִית). The *Ramban*
writes, in his commentary to *Shemos* 13:16, that the cornerstone of our
faith is that the workings of the world are a hidden miracle. He means
to say that the workings of the world seem to be governed by the natural
order of things, but in truth they depend on man's actions, whether for
good or, God forbid, for evil. This is what the *Rosh* meant when he
wrote: "Because they held this true belief [that Hashem took us out of
Egypt], Israel alone of all the nations is the chosen treasure."

(*Orach Yesharim*: R' Simchah Zissel of Kelm,
Da'as Chochmah U'Mussar I, p. 95)

◆§ R' Simchah Zissel of Kelm explained the juxtaposition of, "I am Hashem your God," and, "Who took you out of Egypt," (*Shemos* 20:2) as follows: If you wish to know Who your God is, and how He conducts everything, then contemplate: "Who has taken you out of Egypt." Then you will know and understand "I am Hashem your God" and His ways.

From the story of the Exodus we can learn not only what all our obligations on earth are, and all the elements of our faith, but we may also learn the ways of Heaven and how Hashem acts towards man. For what happened in the Exodus is meant for us, so that we may learn to know and understand the ways of Heaven. That is why we are obligated to remember the Exodus twice daily (in the third paragraph of the *Shema*, the paragraph of *tzitzis*); for it is the basis for the entire Torah. *(Or Yechezkel: Reshimos Talmidim)*

◆§ In this paragraph, the *Rosh* speaks of the Unity of Hashem and His Divine Providence over all things. It is paragraph 26, the numerical equivalent of the Name of Hashem הוי"ה, Blessed is He.
(Or Yechezkel: Main Disciples)

◆§ Reward and punishment, and Divine Providence over each particular detail of the world, operate in two distinct ways. One is the inexorable process of cause-and-effect, which stems from the Divine attribute of Strict Judgment (מִדַּת הַדִּין). The other is the process of Torah which is a manifestation of the Divine attribute of Compassion (מִדַּת הָרַחֲמִים). The latter applies only to those who have gained Torah.

When the *Rosh* writes that Hashem sees people's "innermost thoughts and feelings," he means to say something that is impossible to be understood without Torah, for it is written: "The heart is deceitful above all things, and it is exceedingly weak — who can know it?" (*Yirmeyahu* 17:9). To feel every movement in the arteries of the heart, to know each of its minute turnings, does not lie within the grasp of man. Only the Creator Himself can do this, as it is said: "I, Hashem, search the heart and perceive the innermost feelings" (ibid. v. 10). This unique perception belongs only to the Torah. That is what the *Rosh* means by closing the paragraph with the statement that our belief in Hashem's exact discrimination, in every single detail, is "the foundation upon which the entire Torah rests." It follows that only those who have that attribute of exact, detailed discrimination are able to acquire Torah.
(Orach Yesharim: R' Yerucham Levovitz,
Da'as Chochmah U'Mussar I, p. 28)

❀   ❀   ❀

ء And believe in His Providence upon every detail [of the world].

This means that one is to believe that everything, great or small, is under the direct supervision of Hashem, Blessed is He. If one thinks that anything exists which Hashem does not supervise, one's faith is lacking, because [by so thinking,] one believes that there is some power besides Hashem, Blessed is He, while in truth, all that is done, for good or evil, is the fulfillment of His Will.

ء For whoever does not believe the verse "...Who took you out of the land of Egypt"...

One must believe that besides the very salvation from the servitude to Egypt, there was another act performed: we became servants of Hashem; from then on, we have been in servitude to Him. For the verse, "in order to be a God to you," לִהְיוֹת לָכֶם לֵאלֹהִים (Bamidbar 15:41), came about only through the fact that Hashem "took you out of the land of Egypt."

ء Also does not believe [the beginning of that verse]: "I am Hashem your God..."

With the Exodus, Israel was taken out from the forty-nine depths of impurity, and the reason why Hashem declares: "I am Hashem your God," is also to remove you from your forty-nine depths of impurity, for your benefit. Therefore, believe that you, too, can leave evil and turn to the good and rise from impurity to sanctity; for both [impurity and sanctity] are from Hashem.

ء And [such a flawed belief] is not the perfect Unity.

This would seem to say that to the degree which a man comprehends and recognizes the subject matter of the Exodus, to that extent he comprehends the concept "I am Hashem Your God."

ء This [complete faith] was Israel's unique treasure above all the nations ...

This means that specific Divine Providence guards [and ensures] Israel's spiritual position and level, maintaining the nation on its level where it will be worthy of eternal life.

(Or Yechezkel: Reshimos R' Reuven Melamed)

❧ ❧ ❧

ء And this belief is the foundation of the entire Torah.

With this statement, the Rosh casts light on the Ramban at the end of Parashas Bo [Shemos 13:10]. The Ramban writes: "One who buys a mezuzah for a single zuz (a small coin) and fixes it in his entrance and does it with the proper intent has thereby affirmed ... [that Hashem has taken us out of slavery to freedom...]."

But the scroll of the *mezuzah* does not contain a reference to the Exodus from Egypt. What it does have is the verse: "Hear, O Israel. . ." which indicates Divine Providence over each particular person and object. If one thinks about that verse, which is the foundation of the entire Torah, he will thus be expressing belief in the Exodus and the perfect Unity and Uniqueness of Hashem.

(Or Yechezkel: Main Disciples)

⋖§ Our master, the *Mashgiach* [R' Yechezkel Levenstein], gave his last discourse in the Ponevezh Yeshivah on *Parshas Vayishlach*, 5731. It revolved around the subject of faith and trust explained by the *Rosh*. He read the passage: "Trust in Hashem with all your heart, and believe in His Providence upon every detail [of the world]." The *Mashgiach* explained that the *Rosh* was careful to speak of "His Providence upon every detail," rather than the [more general] Providence expressed by the verse (*Tehillim* 145:9): "His compassion encompasses all His creations (וְרַחֲמָיו עַל כָּל מַעֲשָׂיו)." For the first thing which indicates that a man believes in the perfect Unity of Hashem is his tranquility of soul. Only if one believes that everything is a result of His actions and the consequences follow directly from them in an exact manner, "measure for measure," can he be said to believe that there is Divine Providence over each and every detail. The *Ramban* describes this belief: "If he performs a *mitzvah*, his reward will bring him success; if he commits a sin, his punishment will cut him down — everything by Heavenly decree."

If he has such a belief in Divine Providence over all things, he will live with tranquility of soul. That peace of soul is the first requirement needed to be able to attain stature in Torah and fear of Hashem; and that peace of soul is a result of belief in Divine Providence over each and every detail. Without tranquility, one cannot climb spiritually.

How is such faith implanted in the soul? Only through faith in the Exodus from Egypt.

The *Rosh* wishes to say that one must believe that the sole occurrence which formed the nation of Israel was the Exodus. [It was then that Israel came into existence,] not before then, nor after. Even if a man believes in all that preceded the Exodus and all that succeeded it, but does not believe in the Exodus itself, he cannot be said to believe in "I am Hashem your God" or in Divine Providence over all things. For that is what makes "Israel alone of all the nations the chosen treasure." It is the Exodus and nothing else which brought and raised Israel to the level of Hashem's nation.   *(Or Yechezkel:* Recollections of a close disciple)

~§ *His Providence upon every detail [of the world]*.

[There are two aspects of Divine Providence:

(a) Specific Divine Providence (*hashgachah pratis*), meaning Hashem's supervision over each individual and event.

(b) General Divine Providence (*hashgachah clalis*), meaning Hashem's constant sustenance of all Creation.]

Why has the *Rosh* only associated the fact that "He sees everything in the whole world" with Specific Divine Providence (*hashgachah pratis*)?

Furthermore, why is belief in the Exodus included within the framework of Specific Divine Providence? The *Ramban* (commentary to *Shemos* 20:2) explains that the Exodus revealed for the first time that God is the totality of Will and Desire. Previously, it had been thought that Creation was a matter of necessity [that it had to occur, that it was not brought about by God's Will]. But why is this manifestation of Hashem [the Exodus] not related to the workings of the world in general? Does not General Divine Providence call upon us to recognize that Hashem is all Will and Desire? Moreover, why did the *Rosh* include the faith of Israel within the framework of Specific Divine Providence? Do not the workings of General Divine Providence call forth the need to believe in basic principles of faith?

A new concept is being taught to us, here. Although General Divine Providence obligates man, who lives within its supervision, to have faith, it is not yet sufficient cause for the faith of Israel. General Divine Providence, even if "He sees everything in the world," is not that which obligates Israel to believe.

What obligates Israel to have faith is Specific Divine Providence. Israel is not subject to two kinds of Providence, one general and one particular. With Israel, all depends on [the Specific Divine Providence that stems from] following the precepts of the Torah, fulfilling: "If you walk in My laws" (*Vayikra* 26:3). If a man fulfills the *mitzvos*, then Divine Providence treats him as an individual; that is, he is exclusively subject to the supervision of Specific Divine Providence. For Israel, therefore, existence itself is a matter of Specific Divine Providence. Thus, it follows for the *Rosh* that if a Jew does not believe that "He sees everything in the whole world" along Jewish lines of faith [i.e. that every individual event is Divinely directed in accordance with man's good or bad acts], he lacks the concept of the perfect Unity of Hashem.

Yet there are distinctions between one Jew and another. For one Jew, Specific Divine Providence is seen less clearly, as if it is hidden (בְּהֶסְתֵּר פָּנִים); for another Jew, it is more readily visible. All depends on how closely one draws himself towards Hashem. For the non-Jew, however, if he does not believe in Specific Divine Providence, this will not effect a lack in his existential self, because he is under the supervision of General Divine Providence.   (*Orach Yesharim:* R' Abba Grossbard)

◄§ *Israel. . .above all the nations. . .*
There are two ideas of Divine Providence being discussed here. Non-Jews assume that there is Divine Providence over every creation. But they see the Holy One and His servants as a king who rules his country with the help of a "parliament" and who desires to have his country function according to their legislation. We, however, believe that there is a Divine Providence that emanates from the Holy One alone; it is only He Who oversees each and every detail. Thus, the *Rosh* writes that a man is a heretic if he believes only in Hashem Who created heaven and earth, but does not believe in the Exodus, where Specific Divine Providence was made manifest.

But there is a further point here, namely the revelation of a Specific Divine Providence which relates exclusively to Israel — which is why the phrase "Your God" is used. ["I am Hashem your God, Who took you out of the land of Egypt."] The *Rosh* does not refer to someone who does not believe that Divine Providence operates in the world. What he wishes to tell us is that even if a person believes that Hashem took us out of Egypt, but sees the Exodus as part of the natural order of things, then he does not have the proper view of the perfect Unity of God. We are to believe that Israel is treated in miraculous fashion, above and beyond the workings of nature. That is what is meant by saying: "This [complete faith] was Israel's unique treasure above all the nations."
(*Orach Yesharim:* R' Reuven Melamed,
citing the *gaon* R' Eliahu Lopian)

◄§ *The perfect Unity of Hashem. . .*
Each day, in pronouncing the "Thirteen Principles of Faith," we start with: 1) I believe that the Creator, Blessed is He, creates and directs all creations, and that He alone did, does and will do all that is done. 2) I believe that the Creator, Blessed is He, is unique and there is nothing as unique as Him in any fashion, and that He alone, our God, has always existed and will always exist.

What the *Rosh* writes here sheds light on the above. For he points out that through the Exodus from Egypt, Israel became subject to a special measure of Specific Divine Providence and thus stands apart in its belief in God's uniqueness. That is why we add [in the Second Principle of Faith], "He alone, our God," for Hashem's Unity is affirmed not only by our belief in Creation itself, but also by our belief in His being our God, due to the measure of Divine Providence which we receive in a very individual way. This is what the *Rosh* refers to as "the perfect Unity of Hashem."

This [possibility of affirming Hashem's Unity in the most complete way] came about through the Exodus.

Thus, the *Rosh* also helps us explain the verse: "From the heavens, Hashem looks and sees all of mankind; from where He is seated, He pays attention to all the inhabitants of the Land" (*Tehillim* 33:13-14). R' Moshe Chaim Luzzatto (*Derech Hashem II*, 4:8-9) has written that the Specific Divine Providence over each of the other nations takes effect only through Hashem's agent whom He has appointed over that nation. Hashem Himself only exercises General Divine Providence over those nations and the verse refers to this General Divine Providence by saying that Hashem "sees" all of mankind ["sees" is a general term].

But Israel is in a category of its own, for "God's share is His nation" (*Devarim* 32:9), and He Himself oversees them through Specific Divine Providence. Therefore, when referring to Israel ["all the inhabitants of the Land" refers to the Land of Israel], the verse says: "He pays attention" [a particular term].   (*Orach Yesharim*)

❧ ❧ ❧

❧ *Trust in Hashem with all your heart. . .*

Trust in Hashem is necessary in order to maintain the full measure of the belief in Hashem's Unity in one's heart. For such trust is not, as is generally imagined, that one trusts and is certain that Hashem will grant him good things. Trust consists of relying and trusting in Hashem without knowing what will happen. And one must believe in Divine Providence over each and every detail. He should feel that the eyes of Hashem rest on each corner of the world and range over every man; that the world is filled with His glory. He should believe that Divine Providence depends on each person's actions, on Hashem's perception of his "innermost thoughts and feelings." If he is remiss in these beliefs, he lacks belief in the full Unity of Hashem.

❧ *And believe in His Providence upon every detail [of the world]*.

The *Rosh* means that one should trust in Hashem, but prior to that he should believe in Divine Providence over every individual item, for faith in Divine Providence comes before trust in Hashem. Only after he has gained faith is there hope that he will attain trust.

◆§ *In this way you will fulfill in your heart the perfect Unity of Hashem...*

The basis of belief in Hashem's Unity is the belief that there is nothing besides Him and nothing moves unless He wills it. Thus, belief in Divine Providence over all things is part and parcel of belief in Hashem's Unity.

◆§ *By believing that His eyes roam over the entire world, and His eyes are upon all the ways of man...*

The Holy One's Divine Providence does not involve only that which is seen by all. It involves every action, great and small. Even man's innermost thoughts and feelings lie open before Him and are included in His Divine Providence.

◆§ *Testing the heart and analyzing feelings.*

This image [which implies that our thoughts and feelings are outside of Hashem, and He "perceives" them] is only meant to make an impression on our ear and bring Hashem closer to the realm of our understanding. But true comprehension of Hashem's Unity involves the belief that the thoughts and feelings themselves are included in the Will of Hashem. There is no movement, no stirring of thought in man's heart, without the Will of the Holy One, for He is all-powerful and there is nothing else other than Him.

◆§ *For whoever does not believe the verse, "...Who took you out of the land of Egypt," also does not believe the [beginning of that verse]: "I am Hashem your God."*

The Exodus came about through unlimited Divine Providence over each and every detail. Belief in the Exodus is founded on belief in Divine Providence. Therefore, whoever does not believe in the Exodus does not believe in Hashem's Unity and [His existence proclaimed] in "I am Hashem your God."

◆§ *This [complete faith] was Israel's unique treasure above all the nations,*

The entire Torah involves belief in Divine Providence. If one does not believe in Divine Providence, he lacks belief in the entire Torah. As the *Ramban* said, the entire Torah is a matter of concealed miracles. When we use the term "concealed miracle," we mean to say that there is no such thing as nature or chance. Rather, everything has Him as its source, and He directs the world in accordance with the [good or bad] deeds of man.

෨ᔆ *And this [true] belief is the foundation of the entire Torah.*

We forget these principles, that the Holy One directs the world and that we must submit ourselves and our actions to His direction. When a man thinks that it is he himself who is in charge of his ways and deeds, he cannot be called a believer. (*Or Yechezkel: Reshimos Talmidim*)

෨ᔆ ෨ᔆ ෨ᔆ

෨ᔆ "Perfect Unity" is the understanding that everything that happens in this world is the fulfillment of God's purpose.

෨ᔆ If one does not believe that all that occurs in the world is effected by this purpose and no other additional purpose, one does not possess the concept of Hashem's complete Unity. Complete Unity is synonymous with "single purpose" and that is what is meant by: "Hashem will be One and His Name will be One" (*Zechariah* 14:9). The verse indicates that in the future all will see, and be aware, that all the events that occurred in Creation were paths to such awareness.

(*Or Yechezkel: Emunah*, p. 105)

෨ᔆ *Who took you out of the land of Egypt...*

Ibn Ezra poses a question about the First Commandment: Why do we find, "I am Hashem, your God, Who took you out of the land of Egypt?" Why doesn't it say, "...Who made the heavens and earth, and created you?" His answer is:

> Know that the levels of faith in men's hearts are not identical in their belief in the exalted Name. For the majority believe what they hear from their masters. Those who have seen it written in the Torah which Hashem gave to Moshe stand above them... He who studies the fields of knowledge... will recognize the acts of Hashem in the movements of the heavenly bodies, in the plant world, in the animal kingdom and in the body of man himself... and from the ways of Hashem (in nature), the learned man will know of Hashem... Thus, "I am Hashem" is mentioned for the learned man, and "Who took you out..." has been added so that both the learned and unlearned will understand.

Ibn Ezra wishes to say that "I am Hashem ..." indicates that by studying all of Creation, it is possible to learn and understand that Hashem is the Creator. For Creation in its entirety is a reflection of Hashem. But it requires learning and knowledge to grasp this. And, since the Holy One wanted even the unlearned to know and be aware of His existence (for the possibility of faith has been granted to everyone) Scripture adds: "...Who took you out of the land of Egypt." With the Exodus, the Holy One gave a tangible dimension which showed everyone, even those who did not wish to believe it, that "I am Hashem." To this end, the Holy One gave signs, worked wonders and effected changes in nature. By so doing, all knew and were aware that if He had the power to change the created world, He most certainly must have created it. Once such knowledge is acquired by tangible signs and wonders, it becomes easier to be aware of the Holy One through an understanding of the wisdom reflected by Creation.

(Or Yechezkel: Emunah, p. 31).

◄§ Trust in Hashem... For whoever does not believe...

This statement of the *Rosh* needs a full explanation. For at first he speaks of lofty levels: "Trust in Hashem with all your heart, and believe in His Providence..." Yet, he concludes by saying that "whoever does not believe in "...Who took you out of Egypt" also does not believe in "I am Hashem, Your God; for that is not the perfect Unity of Hashem." Yet, someone with such a lack of faith could be a great heretic! Furthermore, what is the connection? Doesn't the possibility exist where one who does not believe in the Exodus can still, nevertheless, believe in Hashem?

To my mind, when the *Rosh* speaks of Divine Providence over each detail in the universe, he does not mean for us to think of the usual Divine Providence which is on a physical level and applies to all living creatures, including all the nations of the world. Instead, he is referring to Divine Providence as it applies to Israel as a whole; that Israel will take pleasure in Hashem and enjoy the radiance of His Presence, and that they will have everlasting existence. For as the Holy One carefully examines the innermost thoughts and feelings of each person, in terms of that examination, the person gains his portion in the World to Come. That is what the *Rosh* refers to when saying: "He knows all the deeds of man..."

The *Midrash* tells us that the Holy One examined the innermost thoughts and feelings of four-fifths of the population of B'nai Yisrael who, because they did not wish to leave Egypt, died during the three days of the plague of darkness (*Shemos Rabbah* 14:3). They lacked the heart, the will, the soul which desired to leave Egypt, and so they died there. They did not live to acquire all the eternal good that was granted to Israel, as it is said at Sinai: "And you will be a treasure to Me of all the nations... and you will be for Me a kingdom of priests and a holy people" (*Shemos* 19:5-6). For the Holy One examines the innermost thoughts and feelings to determine who is worthy of receiving the eternal good which is hidden away and reserved for the righteous. This is the Specific Divine Providence over Israel, by which Hashem constantly plans and arranges the details of their activities and actions throughout their lives, preparing them for the particular portion that is awaiting each one in the World to Come.

Chazal say that Israel was not worthy of leaving Egypt. By the standards of the Divine attribute of Strict Justice (מִדַּת הַדִּין), they would never have been redeemed. In the natural course of events there was no justification for their redemption, for they were the product of Egypt, just as the fetus is part of the animal. Thus, in expounding the verse; "Who can bring forth the pure from the impure? Only the One" (Iyov 14:4), Chazal say: "Did not Abraham come from Terach, Israel from the nations? How could these things have come about if not through the agency of Him Who is One in the universe?"

For with the Exodus they saw a Uniqueness and a Oneness unlike that of anything else, as it is said, " [Did God ever do miracles for any other nation. . .] like all that which Hashem, your God, did for you in Egypt, before your eyes?" (Devarim 4:34). In Egypt they saw "our God," that aspect of Him which is particular to Israel. Each nation is under the supervision of a particular angel, but the Holy One Himself in His glory is the One Who supervises Israel. Though it seems they were attached inseparably to Egypt, the Holy One took them and attached them to Himself.

The Ramchal speaks of this: "The force of His unique rule [shows itself] in His total independence; nothing binds Him. The order of law and the legislation which He has ordained are dependent on His Will; He is not bound by them in any way. When He so wishes, He submits His will, so to speak, to the deeds of men, and when He so wishes, He thinks nothing of their deeds and grants of His goodness to whomsoever He desires, as it is written: 'And I will grant favor to whomsoever I grant favor' (Shemos 33:19) — even if that person does not act properly" (Da'as Tevunos).

This is evident in the Exodus. Although, on the basis of their acts, Israel did not deserve to be redeemed, nevertheless, they went out from Egypt because He is the Supreme Ruler. He joined them to Himself. He seized them and took them out in love, because of the oath which He had sworn to Avraham, who loved Him, to make them a chosen people and to grant them awareness that He is "your God." This is what is meant by the verse: ". . .Who took you out of the land of Egypt to be a God to you" (Bamidbar 15:41).

This is what the Rosh means. One must believe and have trust in all the levels up to the concept of full Uniqueness which is the concept of "your God." And that we learn from the Exodus from Egypt.

(Or Yechezkel: Reshimos R' Reuven Melamed)

◁§ *For whoever does not believe the verse, "...Who took you out of the land of Egypt..."*

The *Ramban's* comments at the end of *Parashas Acharei Mos* shed further light on this issue. He notes that the main purpose of Torah lies in its perfecting man. It purifies and cleanses his material self. Its force is evident in each limb and organ, of which there are two hundred and forty-eight (רמ״ח), paralleling the two hundred and forty-eight positive commandments (*mitzvos asei*). The perfecting of each particular limb and organ is dependent on its corresponding *mitzvah*.

How, then, could Israel have been granted redemption from Egypt when they were sunk to the depth of the forty-ninth level of impurity, when they were blemished and not cleansed? Besides, there were forces which opposed their leaving Egypt. Their redemption was due to the power of the One and Only, of the Omnipotent. He could take them out with a high hand and bring them to a state of perfection in which they were prepared to receive the Torah. That is what is involved in our obligation to believe in the Exodus. We are to believe that it is in His power to bring us to perfection, and nothing can stand in His way. For there is nothing besides Him, and He is totally free and suffers no restraints.

If one does not believe this, he also has no belief in the verse, "I am your God." *(Or Yechezkel: Reshimos Talmidim)*

◁§ On the surface, we cannot understand why one who does not believe in the Exodus is a heretic with whom we should not associate. Perhaps the explanation is that in addition to the wonders revealed in the redemption from Pharoah and Egypt, Israel was also redeemed from the depths of the forty-ninth level of impurity in which they had sunk. All the doubts and heretical beliefs of all ages were included in the creation of those forty-nine levels. They epitomize the evil that exists in the world. Hashem redeemed us from them and brought us to the realization of His perfect Unity.

If one assumes that man cannot lift himself up and perceive such Unity, and feels that man can only exist in those levels of thought which are included in the forty-nine levels, he does not believe in the verse, "...Who took you out," which states that we went out of the domain of the impure; and thus, neither does he believe in "I am Your God," and therefore lacks a conception of Hashem's perfect Unity.

(Or Yechezkel: Kovetz Inyanim, Elul, 5727, p. 35)

∞§ Trust. . . and believe. . .

At the beginning of his work *HaEmunah V'HaBitachon*, the *Ramban* states that whoever trusts in Hashem (בִּטָחוֹן) is to be called faithful (מַאֲמִין), but not everyone who has faith can be called trusting. How is it, then, that the *Rosh* speaks first of *trusting* in Hashem and follows this up with the need to *believe?* Surely, if one trusts with a full heart he already believes!

Perhaps Rabbeinu Yonah supplies us with an answer. In explaining the verse, "Know Him in all your ways" (*Mishlei* 3:6), he writes: In any act which you wish to perform, remember Hashem, Blessed is He, and look to Him to grant you success in that act. Place your trust in Him and turn your heart to Him, for the deed is not in your hand. Our verse adds something to the previous one: "Trust in Hashem with all your heart" (ibid. v. 5). For there are those who trust in Hashem in general terms and believe that everything is in the Hands of Heaven. They put their trust in Him and not in men — neither in human power nor wisdom.

But they do not apply trust to matters of detail, to each act. That is why we are told, "Know Him in all your ways." This means: Think upon Him in every detail of your actions, in whatever you do, and know in your heart that you do not have the force nor the capability of performing that action; for it is not in your hand but in the Hand of Hashem. Put your hope and anticipation in the kindness (*chesed*) of Hashem. By making this a matter of habit, you will acquire a soul which has a desire for trust. Know that there are those whose eyes turn to Hashem in great matters — when they wish to sail on the seas for some business venture or set out on a long trip. But in minor affairs they do not think of Hashem, deeming the matter insignificant. . . That is why the verse admonishes: "Know Him in *all* your ways" — in both great and small things.

This seems to be what the *Rosh* wishes to say. For the virtue of trust in Hashem comes from grasping the underlying principles which lead to it. The *Chovos HaLevavos* first discusses the Unity of Hashem (שַׁעַר הַיִּחוּד), then examines Creation (שַׁעַר הַבְּחִינָה), then service to God (שַׁעַר הָעֲבוֹדָה) and only after that, trust (שַׁעַר הַבִּטָחוֹן). For if one wishes to trust, there are stages through which one must pass before reaching the most complete level of trust.

On the other hand, trust which stems from a general sense of faith is different and does not require these previous steps. [It gives one an overall philosophy of trust, but not an innate feeling that permeates each act, large or small.] The *Rosh* here teaches that trust should come from a belief in Hashem's Providence over each detail of the universe. This is comparable to Rabbeinu Yonah's view that even though a man possesses a general trust in Hashem, he should strengthen his faith in Hashem's Providence for the minor as well as the major matters.

(Or Yechezkel: Reshimos R' Reuven Melamed)

❧ I am Hashem...

The *Ramban's* commentary to "But I did not inform them of My Name, Hashem" (*Shemos* 6:3) sheds light on the *Rosh*. *Ramban* writes: I appeared to the forefathers with the force of My hand, whereby I plunder the constellations and aid My elect, but by My Name *Yud Hei* (י״ה), through which all existence comes into being, I did not become known to them, for I did not create new creations for them, changing the laws of nature. Therefore, tell Israel that I am Hashem and inform them of the great Name once again. For through it, I will act wondrously with them, and they will know that I, Hashem, do everything.

The Creator, through miracles, revealed anew the entire process of Creation to the generation which left Egypt. They saw that He had not been satisfied to create the world once and for all, and subsequently leave it to function on its own through the laws of nature. But all of Creation, from its beginning, had not for a moment departed from His direct control.

Although our forefathers had attained an understanding of the Creator, they had only experienced Him in terms of His Name *Shin Dalet Yud* (שד״י). They had not experienced Him through feeling that the entire universe in its every detail is under His constant unremitting supervision. This was revealed in Egypt. For the Holy One repaid and punished each man with wondrous exactness for his deeds, in accordance with the fruits of his labor. For each Egyptian was punished in perfect proportion, measure for measure (מִדָּה כְּנֶגֶד מִדָּה), in terms of the acts and the evil by which he had caused suffering to Israel. This is as the Torah states: "...in the matter in which they inflicted evil upon them" (*Shemos* 18:11; see *Rashi* there).

It is in such a light that the *Rosh* has written that whoever does not believe in the Exodus, in that revelation of the Divine Providence in each detail, clearly does not believe in the full meaning of "I am Hashem your God." For the full name of the Holy One is His great Name, which indicates that He is the sole Supervisor in the fullest sense of "One and Only." If one does not admit that His directing of the universe is continuous, encompassing every detail and every moment, one does not accept the Name *Yud Hei Vav Hei* (י־ה־ו־ה) which is His full and true

Name. Man's entire task, and the purpose of life towards which he should strive, is to understand and be aware of His great Name, and to realize that through this Name, He directs His worlds without a pause; for this realization and true appreciation is the purpose of all Creation.

(Or Yechezkel: Reshimos Talmidim)

ఆ *This [true] belief...*

How hard one must labor and keep in mind that "there is nothing other than Him." That is the basis of belief in the Exodus — to realize, truly, in a tangible sense, that there is no force besides Him. Belief in a Creator and a Director of the universe is obvious. That is not such a difficult task. But what is difficult is grasping the true concept of Hashem's Oneness and Uniqueness, the realization that there is no force of nature or power other than Him. To attain this, one must uproot all the forms of idolatry, as *Chazal* (quoted by *Rashi*) teach on the verse, "You shall destroy, indeed destroy"(*Devarim* 12:2): "This indicates that when one destroys idolatry one must search and tear out its roots." That is a difficult task. And that was the purpose of all the many miracles at the time of the Exodus: to expose and uproot the bases of all forms of idolatry.

(Or Yechezkel, Iggeres 69)

❖ Monday ❖

27

לְהַרְחִיק גַּאֲוָה וָכַעַס, וּגְעַר בְּיֵצֶר הָרָע הַמַּשִּׂיאֲךָ
לָלֶכֶת בְּדַרְכֵי לִבְּךָ. וְאַל יֵשָׁט, כִּי דְרָכָיו
[נ"א וְאַל תֵּשָׁט אֶל דְרָכָיו כִּי דַרְכֶּיךָ] זַךְ וְיָשָׁר.

Stay far from pride and anger. Oppose the evil
inclination (*yetzer hara*) that entices you
to follow the ways of your heart. Do not deviate,
for His ways are pure and upright. [variant: Do not
deviate into his — the yetzer hara's — ways,
for your own ways are pure and upright.]

❧ *Stay far from pride and anger.*

The *Rosh* has taught us a lesson. His advice is: "Do not deviate"
Essentially, this means not opening the door for the evil inclination
(*yetzer hara*). For the *yetzer's* advent involves a two-stage approach.
First he finds an opening, and then he engages his host with a flood of
idle words. And thus, with his great cunning, he enters into a person
and becomes a resident. Thus *Chazal* teach (*Bereishis Rabbah* 22:6): "R'
Yitzchak says: At first he is a guest and afterwards he becomes the
owner of the house."

(*Orach Yesharim*: R' Yerucham Levovitz, *Da'as Torah I*, 18)

❧ Of all his prescriptions, why has the *Rosh* repeated only the one
about pride and anger? He would seem to have indicated something
new — to stand far away from pride even though one's intention is for
the sake of Heaven. The *Rosh* wishes to caution us even against pride
which springs from a good thought. For on the surface we would have

supposed that one is obligated to have such pride, as it is stated of Yehoshaphat: "And his heart was proud in the ways of Hashem" (*Divrei HaYamim II* 17:6). However, such calculations may lead us astray. For one may be drawn into anger when others do not listen and accept what he teaches and are not quick to obey what he has to say with regard to serving Hashem.

And even when one sets out to perform a good deed, he should place his trust in Hashem to help him succeed, accomplish his task, confer benefit upon others, raise the glory of Torah and the level of awe amongst others without having recourse to pride, even for the "sake of Heaven." This is sufficient reason for repeating the admonition to stay as far away as possible from pride and anger of all sorts.

> (*Orach Yesharim*: R' Avraham Yaffen,
> *HaMussar V'HaDa'as: Elul*, p. 45)

➳ *Oppose the evil inclination...*

A person who has attained an elevated level in his service to Hashem, who thinks about what he is doing, comes to the conclusion that he should do what is good and correct, and agrees to take upon himself resolutions which he feels are good and necessary for serving Hashem. Thereafter, when the time comes to put his resolutions into practice, the evil inclination (*yetzer hara*) throws him into confusion with vain and false arguments in an attempt to put aside these resolutions. It is to such that the *Rosh* says: "Do not deviate into his ways"; the *yetzer hara* would trick you into thinking that your resolutions are of no use in promoting service to Hashem. To which the *Rosh* notes: "...for your own ways" — the resolutions which you chose to accept upon yourself — "are pure and upright." That is the truth of the matter, and don't abandon the truth because of empty desires and vanities.

> (*Or Yechezkel: Mekor HaChaim* and *Reshimos Talmidim*)

➳ In paragraphs 1 and 6, the *Rosh* prescribes: "One should remove oneself as far as possible from pride... and so, too, from anger." That is, one should not have a tendency towards pride. It is of this sort of tendency that the *Ramchal* has written: "There are other haughty men whose arrogance is buried in their heart, and they do not put it into action" (*Mesilas Yesharim*, Chapter 11). In other words, it is pride in potential. But here the *Rosh* speaks of pride that is put into action, and he teaches us how to remove oneself from it in action: namely, to "oppose the evil inclination (*yetzer hara*)."

The Gaon of Vilna has written: "Man's evil inclination overcomes him in two aspects — desire and anger. In his youth, one follows the desires of his heart, and in his mature years, the *yetzer hara* overcomes him with a pompous heart, great anger and sufferings" (*Aderes Eliahu* to *Bereishis* 4:23).

That is the pride of which the *Rosh* cautions us and says: "Oppose and prevent the *yetzer hara* that entices you to follow the ways of your heart." (*Orach Yesharim*)

ๅ§ As long as one does not keep pride and anger at a distance, he does not know the ways of his heart. He thinks that his heart is good and correct. But when he keeps them at a distance, he will be aware of, and sense, the tendencies and ways of his wicked heart. Then he will understand the significance of "pure and upright."
(*Or Yechezkel: Mekor HaChaim*)

ๅ§ Here we have a fresh piece of advice on how to avoid anger, for the *Rosh* has found that the root of anger is our assumption that justice is on our side. So, too, one is arrogant because he assumes that he, and only he, sees the truth. Thus, the *Rosh* says: "Oppose the evil inclination which entices you to follow the ways of your heart." It could be that you are completely mistaken and your thinking is askew. What you see as "straight" is really the doing of the evil inclination. For "bribery blinds the clear sighted" (*Shemos* 23:8), that is why you perceive that crooked is straight. (*Or Yechezkel*: Main Disciples)

ๅ§ *[Variant reading:] Do not deviate, into his — the yetzer hara's — ways, for your own ways are pure and upright.*

The *Rosh* prescribes "Do not deviate into his ways." He is warning us not to have dealings with the *yetzer hara*. The *Rosh* is not speaking about the *yetzer hara*'s enticing a person to sin, but of his casting doubt on one's good deeds. For example, when a person wants to do a *mitzvah*, the *yetzer hara* tells him not to hurry with what he is doing, but to think it through carefully, and the like. It is with this in mind that the *Rosh* warns us not to converse with the *yetzer hara*.

For one must know with certainty that what he does is most definitely pure and upright without a shadow of a doubt. And one must act immediately and speedily. That which is definitely good need not be weighed, since there is no doubt about the need to do it. The acts of the righteous are always performed with swiftness. To the righteous, all the *mitzvos* of Hashem are matters of definite certainty; they fall under no kind of doubt. Their swiftness indicates that the righteous do not pause for a moment to listen to the arguments of the *yetzer hara*. A lack of swiftness already shows that one has descended lower than the level of absolute certainty, and this creates an opening through which the *yetzer hara* can enter.

(*Orach Yesharim*: R' Yerucham Levovitz, *Ma'amarim*, 5693)

28

מִדְּבַר שֶׁקֶר תִּרְחָק.
וְאַל תּוֹצִיא שֵׁם שָׁמַיִם לְבַטָּלָה וְלֹא בְּמָקוֹם מְטוּנָּף.

Distance yourself from falsehood.
Do not pronounce the Holy One's Name in vain
or in an unclean place.

✅ Why does the *Rosh* connect his warning about falsehood with a warning about pronouncing the Holy One's Name in vain?

Rabbeinu Yonah has explained extensively that there are several sorts of falsehood (see *Sha'arei Teshuvah*, *Sha'ar* III, 178). The *Rosh* has repeatedly given prescriptions against falsehood and admonished us to keep our word (in paragraphs 3, 28, 30, 43, 103, 130), but these prescriptions are couched in different terms.

In paragraph 3, he told us to stay away from falsehood and deceit, and listed it as one of the bad characteristics; it includes defrauding and deceiving people for financial gain.

But there is a falsehood involved when a man relates imaginary incidents and does not harm another at all. Rabbeinu Yonah (loc. cit.) warns that such behavior will eventually bring him to bear false witness against another. At the moment, he seems only to desecrate Heaven and his own lips. Yet, it is to this that the *Rosh* seems to refer here, and that is why he links falsehood with the prohibition to pronounce the Holy One's Name in vain or in an unclean place. Rabbeinu Yonah has also listed speaking insincerely as a category of falsehood. The *Rosh* has taken up such falsehood in paragraph 103 — "Do not entice another with a smooth tongue and flattery, and do not speak with a contradictory heart."

There is another sort of falsehood — creating a false impression (*g'neivas da'as*), of which *Chazal* say: "It is forbidden to give a false impression to anyone, even a non-Jew" (*Chullin* 94). The *Rosh* speaks of such deception in paragraph 130: "Do not utter a false or unreliable word. Prove trustworthy to every man, even a non-Jew."

Not fulfilling a promise is also counted as a category of falsehood. The *Rosh* refers to this in section 30: "Use an honest measure" (see *Tosafos Yom-Tov*). (*Orach Yesharim*)

⮬ He who accustoms himself to speak falsely to other men will utter falsehoods to the Holy One, as it is written: "With their mouth and their lips they honored Me, but their heart they kept distant from Me" (*Yeshayahu* 29:13). Eventually, he will reach the point where he will pronounce Hashem's Name in vain and in an unclean place. This explains why the *Rosh* connects the warning about falsehoods with the warning on pronouncing the Holy One's Name in vain.

(*Or Yechezkel: Reshimos Talmidim*)

29

הָסֵר מִמְּךָ [נ"א משענת הקנה הרצוץ] מִשְׁעֶנֶת בְּנֵי אָדָם
וְהַצְנֵעַ לֶכֶת עִם בּוֹרַאֲךָ. וְאַל תָּשִׂים זָהָב כִּסְלֶךָ,
כִּי זֹאת תְּחִלַּת עֲבוֹדַת עַכּוּ"ם,
וּפַזֵּר מָמוֹנְךָ כַּאֲשֶׁר הוּא רְצוֹנוֹ.
כִּי בְּיָדוֹ לְמַלֹּאות חֶסְרוֹנְךָ וְלָתֵת טֶרֶף בְּנֵי בֵיתֶךָ.

Remove yourself from reliance on human beings
[variant: reliance on a broken, weak reed
i.e. on human beings], and walk modestly
with your Creator. And do not make gold
your infatuation, for that is the beginning
of idol worship. Instead, distribute your money
in accordance with Ha-shem's Will, for He
has the power to supply what you lack
and give sustenance to your household.

Remove your hope and reliance from that which you thought to depend on and be helped by — from that thin, broken, battered reed, which is to say, dependence on human beings. On the contrary, conceal yourself to walk with your Creator, the Holy One, Blessed is He. Do not let your strategies and faith be centered on gold and possessions, for that is the beginning of idol worship, since these things turn one's forces and thoughts away from the Holy One, Blessed is He. Rather, spend your money willingly and easily on every purpose that the Holy One, Blessed is He, wants; for the Holy One, Blessed is He, has the power and strength to restore any loss or lack that you experience, and give you all your food, and provide for all the needs of your household.

≈§ Remove yourself from reliance on human beings.

The first step when dealing with any bad trait is distancing oneself from it. But this requires great consideration, understanding and thought in order to successfully execute the action. For example, in distancing oneself from the desire for honor, one must learn not to perform any action for the sake of honor, whether it is a complete action or some addendum to an action. The intelligent approach is to accustom the soul, bit by bit, to acutely recognize sharply the deceit and treachery of honor, as the *Rosh* has written in *Orchos Chaim*: "Remove yourself from reliance on a broken, weak reed, i.e. in human beings." For whoever ponders the matter sees that being honored by men neither helps nor hinders.

Few respect the morally superior person. Instead, they seem to fawn over the wealthy from whom they hope to see gain, and honor the powerful from whom they will receive protection. This being the case, the pursuit of honor is an illusion.

There are many witnesses of the vanity and deceit of seeking honor of this sort, if one just thinks about it and becomes aware of the workings of his soul.

Bit by bit, the truth of the matter will make its mark on him. For the soul accepts a truth. All the more so when we add faith in the teaching of *Chazal*: "Whoever flees from honor, honor pursues him."

The same principles apply to all the other moral traits.

When one's faith is founded on thought, then his thought will be strong, and his faith will be embedded in his heart like a secure tent-peg which cannot be moved.
(*Orach Yesharim*: R' Simchah Zissel of Kelm, *Pinkas HaKabalos*, p. 164)

❀ ❀ ❀

ᴥᴐ Remove yourself from reliance on human beings [variant: reliance on a broken, weak reed].

Thereby you will accustom and strengthen yourself in the virtue of reliance [on God]. For if you do not do so, your heart will rest on the support of man, [and you will assume] that men support the righteous, that they certainly would not abandon a pious man to let him die of hunger.

ᴥᴐ And walk modestly with your Createor.

How is this related to dependence on men? The *Rosh* is admonishing us not to be righteous in public. For when people see someone cloaked, as it were, in a mantle of holiness, they support him extensively, and this is a great crutch. This causes him to lose his trust in God. Therefore, he should walk modestly and not let his deeds be publicized. For without modesty he can still be said to depend on men, and once again falls upon trusting extraneous factors.

ᴥᴐ And do not make gold your infatuation. . ..

There are many things upon which man depends in the course of his life and only later realizes that they were powerless to help him. But it is rare that he should see the weakness inherent in money. For he takes it as a given that he can buy anything with money. That is why the *Rosh* has especially singled it out. Should you ponder the issue, you will realize that man will never get any more worldly benefit than that which has been allotted to him on Rosh Hashanah. For God has many ways to deprive him of the benefits which he might have acquired with money.

ᴥᴐ For that is the beginning of idol worship.

Money is the starting point of idolatry, because all are close to it. But idolatry itself is a lack of strong faith in Divine Providence, with the result that one leans on man as a crutch. As the *Chovos HaLevavos* put it: "He who does not know his master will not serve him, but will serve someone who knows him" (*Sha'ar Yichud HaMa'aseh*, Chapter 4). Such a man is plagued by idolatry itself and cannot receive the Torah and the success which springs from it, because he is truly incapable of relating to the Torah.

ᴥᴐ Instead, distrubute your money. . .

Should a person argue that he is saving his money because it is God's Will that he not become dependent on man for his needs, this is subject to a test. Does he spend his money in the performance of *mitzvos*? For that, too, is God's Will. If he does not, this indicates that he saves his money because he loves it, not because he wishes to fulfill God's Will.

ᴥᴐ In accordance with Hashem's Will. . .

Spending money in accordance with Hashem's Will does not necessarily mean just spending it for *mitzvos* such as *tzitzis* and *tefillin*. But if you feel that your soul will benefit if you part with some of your money, that it may help you gain spiritual advancement, or break your desire for money, that falls under the category of "Hashem's Will," and you may spend your money freely.

(*Or Yechezkel: Reshimos R' Reuven Melamed*)

❀ ❀ ❀

❧ Remove yourself from reliance on human beings [variant: reliance on a broken, weak reed], and walk modestly with your Creator,

The *Rosh* prescribes that one have trust, and teaches us that this trust goes hand in hand with modesty. For it is possible that a person will exercise trust just in order to gain people's respect, so that they should say that he trusts in God. Furthermore, trust must be accompanied with modesty and express itself privately; for should one become known as a person who trusts in God, others will take pains on his behalf, and his trust will then not be of the proper sort, but will become just another means for gaining his desires. (*Or Yechezkel*: Main Disciples)

30

דַּע אֶת אֱלֹהֵי אָבִיךָ. וּדְבָרֶיךָ בְּמֹאזְנֵי צֶדֶק תִּשְׁקֹל
וְהִין צֶדֶק יִהְיֶה לָךְ. וְיַקַּל בְּעֵינֶיךָ, הוֹצָאַת מָמוֹנְךָ
מֵהוֹצָאַת דְּבָרֶיךָ. וּפִיךָ אַל יְמַהֵר לְהוֹצִיא דָּבָר רַע
עַד אֲשֶׁר תִּשְׁקְלֵהוּ בְּמֹאזְנֵי שִׂכְלֶךָ.

Know the God of your father. Weigh your words
on the scales of justice and use an honest
measure. The expenditure of money
should be easier for you than the expenditure
of words. Your mouth should not rush
to utter a bad word, until you have weighed
it on the scales of your intelligence.

Know the God of your father, and whatever you wish to say, weigh it carefully in accordance with the just balance of your intelligence, so that you will not come to say anything that is not correct (i.e., not proper or inappropriate). Keep your word, and do not change what you have said in order to go back on a promise. It should be much easier and more comfortable for you to spend your money than to give forth your words. Therefore, do not be in a rush to utter even one harsh word, even if it is necessary, unless you weigh it thoroughly with intelligence and understanding.

◆§ *Know the God of your father. Weigh your words on the scales of justice.*

For some time now, on each Yom Kippur, I have given thought as to how all these resolutions (קַבָּלוֹת) might be included in one item. And I thought that this item might be: to know what one is saying, whether it be in everyday matters, in prayer, or in learning Torah. This is an important principle.[1]

The suggestion of the *Rosh* will be very helpful here: that one accustom himself to know what he is saying. This means that a man should not be a babbler — speaking in a mixture of topics when his mind is not settled. He should, rather, concentrate on the contents of each topic, whether it is in everyday matters or whether in heavenly matters — whether in prayer or in learning Torah. If he accustoms himself to this, he will begin to know what he is saying, word by word, without the admixture of an extraneous thought.

This is, however, a very difficult task. But, praise God, I have found advice to somewhat lighten the task for the one who is trying to acquire such a habit. We will (may it not be considered a vow) begin bit by bit, and hopefully, with the help of God, we will find it very valuable and march on from there. . .. At any rate, we will (may it not be considered a vow) begin bit by bit to accustom ourselves not to mix topics, even in thought, and especially during learning and prayer.

It is worthwhile to study paragraph 30 of the *Orchos Chaim* each day: "Know the God of your father. Weigh your words on the scales of justice." That is the direct opposite of speaking in a jumble. (*Orach Yesharim*: R' Simchah Zissel of Kelm, *Pinkas HaKabalos*, p. 14)

◆§ *The expenditure of money should be easier for you than the expenditure of words.*

It is a matter of marvel to see the many stages through which a person

---

1. It was a practice in the Mussar Movement for a person to make special resolutions governing his behavior, in order to promote his spiritual growth.

must go before speaking. Speech should come only after much thought and contemplation. Then comes the fruit of such labor: an utterance. The practical significance is that one's utterances should not come easily. This is what *Chazal* mean by saying: "The righteous say little. . . and the wicked say a lot" (*Bava Metzia* 87a). It is this that the *Rosh* has in mind when he writes: "The expenditure of money should be easier for you than the expenditure of words." (*Orach Yesharim*: R' Yerucham Levovitz, *Da'as Chochmah U'Mussar* III, p. 30)

⇥ *Your mouth should not rush to utter a bad word, until you have weighed it on the scales of your intelligence.*

Even if it is something that needs saying, you must weigh it well, and consider whether it must absolutely be said. Do not, then, rush to say something before it is perfectly clear to you that it should be said. Following the variant of the *Beis HaTalmud* of Kelm we find: "Your mouth should not be in a rush to utter a word until you have weighed it well." [This variant omits the word "bad"] According to this, not only a reprimand, but even the most dignified utterance should be carefully weighed. Rabbeinu Bachya has written that we use the crown of the Holy One when we speak. One ought to ponder the concept of the "speaking soul" (see *Onkelos* to *Bereishis* 2:7) which is the basis of man. He should weigh every word that he says in the balance of his mind. And the elevated levels of responsibility which the *Rosh* enjoins us here should stir us to action.

(*Orach Yesharim*: R' Yosef Shlomo Kahaneman, Rav of Ponevezh)

31

וִדּוּי עַל עֲוֹנוֹתֶיךָ עֶרֶב וָבֹקֶר אַל יֶחְסַר. וְזִכְרוֹן צִיּוֹן
וִירוּשָׁלַיִם בְּשִׁבְרוֹן לֵב וּבִדְאָגָה וּבַאֲנָחָה וּבְדִמְעָה.

Don't neglect the confession of your sins evening and morning, nor the remembrance of Zion and Jerusalem with a broken heart, with concern, sighing and tears.

⇥ *Don't neglect the confession of your sins evening and morning.*
This is a continuation which follows the admonition about speech;

for man ordinarily pays no attention to his spiritual state. However, if he weighs his words constantly on the balance scales of his intellegence and contemplates his deeds and repents, then — and only then — will he continuously stir himself to bring himself closer to God and thus will he ascend higher and higher.

(*Orach Yesharim*: R' Yosef Shlomo Kahaneman, Rav of Ponevezh)

✥ Here, the *Rosh* urges a man to admit his sins twice daily, evening and morning, without fail. Below, in the list of prescriptions to be studied on *Shabbos* (paragraph 21), he writes: "One should confess his sins each night before going to sleep except when it is forbidden to eulogize or to fast." There, he urges one to admit his sins only once a day and he also makes an exception for days when it is forbidden to fast or hold a eulogy.

Perhaps his statement, "one should confess his sins," there, does not mean that he should say [the fixed formula of confession], "I have erred, I have transgressed, I have sinned (חָטָאתִי, עָוִיתִי, פָּשַׁעְתִּי)," but refers instead to what the *Rambam* writes: "It is of the ways of repentance that he who repents should constantly cry out before God with pleas and weeping" (*Hilchos Teshuvah* 2:4). That is why the *Rosh* (in the prescriptions assigned to *Shabbos*), after stating "One should admit his sins each night...," immediately adds: "He should grieve over his sins, and the length of the exile...." It is of such admission of sins that he writes that one should admit them only once a day before he retires and he need not admit them on days when it is forbidden to fast or hold a eulogy.

(*Orach Yesharim*)

32

זְכֹר יוֹם הַמָּוֶת תָּמִיד.

וְצֵידָה לַדֶּרֶךְ הָכֵן.

וְשִׂים בֵּין עֵינֶיךָ שְׁנֵי אֵלֶּה תָּמִיד

וְיִהְיוּ מְזוּמָּנִים לְךָ לְיוֹם הַפֵּירוּד

וּמְטָתְךָ בְּדִמְעָה תַמְסֶה. וְיִבָּהֲלוּךָ רַעְיוֹנֶךָ

מִדֵּי זָכְרְךָ חֶרְדַת רַבָּן יוֹחָנָן זִכְרוֹנוֹ לִבְרָכָה.

Constantly remember the day of death, and prepare provisions for the journey. Place these two things [the remembrance and the preparation] constantly between your eyes, and they [your provisions] will be ready for you on the day of departure. Soak your bed with weeping [over your sins]. Let your thoughts be disturbed when you remember the trembling fear of Rabban Yochanan [ben Zakkai], of blessed memory [on his deathbed; see *Berachos* 28b].

TOSAFOS YOM TOV
Remember regularly, throughout the day, that you must certainly die, and prepare for yourself provisions for the journey to the World to Come. Those provisions are the Torah which you have learned, the good deeds which you have done, and your regret and repentance over the mistakes, sins, and crimes which you have committed. Pay attention carefully and regularly to these two things: namely, regularly remembering the day of death and preparing provisions for the World to Come, and these will be ready for you on the day when you leave this world.

◆§ *Constantly remember the day of death . . .*
Remember that your life here is not for generations upon generations.

◆§ *And prepare provisions for the journey.*
Show concern for your needs after your life has been completed here, so that you will not go hungry for bread [in the World to Come].

◆§ *Place these two things [the remembrance and the preparation] constantly between your eyes. . .*
Remember constantly the task that you have, to prepare what you need for the end of your days.

◆§ *And they [your provisions] will be ready for you on the day of departure.*
This is the method in which one prepares himself for departure from this world. At the outset, he must make himself strong. Yet, he should be aware that there is no end to the heights demanded from him. Even Rabban Yochanan ben Zakkai trembled, for there is punishment in *Gehinnom* even for those who achieve greatness. On any level that a

man finds himself, life and death, good and evil stand before him intermingled, so that the one cannot be distinguished from the other.

We find that the Sages stood in great fear of Hashem's judgment, Blessed is He; and that trait had always been the norm among the Jewish people until recently. As R' Yisrael Salanter writes, "Previously, as I knew it, everyone was seized by shuddering when the announcement was made that Rosh Chodesh Elul was forthcoming" [i.e. that Rosh Hashanah, the Day of Judgment, was only a month away]. Death, too, should remind a man of that judgment of which Rabban Yochanan ben Zakkai had such fear. And at a funeral, when we accompany each man to his personal day of judgment, we should remember and sense the judgment which awaits each of us, as the Rosh writes: "Constantly remember the day of death."

(Or Yechezkel: Kovetz Inyanim, 5729, p. 36, and Elul 5727, p. 55)

◆§ Constantly remember the day of death, and prepare provisions for the journey.

The Rosh has made two points here. First — to remember the day of death, and what follows from that — to prepare provisions for the journey. The source is in Avos (3:1): "Akavia ben Mahalalel says, Keep your eye on three things and you will not come to transgression."

R' Yisrael Salanter explained, in mussar terms, how one works towards this goal and how one prepares provisions for the journey "in the sense that whoever is joined to life has hope," specifically through the study of mussar. For with that, he is joined to life and the hope exists that he will return in teshuvah (repentance).

We don't sense the day of death and don't feel that life can cease because our soul is eternal; it lives forever. Thus, we don't possess that sense that life will cease. That is why the wisest of men (King Shlomo) has said: "It is better to go to a house of mourning than to a banquet house" (Koheles 7:2); for thereby, "the living will take it to heart" (ibid.) that one can die — that is, his body can die. For the soul does not feel the passage of time, since it is above the realm of time; it is eternal. Only by taking it to heart constantly does the soul understand and feel the sense of mortality.

Two more points are included here. "Constantly remember the day of death" — this involves self-control, awareness of the freedom of choice. "Prepare provisions for the journey" — this is the power of teshuvah (repentance). Even Rabban Yochanan ben Zakkai was afraid; along which road would they lead him? Which force would prevail? A fearsome thought!

(Orach Yesharim: R' Yosef Shlomo Kahaneman, Rav of Ponevezh)

◆§ Remember. . . and prepare

Remembering the day of death is one of the proven methods of attaining fear of Heaven, which comes in the wake of true awareness of the fact that the day of death will come, and in the sense that one lacks "provisions for the journey."

The talmidei Rabbeinu Yonah present the same picture in Berachos: " 'They run to the pit of the grave and I run to the World to Come.' When I see the days and seasons passing, I feel that each day I am running and am coming closer to death. That is why I prepare provisions for the way."

One must always remember the day of departure and how great is the obligation to prepare provisions for the way. A person must, of necessity, be overcome by a sense of alarm when he remembers that even that towering cedar of a man, Rabban Yochanan ben Zakkai, with all his awesome greatness, wept and took fright at the thought of the punishment in Gehinnom. Even though he saw the Heavenly fire and the angel who spoke from within the fire, even though he heard the heavenly voice which called him in invitation, nevertheless, all this did not calm him. He stood in dread of Heavenly judgment.

(Or Yechezkel: Reshimos Talmidim and Kovetz Inyanim, 5720, p. 35)

◆§ R' Simchah Zissel of Kelm would say that he who remembers the day of death has, in a way, been granted a Heavenly revelation; for he grasps what others do not. The day of death is not known to us, as the Zohar says: "Man goes about in this world and imagines that it belongs to him and he will remain in it for generations." If, then, one remembers the day of death, he has attained what others have not. This holds true for the study of mussar, as well.

(Or Yechezkel: Reshimos Talmidim)

◆§ And prepare provisions for the journey.

In paragraph 51, the Rosh repeats the admonition to remember the day of death, but with different phrasing: "Do not forget the stroke of death which will come suddenly. And bear in mind that one will stand in judgment."

We might interpret the two paragraphs as follows: Here, he urges man to hurry to perform mitzvos to the best of his ability, before his day comes, and not to let time slip by. Thus, he goes on to say "and prepare provisions for the journey," which is not found in paragraph 51. There, the emphasis is on the fear of Hashem: the Rosh admonishes man to fear Hashem, for he shall be judged. Thus, paragraph 51 continues: "and bear in mind the judgment [which follows]."

In the same vein, paragraph 52 follows with: "and do not avoid transgressions because of the punishment, but serve only because of love." Although one is to be constantly aware of the final judgment, his service to God should not be motivated only by fear of punishment. He should attempt to serve his Creator from pure love, and not just for the reward.   (*Orach Yesharim*)

◢§ The trembling fear

The *Rosh* offers advice as to how one can increase his fear and dread of the final terrifying day of judgment. To that end he says: "Remember the day of death constantly. . ." and he adds another piece of advice: to contemplate the trembling fear possessed by Rabban Yochanan ben Zakkai and see it as an example of how one should fear the day of judgment. It is as if he says to the simple soul who has no fear of judgment, "Look at how fearful Rabban Yochanan ben Zakkai was." In truth, all of Creation itself bears witness that judgment exists. But the simple soul is far from such awareness. One must be told to contemplate the fear and terror as seen by the example shown by great and righteous men. From them he will learn how to plant faith deep within himself.

(*Or Yechezkel: Kovetz Inyanim, Elul*, p. 17)

◢§ Remember the trembling fear of Rabban Yochanan. . .

Rabban Yochanan ben Zakkai felt fear because he did not know in which direction he would be led. Could he not have repented for whatever sins he may have done? No! For God's judgment is deep and hidden. There are also demands made with regard to those matters which a man does not see as sins, but which in Heaven are considered sins. And if he is unaware of such sins, how can he repent?

At first, Rabban Yochanan ben Zakkai said: "Now that they are taking me before the King Who enthrones kings, the Holy One, Blessed is He. . ." He feared lest he not find favor before the Holy One. This would be terrible; even the sufferings of *Gehinnom* would not help (Heaven save us), for His anger is eternal.

Fear of Heaven means the awe of His majesty. A man has no idea what the King will demand. Even if he imagines himself to be whole and perfect; even if others view him as righteous, nevertheless, when he stands before the Royal Judge, he is in a pitiful state. The levels are measured by a rod marked off in infinitely fine gradations, and it is possible that he will not find favor before God and will be found lacking levels of perfection.

Then, Rabban Yochanan ben Zakkai added: "And besides, there are two paths and I do not know along which one I will be led." Even if

God would not be angry, there are two paths, and one leads to *Gehinnom*. For whoever is not perfect in his actions must purify himself in *Gehinnom*.

(Or Yechezkel: Reshimos Talmidim)

&3 *Soak your bed with weeping [over your sins]. Let your thoughts be disturbed when you remember the trembling fear of Rabban Yochanan...*

The *Rosh* most likely knew the character of the thought process made by Rabban Yochanan ben Zakkai. Why does he tell us to learn from Rabban Yochanan ben Zakkai's fear? Let him present the same reckoning, and each one will apply it to himself and thereby arouse himself.

Here, the *Rosh* has added another row of bricks to the wall of *mussar*. Generations have diminished in stature, hearts have become smaller. Today, the reckoning of Rabban Yochanan ben Zakkai does not awaken us from our deep sleep. We need to see the weeping, frightened Rabban Yochanan ben Zakkai himself before our eyes. Then we will make the comparison and realize: If the flames have fallen upon the mighty cedars, what will become of us, the hyssop that clings to the walls? That is why the *Rosh* says: "Soak your bed with weeping when you think of the trembling fear of Rabban Yochanan ben Zakkai."

The *Rosh*, with a heart that was as broad as a great assembly hall, could limit himself to this comment. But what about our own generation? We who are orphans, children of orphans, we who are of impoverished intellect, and lacking sensitivity. We need to be spurred on by a large picture which joins them all — King David, who said, "My flesh prickled through fear of You, and of Your laws I was afraid" (*Tehillim* 119:120); Ezra the Scribe, who said, "My God, I am [too] ashamed and disgraced, my God, to lift my face towards You" (*Ezra* 9:6); Rabban Yochanan ben Zakkai, who wept and said: "If before a king of flesh and blood..." (*Berachos* 28b); the *Rosh*, who wrote, "Soak your bed with weeping..." R' Chaim of Volozhin, who fainted in terror when he reached Ezra's prayer (quoted above); R' Yisrael Salanter, who trembled in fear at the approach of the Days of Judgment!

When we make the sum total of this overwhelming reckoning, perhaps our feelings will be aroused and we will rise from our slumber and open the gates of our heart.

(Orach Yesharim: R' Yehudah Leib Chasman, Or Yahel III, p. 285)

&3 How awesome is the statement of the *Rosh*: "Soak your bed with weeping" — weeping without pause, until the sea of tears bursts forth and overflows your bed; until you are dissolved in them! And why tears? Because you think of the fear of Rabban Yochanan ben Zakkai. If he was afraid, what are we to say, how can we justify ourselves? That is, indeed, what we all say (in the Yom Kippur prayers): "Behold I [stand] before You like a vessel filled, with shame" — truly filled, to the brim with shame and disgrace and nothing else. (Ibid.)

◦§ On Rosh Hashanah, when all the world passes before the Creator, each man is judged not only with respect to his good and evil actions, but he is held accountable as to whether or not he has performed his personal destiny in life; whether he has fulfilled the unique purpose for which he was created. On this account, all have cause to worry. Our future depends on the extent to which we have completed our foreordained task or have failed in so doing.

This is exactly what the *Rosh* meant when he wrote: "Soak your bed with weeping... when you remember the trembling fear of Rabban Yochanan ben Zakkai." The Alter, R' Simchah Zissel of Kelm, used to point out that Rabban Yochanan ben Zakkai began to weep specifically when he saw his disciples. For he trembled and felt fear lest he had not fulfilled his duty towards them, lest he had not cared for each one to the fullest extent. (*Or Yechezkel:* R' Eliahu Lopian, *Lev Eliahu III*, p. 362)

◦§ It is one of the amazing aspects of Creation that only those who fear Heaven possess true love of life and fear of death. The ordinary individual does not attach much importance to death, and casually agrees to it. For who is it that actually fears death, and constantly remembers the day of death, and prepares provisions for his soul? Only one who fears Heaven is concerned about such matters. In the words of the *Rosh*, "Constantly remember the day of death ... Let your thoughts be disturbed when you remember the trembling fear of Rabban Yochanan ben Zakkai."

The righteous, who love life, live with constant fear of, and concern about, the day of death; they feel the need to prepare provisions for the way. But the ordinary man just lives his life, and his coming death makes no impression upon him. He does not seek out advice nor correct his acts, even in extreme old age. One must possess the fear of Heaven to feel the value of life, to have the proper view of death and fear it.

By nature, man tends to defuse the whole topic of death: "For man also loves his delights and needs to satiate his appetites, even though 'death's ways are its end' (*Mishlei* 14:12) and 'its steps bolster the grave' (ibid. 5:5)." Fear [of Heaven] saves man from such a state. Fear makes one sensitive to the value of life. That is what the Torah means when it urges us: "And you shall choose life" (*Devarim* 30:19).

(Or Yechezkel: Kovetz Inyanim II, 5729, p. 57)

33

חֲבֵר טוֹב הֱיֵה לְיִרְאֵי ה׳. הִתְחַבֵּר בְּחֶבְרָתָם. וּמֵחֶבְרַת פּוֹעֲלֵי אָוֶן הַרְחֵק, וֶאֱהוֹב הַמּוֹכִיחִים.

Be a good friend of those who fear Hashem. Keep their company, and stay away from the company of those who act unjustly. And love those who admonish [you].

◆§ One might say that the *Rosh* intends to tell us that the value and advantage in keeping company with those who fear God is that they admonish us. In order to "love those who admonish," you must be a good friend of the God fearing and stay away from those who act unjustly. For one scoffing remark drives off a hundred admonitions. This is why the *Rosh* placed these two injunctions [about friends and about the love of admonishment] side by side.   (Orach Yesharim)

34

טוֹב וְיָשָׁר לְךָ לְהַמְעִיט בְּעֵינֶיךָ פְּעֻלּוֹתֶיךָ הַטּוֹבִים וְהַגְדֵּיל פְּשָׁעֶיךָ. [נ״א וּלְהַגְדֵּיל בְּעֵינֶיךָ פְּשָׁעֶיךָ] וּלְהַרְבּוֹת חַסְדֵי בּוֹרַאֲךָ, וְיוֹצֶרְךָ מִבֶּטֶן, וְנוֹתֵן אָכְלְךָ בְּעִתּוֹ. וְלֹא תִהְיֶה מְשַׁמֵּשׁ עַל מְנַת לְקַבֵּל פְּרָס בַּעֲשׂוֹתְךָ מִצְוֹתָיו.

It is good and proper for you to denigrate your good deeds in your own eyes and to emphasize your sins [variant: **and to emphasize your sins in your eyes**], **and to magnify the kindnesses of your Creator, Who formed you from the time you were in the womb and Who gives you your food in its proper time. And when you perform His *mitzvos*, do not serve in order to receive a reward.**

⮜ *It is good and proper for you to denigrate your good deeds in your own eyes.*

When one contemplates the greatness of man's obligation to serve his Creator, and realizes that the evil of one who rebels against Him is boundless, he sees that no matter how much he adds in his service towards God and in his acts of repentance, it still is meager [compared to what he owes], and therefore [his righteous acts] will seem small in his own eyes.

(*Orach Yesharim*: Rabbeinu Yonah, *Sha'arei Teshuvah* 1:16)

⮜ *Magnify the kindnesses of your Creator...*

When you minimize your good deeds and magnify your sins in your eyes, then you will see the Creator's acts of kindness. You will not serve in order to gain a reward, for you will realize that you deserve nothing [and everything He gives you is only from His kindnesses].

But if you magnify your good deeds and play *down* your sins in your eyes, you will not see the acts of kindness of your Creator. You will think that everything is coming to you as payment for your good deeds. It is comparable to an employer who pays a worker; in such a situation, there is no kindness involved.

(*Or Yechezkel: Reshimos R' Reuven Melamed*)

⮜ *And when you perform His mitzvos, do not serve in order to receive a reward.*

And I, when I was young, once asked my uncle Rabbeinu Asher (the *Rosh*), "How is it that in the *Seder Kedushah* (וּבָא לְצִיּוֹן) we say: 'Be it Your Will that we keep Your statutes in this world in order to be found worthy, live, see and inherit good and blessing for the days of the *Mashiach* and the World to Come (כְּדֵי שֶׁנִּזְכֶּה וְנִחְיֶה וכו')? What greater example could there be of serving in order to receive a reward?"

He answered, "I do not use that phrasing, but I [omit the expression, "in order to," שֶׁ כְּדֵי, and] say, ['Be it Your Will that we keep Your statutes

in this world,] and may we be found worthy and live. . .' all in the terms
of petition and prayer."

My other uncle, R' Chaim, gave me a different answer. He said that
[even if we include the expression, "in order to. . ."], this is not considered
serving in order to get a reward. One puts himself in that category only
if, on seeing his wishes unfulfilled, he regrets having served.

(Sefer HaChasidim Tinyana, by the nephew of the Rosh,
paragraph 51; see, too, paragraph 89)

◆§ The essential purpose of Creation is to benefit man. If so, the most
important service and the most acceptable one is that which is done
for a reward; that is, when a person serves so that Hashem might benefit
him. And with that, Hashem will, so to speak, have a sense of satisfaction
[from seeing the purpose of Creation fulfilled]. Indeed, if a person does
serve for reward purely with the intention to have God "feel" satisfaction
when He benefits His creatures in return for their service, that would be
the highest category of Divine service. But if, on the contrary, a person
thinks only of the pleasure *he* will have, this is an inferior level of service,
and we have been admonished to refrain from it.

(Orach Yesharim: R' Chaim of Volozhin, Ruach HaChaim 1:3)

35

יוֹמָם וָלַיְלָה זִכְרוֹ מִפִּיךְ אַל יָמוּשׁ. בְּשָׁכְבְּךָ תִּשְׁגֶּה
בְּאַהֲבָתוֹ, וּבְקוּמֶךָ, וּבְהִילוּכְךָ תִּמְצָאֶנּוּ, וַהֲקִיצוֹת
בּוֹ תְּשַׁעֲשֵׁע, וְהוּא יְיַשֵּׁר אוֹרְחוֹתֶיךָ.

Day or night, mention of Him shall not depart
from your mouth. When you lie down to sleep, be
infatuated with love for Him, and when you rise
up and walk about, you should find Him. In your
waking hours you should find delight in Him,
and He will straighten your paths.

◆§ *Day or night . . .*

When one bears in mind throughout the day that there is nothing
other than Him, that there is nothing in the world aside from His Will,
then one will neither have questions nor doubts which weaken his love

of Hashem. For from the very beginning, anything that happens is perceived as stemming from His Will; day and night the awareness of Hashem is before him; he is constantly absorbed in His Love and Will. Then, automatically, he drops the belief that his own striving and deeds are the determining factor. He accepts God, constantly, as King. And one does not question the acts of a king, for the king's will is subject to no higher authority. (Or Yechezkel: Reshimos Talmidim)

⋖ Be infatuated with love for Him...

The Kitzur HaSh'lah says that whenever one speaks of what he wishes to do, he should say, "If Hashem wills" (אי"ה), or, "with Hashem's help" (בעז"ה), to plant in his heart the awareness that he is not independent but is in the hands of the Holy One. Thereby, he fulfills what the Rosh says: "Mention of Him shall not pass from your lips day or night," for at all times he makes mention of Hashem, and His Name does not pass from his lips.

But that which follows: "When you lie down to sleep, be infatuated with love for Him" — that is a very lofty plane in service to and love of Hashem. That is a matter which involves the heart and soul and cannot be achieved by speech alone. It requires long, drawn-out labor.

(Orach Yesharim)

36

כַּוֵּן בִּתְפִלָּתְךָ כִּי הַתְּפִילָה הִיא עֲבוֹדַת הַלֵּב.
וְאִם בִּנְךָ יְדַבֵּר לְךָ וְלֹא מִלְּבּוֹ, הֲלֹא יִחַר לְךָ,
וּמַה תַּעֲשֶׂה טִפָּה סְרוּחָה לִפְנֵי מַלְכּוֹ שֶׁל עוֹלָם.
וְלֹא תִהְיֶה כְּעֶבֶד שֶׁמָּסְרוּ לוֹ מְלָאכָה נִכְבֶּדֶת
לְטוֹבָתוֹ, וְחִבְּלָהּ. וְאֵיךְ יַעֲמֹד לִפְנֵי הַמֶּלֶךְ.
וּמַה טּוֹב לְבַקֵּשׁ סְלִיחָה, עַל אָמְרְךָ
סְלַח לָנוּ, בְּלֹא כַּוָּנָה. וְאִם אִי אֶפְשָׁר בְּכָל
הַתְּפִילוֹת, בְּרָכָה רִאשׁוֹנָה שֶׁל שְׁמוֹנָה עֶשְׂרֵה.
וּפָסוּק רִאשׁוֹן שֶׁל קְרִיאַת שְׁמַע אַל יֶחְסָר.
כִּי לֹא יָצָא חוֹבַת הַתְּפִילָה מִי שֶׁלֹּא כַּוֵּן בָּהֶם.

Have proper intention (כַּוָּנָה) in your prayer, for
prayer is the service of Hashem from the heart.
If your son were to speak to you,
but not from his heart, would it not anger you?
How, then, can a putrid drop [a human being]
act this way before the King of the universe?
Do not be like a servant who
has been given an honorable task
for his own benefit, and then spoils it.
How, then, can he stand before the King?
How good it is to seek forgiveness for
the fact that you say, "Forgive us!" [in the
Shemoneh Esrei] without proper intention.
And if it is impossible [to have proper intention]
throughout all the prayers, [then have it]
during the first blessing of the Shemoneh Esrei.
Do not omit [proper intention in] the first verse
of the Shema. For he who does not have
proper intention when saying these
does not fulfill the obligation of prayer.

⋖§ Have proper intention in your prayer . . .

Know that these acts of service, such as the reading of the Torah,
prayer and other mitzvos, have only a single purpose. They are meant
to have you become involved in the mitzvos of God, Blessed is He, and
to turn away from worldly dealings, as if you became involved with
Him and freed yourself from everything else.

But if you pray with moving lips and with your face to the wall, yet
think about buying and selling; if you give voice to your reading in the
Torah, but your heart is on the building of your house and you don't
pay attention to what you are reading. . . do not imagine that you have
reached the desired goal. On the contrary, you will resemble those of
whom it is said (Yirmiyahu 12:2): "You [Hashem] are close to them in
their mouths, but distant from them in their thoughts."

(Orach Yesharim: Rambam, Moreh Nevuchim 3:51)

৵§ Let all your limbs stand like men in battle — alert, anxious to obey the command of their leader. They pay no attention to any pain nor think about any loss which may occur. Let the words of the tongue correspond to the thoughts of the mind and do not let the words exceed the thoughts. Let one not utter his prayer mechanically and habitually, like a parrot, but, each word should be accompanied with the proper thoughts and intent before Hashem.

(Orach Yesharim: Kuzari 3:5)

৵§ For prayer is the service of Hashem from the heart.

A specific organ of each of our two hundred and forty-eight organs is designated for each mitzvah. The organ designated for prayer is the heart. The task of the heart and its purpose is prayer. That is what the Rosh meant by: "Have proper intention in your prayer, for prayer is the service of Hashem coming from the heart."

Prayer that comes from the lips only but not from the heart does not fulfill the mitzvah of prayer, nor does it achieve the desired goal. Even if the person hears what his lips say, and understands what he hears, but only with his mind, that is not enough. His heart must hear what his lips say. His heart should labor and absorb what he says. That is the only way he will derive great benefit and strengthen himself through prayer.

R' Yerucham, the Mashgiach (spiritual dean) [of Mir Yeshivah], would say that prayer without proper intention (כַּוָּנָה) could be likened to putting on tefillin around the neck, an act whereby one does not fulfill the mitzvah at all. And furthermore, the mitzvah was turned, thereby, into a disgrace.

Similarly, proper intention of prayer is in the heart, and if it is not there, man has not fulfilled the mitzvah of prayer.

What is the form of proper prayer? The Torah writes: "...and to serve Him with all your heart" (Devarim 11:13). Chazal explain: "What is service of the heart? Prayer!" This means that the very definition of prayer is "the service of the heart." Of necessity, prayer must be associated at least with the heart. If the heart is not involved, you will not have prayer. For proper intention is the soul of prayer, and it is meant to bring the heart to the state of prayer. One can only feel that he stands in the presence of and serves before the King if he prepares himself before the prayer, if he works on his heart and prepares it for prayer. That is what is called "the spirit of prayer (רוּחַ הַתְּפִילָה)," which is the proper form of prayer.

(Or Yechezkel: Reshimos Talmidim)

◆§ *If your son were to speak to you, but not from his heart, would it not anger you?*

Imagine that a man comes before you, one who is seeking a favor from you and, though he speaks to you, you know that he is only mouthing words, without even thinking about them. You would certainly be angry and would refuse to help him. How then can you act similarly in your prayer? Not only is your prayer wanting because it lacks proper intention, but you will bring anger upon yourself. When one puts forward a request to a friend or to the authorities, that request should itself be the cause for a favorable reply. Now, if the request is a half-hearted one, it stands to reason that not even half a reply will be forthcoming. The answer will depend on the measure of the petitioner's efforts in proving the real necessity of his request. If his heart is not evident, he will not accomplish a thing.

This should tell us that each of us must strengthen his fellow man on this point. If he doesn't do so, he has no true appreciation of the importance of the issue. For even man made of flesh and blood will feel angry when confronted by a man who does not speak from the heart. How, then, can we not feel upset about such negligence in the Divine service of prayer?

(*Or Yechezkel: Kovetz Inyanim*, 5729, p. 32; *Reshimos Talmidim*)

◆§ *How, then, can a putrid drop [a human being] act this way before the King of the universe?*

It would be disrespectful to behave in this way to a friend. How, then, can one act in such a way before the King of kings? Man, when he deals with matters of the here and now, tries to keep his promises and does not wish to be numbered among those who act unjustly and lie. But when we turn to non-mundane matters, to the service of the spirit, we do not sense that we are liars before Hashem, Blessed is He.

There are several reasons for such behavior. From childhood on, we have become accustomed to saying before Hashem, things that we do not believe. And because this has become a matter of habit, it seems natural and we are no longer aware that we mouth falsehoods. In addition, our reasoning deceives us: we think the only requirement is to say words, even though our hearts and lips are not at one. We think that the substance of prayer consists of orally proclaiming the acceptance of the yoke of the Majesty of Heaven, even though it is not in our heart.

There is a third reason, too. We lack true faith and are not really aware that when we stand during *Shemoneh Esrei*, we are standing in

His presence and petitioning Him. That is why we think lightly of saying what is far, far from our heart's thoughts. If we were to believe and be aware that the Holy One hears every utterance and knows every hidden thought, that He senses the gap between heart and lips and that our words spring only from the lips, we most certainly would avoid speaking falsely before Him.

(Or Yechezkel: Emunah, p. 167; Reshimos Talmidim)

ङ Do not be like a servant who has been given an honorable task for his own benefit, and then spoils it.

Prayer is a task of honor. It has been given to man for his benefit. Take care not to spoil it. In prayer we aim in truth to give *praise* (שֶׁבַח) and offer *thanks* (הוֹדָאָה) to Hashem, Blessed is He, for all that He has done, and ask that He supply all our needs. When we pray without proper intention, the basic *halachah* requires us to repeat our prayers [since we did not fulfill the *mitzvah*. However, in our day, one does not repeat the prayer even if he recited it without proper intention. See *Shulchan Aruch, Orach Chaim* 101:1]. We, however, do not really have proper intention. Our error may be found in our basic misconception that all that is necessary for prayer is the *wish* to pray. That is foolish. Picture a man who asks something of another and the benefactor-to-be knows that the suppliant's heart is not in the request. He will not grant him his wish. How, then, can we pray before the Creator and, while we are praying, think about other matters?

(Or Yechezkel: Kovetz Inyanim, Elul p. 85; Reshimos Talmidim)

ङ [Then have it] during the first blessing of the Shemoneh Esrei . . . the first verse of the Shema.

Accepting the yoke of the Majesty of Heaven has two aspects. We must accept the yoke — that is the *mitzvah* of reciting the *Shema* morning and evening. And then we must be on constant guard not to throw off that yoke; not to neglect even the simplest of commandments. We must keep these two aspects in mind in accepting the yoke.

To accept the yoke of Heavenly Majesty while reciting the *Shema* is also not a simple affair. To fulfill the commandment as prescribed by the *Shulchan Aruch* [Orach Chaim, Chapts. 60-61] requires our very special attention. We must direct our thoughts to understanding the meaning of the first verse. Failing to do so nullifies the act. If one has recited the *Shema* from beginning to end, but has not had the proper intention when saying the first verse, he must repeat the *Shema* with the proper intention. To have such proper intention, one must possess a "tranquility of soul" at least during the time he is praying. Attaining this state does not come easily for a man who is not in the world of Torah but immersed in the hustle and bustle of life.

What does that first verse mean? It means: "Israel, accept the fact that the Master of all — He Who was, is and will be — directs us; that there is nothing besides Him — the Master of all, He Who was, is and will be — in the heavens, on earth, and in the four directions." Preferably, one should continue to concentrate on these thoughts through the end of the second verse of the *Shema*. He should reach the level of wholehearted acceptance of this principle even to the point of suffering martyrdom for it. This set of beliefs, this acceptance of the yoke of the Majesty of Heaven, serves as the basis for the acceptance of the *mitzvos* which is formulated in the second paragraph of the *Shema*.

(*Or Yechezkel: Kovetz Inyanim*, p. 71)

◄§ In *Pirkei Avos* (2:18) we are told: "Take care with reciting the *Shema* and prayer (*Shemoneh Esrei*)". The *Yavetz* elaborated upon this maxim at length. The gist of his remarks is that the *Shema* and *Shemoneh Esrei* are essential and indispensable.

We may compare this to man's physical existence. Many foods are good for the body. But even though his entire diet is of service to him, man cannot live without bread and water. If he fills his home with gold and silver, but lacks bread and water, he will certainly starve to death. *Mitzvos* present a similar picture. All *mitzvos* are beneficial to the spirit. But without the *Shema* and prayer, it is impossible to exist. If he is sinfully negligent with regard to them, his lot is evil and bitter. They are the key to a person's success; without them there is no hope that he will merit achieving the end for which he was created.

And there is something more. The foundation of the *Shema* is the acceptance of the yoke of the Majesty of Heaven — the first principle which every Jew must take upon himself. *Shemoneh Esrei* (prayer) is the expression of praise to the Holy One and the awareness of our need for Him. It is then that man asks for his sustenance from Hashem, Blessed is He. This expresses the principle of faith in Divine Providence, and the awareness that there is no other than Him; for without Him we can receive nothing. That is why prayer stands on such a high pinnacle; it expresses the basic principles of faith in Hashem and in His Providence.

(*Or Yechezkel: Emunah*, p. 175)

◄§ If we think about it, we will realize that most people do not properly perform the *mitzvos* of reciting the *Shema* and praying. For the first verse of the *Shema* requires proper intention of the heart (כַּוָּנַת הַלֵּב); to see the Holy One as the Master of all; Who was, is, and will be; Who rules the four points of the compass. Without great effort and without contemplation of the issue of faith, and of the Exodus from Egypt, one will be far from that desired proper intention of the heart, for the heart of man is steeped in heresy and apostasy.

It is certainly difficult to say the first blessing of *Shemoneh Esrei* as one should. Do not imagine that it is easy. I have experience, and yet if I do not make a great effort, I know that after a few sentences I am far removed from the proper intention. To prevent this, one should pray from a prayerbook. Without plans and stratagems it is indeed difficult to become careful when reciting the *Shema* or praying.

(Or Yechezkel: Emunah, p. 309)

◆§ If one can have proper intention (כַּוָּנָה) during the *Shemoneh Esrei* prayer, he may pray; if he cannot, he should not pray (*Rambam, Hilchos Tefillah* 4:15). The *Poskim* have ruled that if he can have proper intention for the first blessing (which ends with מָגֵן אַבְרָהָם, "Shield of Avraham"), that is sufficient (*Shulchan Aruch, Orach Chaim,* 101:1).

And yet, since this prayer is essentially man's request before God for his needs, and is accompanied with his heart's faith that all rests in God's Hand, that He is the Master of all, and that it is only from Him that man can ask for his needs, why is the first blessing more relevant to these thoughts than any of the other blessings? Why is it enough for a person to have proper intention for the extent of the first blessing only? And why is it that if he had proper intention only during the first blessing, it is considered as if he had proper intention during the entire *Shemoneh Esrei*?

The answer is that the first blessing is the basis of faith. And this is so, because it declares that Hashem is the God of Avraham, Yitzchak and Yaakov. They were the first to be aware of their Creator; they understood that the world has a Director, that He is the First Cause and there is nothing beside Him.

For by speaking of the God of his Forefathers, man fixes this belief in his heart. It is obvious that his heart knows that in asking for his needs he cannot turn anywhere except to Him. Therefore, even if he does not have proper intention during the utterance of the following individual requests, he may, nevertheless, pray, since his faith has been established in the first blessing, which is the basis for the others.

(Orach Yesharim: R' Simchah Zissel of Kelm)

37

לְמֹד פַּרְשִׁיּוֹתֶיךָ עִם הַצִּבּוּר, שְׁנַיִם מִקְרָא וְאֶחָד
תַּרְגּוּם וּפֵרוּשׁ רַשִׁ"י ז"ל, וּתְדַקְדֵּק בּוֹ כַּאֲשֶׁר תּוּכַל
וְכֵן יִהְיֶה לְךָ בִּגְמָרָא, כִּי הָעוֹסֵק בַּגְּמָרָא מִדָּה
טוֹבָה וְנוֹתְנִין עָלֶיהָ שָׂכָר. וְאֵין לְךָ מִדָּה טוֹבָה
הֵימֶנָּה וּתְנַן תַּלְמוּד תּוֹרָה כְּנֶגֶד כֻּלָּם.

Study your [weekly Torah] portions along with
the community [by reading] the text of the Torah
twice and the translation [of *Onkelos*] once,
and the commentary of *Rashi z"l*.
Study it carefully as best as you can and so shall
you do with *Gemara;* for to occupy oneself with
Gemara is a good trait, and reward is given for it.
There is no better trait than this,
as the *Mishnah* says: "The study of Torah is equal
to all [the good deeds] combined" [*Peah* 1:1].

TOSAFOS YOM TOV

During the week, study that portion of the Torah which will be read in synagogue on Shabbos morning at the end of that week. Read each verse twice, and the Aramaic translation of that verse once, and take care to finish the Torah portion before the reader finishes reading it in the synagogue.

Also study the commentary of *Rashi* on that portion of the Torah. Examine his commentary with the greatest possible depth and exactitude, in order to discern, as well as you are able, what was actually *Rashi's* true intention.

Likewise, when you study *Gemara*, study in such a way that you will be sure that you have correctly understood. Examine it with depth and exactitude, as best as you can. For when someone studies *Gemara*, and devotes himself to studying it carefully and efficiently in order to understand everything correctly, he makes himself beloved, and receives the best and most complete fulfillment — more than is received from studying any other part of the Torah. And the Holy One, Blessed is He, gives a special reward for studying *Gemara* for there is no field of Torah that is better to study than *Gemara*.

The *Mishnah* states that Torah-study is accounted by the Holy One, Blessed is He, as equal to the finest of the good deeds, so that He can reward someone who studies Torah for his studying. And it is certainly impossible to understand the Torah correctly without the *Gemara*.

∽§ *Study your [weekly Torah] portions along with the community...*

The *Rosh* has seemingly repeated this prescription in his section for *Shabbos* (paragraph 15): "One should study the weekly Torah portion each week, twice in the Hebrew, once in the Aramaic translation [of *Onkelos*], and with the commentary of *Rashi*." But here he states that one should do so "along with the community," whereas there the point is made about learning it each week.

Let us consider the comments of the *Ma'adanei Yom-Tov* (*Berachos* 1:38). The *Beis Yosef* concludes that according to the *Rambam*, the two-time review of the weekly Torah portion should not include the reading that one hears during the *Shabbos* service. One must review the portion on his own twice more, even if he hears it in the public reading. The *Ma'adanei Yom-Tov* feels that this view holds true only preferably (לְכַתְּחִלָּה). For optimally it is not sufficient to merely read; one should study what one reads. But if we are speaking of the second-best method, according to the strict *halachah* (בְּדִיעֲבַד), the public reading can be considered as one of the two reviews.

Perhaps the Rosh in his section on *Shabbos* addresses this point. He did not quote the version of the *Gemara* verbatim [i.e. he left out the phrase "with the community"], because he wished to point out that one should *learn* the weekly portion twice and not rely on the public presentation, which is only a *reading*.

We have already suggested that the *Shabbos* section contains prescriptions which go beyond the letter of the law (לִפְנִים מְשׁוּרַת הַדִּין). The above analysis fits in well with this hypothesis. [Here, in paragraph 37, the *Rosh* presents the basic requirements: to read the portion twice, even if one of the readings is simply to verbalize along with the public reading. But in the *Shabbos* section he prescribes going beyond the letter of the law by doing two studious readings in addition to the public reading.]

The *Rambam* discusses the topic of reviewing the weekly portion in *Hilchos Tefillah* (*Laws of Prayer*), near *Hilchos Krias HaTorah* (*Laws of Torah Reading*). The *Rosh* here, however, placed the topic of reviewing of the Torah reading in the same paragraph with the comment, "And so shall you do with *Gemara.*" This would seem to indicate that here, the *Rosh* is referring to the Rabbinically established minimum for performing the *mitzvah* of Torah study. Perhaps, in the *Shabbos* section, when he repeats the prescription about reviewing the Torah reading, he is indicating that this is also an aspect of the *mitzvah* of the public Torah reading. He thus stipulates that even one who is constantly involved in studying the Torah is obliged to fulfill this *mitzvah,* as well.

The *Tosafos Yom-Tov* writes: "One should take care to complete his review of the portion before the Torah reader finishes the reading in the synagogue." He seems to have based his remarks on the teaching of Rabbeinu Yonah, who says that one should read the weekly portion at home before it is read in public in the synagogue (*Berachos* 8b). The *Or Zarua* expresses the same opinion at the beginning of *Hilchos Shabbos.*

This, however, does not seem to be the position of the *Rosh.* For in his commentary on *Berachos,* on the basis of a *midrash,* he states that even as a first choice (לְבַתְּחִלָה) one should complete his review of the Torah reading before the *Shabbos* meal. He makes no mention of trying to complete it before the public reading of the Torah.

(*Orach Yesharim*)

◂§ *And the commentary of Rashi z"l.*

The commentary of *Rashi* is based on explaining the plain meaning of each verse. *Rashi's* interpretations are drawn exclusively from *midrashim* and the tradition transmitted by *Chazal,* as is known. The *Rosh* instructs us to "study your [weekly Torah] portions along with the community [by reading] the text of the Torah twice and the translation [of *Onkelos*] once, and the commentary of *Rashi* z"l. Study it as carefully as you can and so shall you do with *Gemara...*" These instructions were not directed towards someone else, but to himself. So he said and so he acted. Even though there was no lack of great commentaries on the Torah in his day, he specifically named *Rashi* as the commentary to "study carefully as best as you can." In my opinion, his following words: "And so shall you do with *Gemara,*" refer to *Rashi's* commentary on the *Gemara.* For it is indeed the most wonderful commentary of all those that have been handed down to us from the generations gone by; it is "a metropolis in which everything [one needs] can be found."

(*Orach Yesharim:* R' Yerucham Levovitz,
Introduction to *Da'as Torah, Bereishis*)

ᴥᎦ Study it carefully . . .
One who studies *Chumash* and *Rashi* for years in a consistent manner, with deep understanding, attention and intellectual analysis, will gain great understanding, will grow to his full potential and will be blessed. I am a simple soul and I speak to myself and those like myself. I see the beginning of the glory of Israel, the exalted benefit reaped by every Jew who studies *Chumash* with *Rashi* regularly, week after week, without a break. For he thus becomes a man of order and discipline. (ibid.)

ᴥᎦ For to occupy oneself with Gemara is a good trait, and reward is given for it.
Since the *Rosh* writes of the one who engages in the study of *Gemara* that "there is no better trait," why must he inform us that there is a reward? We are told in the *Mishnah*: "Rebbe says: Be as careful with a minor *mitzvah* as with a major one. For you do not know what reward is given for *mitzvos*" (*Avos* 2:1). And Rabbeinu Yonah has written in his *Sha'arei Teshuvah* that the reward for the simplest *mitzvah* is so great and wonderful that it cannot be described or measured. Most certainly, then, this holds true for the study of *Gemara*, of which the *Rosh* says: "There is no better trait."

Perhaps the answer is that the pleasure of *Gemara* study is so great that the study itself could be its own reward. For the pleasure of such study is truly like the pleasure of *Gan Eden*. The *Rosh* wishes to tell us a surprising fact: that for enjoying this marvelous pleasure, we also receive [additional] reward! May He be blessed, Who chose us from all the nations and gave us His *Gemara*.

(*Orach Yesharim*: R' Eliahu Lopian, end of *Lev Eliahu, Shemos*)

⚜ Tuesday ⚜

38

מִכָּל מַאֲכָל אֲשֶׁר יֵאָכֵל וּמִכָּל מַשְׁקֶה אֲשֶׁר יִשָּׁתֶה,
אַל תִּהְיֶה בְּלֹא בְּרָכָה תְּחִלָּה וְסוֹף. וְכַוֵּן בָּה כַּאֲשֶׁר
תּוּכַל. וְכַסֵּה רֹאשְׁךָ כְּשֶׁתַּזְכִּיר אֶת ה', וְיִזְמוֹ
[נ"א וּתְסַגוֹר] עֵינֶיךָ. כִּי מִדֵּי דַבְּרוֹ בּוֹ, אַל תְּהִי
כָּאָמוּר: "בְּפִיו וּבִשְׂפָתָיו כִּבְּדוּנִי, וְלִבּוֹ רִחַק מִמֶּנִּי."

Any food that may be eaten or drink that may be
imbibed should not be [ingested] without a
blessing before and after. Concentrate on it as
best as you can. Cover your head when you
mention His Name, and close your eyes.
For when one speaks of Him [during prayers or
blessings], it should not be like the verse
(*Yeshayahu* 29:13), "With one's mouth and one's
lips they honored Me, but one distanced his heart
from Me [i.e. their prayers were insincere].

⋖§ *Cover your head when you mention His Name, and close your eyes.*
Our Master, the *Mashgiach* (R' Yechezkel Levenstein), was very
careful to put on his hat before every blessing, even the short blessings
like the *Shehakol* ("...through Whose Word everything came to be") or
the *Asher Yatzar* ("...Who created man with wisdom..."). Covering the
head with a hat or *tallis* (as opposed to a *yarmulke*) makes man's heart
submissive and brings on the fear of Heaven (*Beis Yosef*, *Orach Chaim*,
Chapter 8). It also serves as a preparation for the blessing or prayer.
   He would often say that, if one does not prepare himself before the
act and during the act, his prayer will only be a matter of mouthing

words. His heart will be elsewhere, and all his service will rest, Heaven forbid, on an unreal base.   (*Or Yechezkel: Reshimos Talmidim*)

⋙ We are directed to train and habituate our body to serve the One Who sees but is not seen. The angels all serve Him in such fashion, for they ask: "Where is the place of His glory?" [אַיֵּה מְקוֹם כְּבוֹדוֹ], and they are aware of Him to the fullest possible extent. Man, too, who is but a physical being, must also be aware and still "see" Him, even though He is invisible. Man must be capable of serving Him. That is why the *Rosh* says that one should close his eyes when praying or pronouncing blessings. When he shuts his eyes, he will not be disturbed by physical vision and he can be an honest servant to Him Who sees but is not seen. The "whispered prayer" [*Shemoneh Esrei*] should also be executed in this manner. It accustoms one to strip away the material.

(*Orach Yesharim*: R' Yerucham Levovitz,
Da'as Chochmah U'Mussar III, p. 203)

⋙ He should strip himself of the material. For that which one sees — namely, the revealed [physical] world — causes confusion in prayer; for it detracts from the essence of prayer. That which is seen hinders one's awareness of the existence of the unseen. The *Rosh* tells us to close our eyes and push away the reality that is visible from before our eyes. In that way, it is more likely that we will achieve our goal. For then, the existence of the unseen will take the place of the seen.

The statement of the *Rosh* cannot, at face value, apply to every person, nor in all instances. Sometimes one can concentrate better with his eyes shut; other times, when his eyes are on the prayerbook. The *Rosh* wishes to tell us that prayer is built on the reality of the unseen. That is why he advises us to push away the sphere of the seen. In this way we may more closely approach the essence of prayer.

The *Tur* teaches that when praying, one "should envision the Divine Presence opposite him, as the Psalmist writes, 'I have placed Hashem opposite me always' (*Tehillim* 16:8). The reasoning behind this teaching is the very foundation of prayer. For, if one lacks the sense of standing before the Divine Presence, if he has no awareness of the realm of the unseen, his actions are not truly "prayers."

(*Orach Yesharim*: R' Yerucham Levovitz —
Da'as Chochmah U'Mussar I, p. 139)

⋙ *For when one speaks of Him [during prayers or blessings], it should not be like the verse (Yeshayahu 29:13), "With one's mouth and one's lips they honored Me, but one distanced his heart from Me."*
Rabbeinu Yonah writes in *Sha'arei Teshuvah* that one cannot

achieve fear of God without strategy and deep thought, without "waging great campaigns." It is never acquired without study, contemplation and effort. The "fear" that one has without such constant application is only a "commandment learned by rote from other people" (מִצְוַת אֲנָשִׁים מְלוּמָּדָה).

However, the Alter of Kelm posed a question on this point. *Chazal* have said that a man should always engage in study and the performance of *mitzvos*, even if he does not do so for the sake of learning or *mitzvos*, but for some ulterior motive. For such involvement will lead him to the study and the performance of *mitzvos* for the proper reasons (*Nazir* 23b). Why, then, is such severe punishment given for "fear. . . learned by rote from other people?"

Learning that is not properly motivated is permitted, he answered, when it leads to learning that is. But "fear learned by rote" never leads to true fear of Heaven. Hence, there is no reason to allow it.

(*Or Yechezkel: Kovetz Inyanim, Elul 5727*, p. 58)

⇜§ "Rote" means the force of habit. It draws people and attracts them.

Man possesses a tendency, an inclination (יֵצֶר) to habit. Therefore it is a mistake to assume that because one has thought profoundly about the fear of Heaven and acquired feelings of true fear, his fear can no longer become a matter of habit. For the tendency towards "fear learned by rote" is always there, ready to govern one's actions. Man must constantly increase his contemplation in order to overcome that which has become habit.

(Ibid.)

39

נְטוֹל יָדֶיךָ לִתְפִילָה וְלַאֲכִילָה, וּבְעֵת צֵאתְךָ
מִצְרָכֶיךָ בָּרֵךְ אֲשֶׁר יָצַר, וְעַל נְטִילַת יָדַיִם
לֹא תְבָרֵךְ. אִם לֹא קִנַּחְתָּ אוֹ שִׁפְשַׁפְתָּ וְתִרְצֶה
לְהִתְפַּלֵּל מִיָּד אָז תִּתְפַּלֵּל [נ"א תברך]
אֲשֶׁר יָצַר וְעַל נְטִילַת יָדַיִם.

Wash your hands for prayer and for eating [bread]. When you have fulfilled your bodily functions recite the *Asher Yatzar* blessing ["...Who created man with wisdom..."], but do not recite the blessing for washing hands, unless you have wiped yourself or rinsed yourself and wish to pray immediately — then you should recite *Asher Yatzar* and the blessing for washing hands.

TOSAFOS YOM TOV

Wash your hands before prayer and before eating [bread]. Likewise, wash your hands after fulfilling your bodily functions, and recite the *Asher Yatzar* blessing. Do not recite the blessing for washing your hands unless you have cleaned yourself and wiped yourself and you are going to pray immediately. In that case, recite the blessing for washing hands and the *Asher Yatzar* blessing. (However, some Poskim rule that one should not recite the blessing for washing hands even if he is going to pray immediately, but only [before eating bread or] when he washes hands upon rising in the morning; and this is the accepted ruling.)

40

גְּדִילִים תַּעֲשֶׂה לָּךְ, עַל אַרְבַּע כַּנְפוֹת כְּסוּתֶךָ.
לְמַעַן תִּזְכּוֹר וְקַדֵּשׁ עַצְמְךָ בְּכָל דְּבָרֶיךָ.
וֶהֱוֵי צָנוּעַ בְּבֵית הַכִּסֵּא. וְעִם בֵּיתֶךָ, כִּי אֲפִילוּ
שִׂיחָה קַלָּה שֶׁבֵּין אִישׁ לְאִשְׁתּוֹ, עָתִיד לִיתֵּן עָלֶיהָ
אֶת הַדִּין, וְאַל תִּנְהַג עַצְמְךָ בְּקַלּוּת רֹאשׁ.
וִיהִי מוֹרָא שָׁמַיִם עָלֶיךָ,
וְהִשָּׁמֶר מִלְהִסְתַּכֵּל בְּאִשָּׁה וַאֲפִילוּ פְּנוּיָה.
וּמְזוּזוֹת עַל פִּתְחֵי בֵיתֶךָ אַל יֶחְסָרוּ.

Put *tzitzis* on the four corners of your garment
so that you may remember [all the *mitzvos*]
and sanctify yourself in all your activities.
Be modest in the bathroom and in your home, for
a man will have to account for even a lighthearted
conversation between himself and his wife.
Do not act in a lightheaded manner; and
the fear of Heaven should be upon you.
Take care not to gaze at a woman,
even an unmarried one.
Mezuzos should not be missing
on the doorways of your home.

◆§ *Do not act in a lightheaded manner; and the fear of Heaven should
be upon you.*

Lightheadedness is the antithesis of fear of Heaven. Lightheadedness
completely strips man of the fear of Heaven, and carries him away from
it. That is why the *Rosh* has written: "Do not act in a lightheaded
manner; and the fear of Heaven should be upon you." Lightheadedness
means tossing off the yoke of the Majesty of Heaven. Man acquires
lightheadedness because he lacks the fear of God.

The *Rosh* teaches us that fear of Heaven is the sole protection against
lightheadedness, because it is its exact antithesis.

How can a person acquire the fear of Heaven? The first step in his
penitence is to retreat from and leave his present state. His first act of
sacred service is becoming serious [literally, heavy headed, כּוֹבֶד רֹאשׁ].
Being serious is the prelude to fear of Heaven.

The Alter of Kelm spoke to the point about this issue. "Lightheadedness," he said, "is exactly that — a light head. 'Seriousness' is also exactly
what the expression implies: a heavy head. When a person's brain is
empty, he is lightheaded... Let there be but a faint breeze of impurity
and desire, and he responds and submits to it. But the man with the
'weighty head,' the serious man, is filled to overflowing with Torah,
with wisdom and with fear of Heaven. Even fierce winds cannot move
him easily. He will certainly remain firm in his position, and fear God."

(*Orach Yesharim*: R' Yerucham Levovitz, *Da'as Torah III* 1, p. 116)

41

סוֹד אַחֵר, אַל תְּגַל. גַּם אֶל הַדְּבָרִים אֲשֶׁר יְדַבְּרוּ
לְפָנֶיךָ שֶׁלֹּא עַל דֶּרֶךְ סוֹד, טוֹמְנֵהוּ בְּקִירוֹת לִבֶּךָ.
[נ"א טמנם בקרב לבך] גַּם אִם תִּשְׁמָעֵנוּ מֵאַחֵר
אַל תֹּאמַר כְּבָר שְׁמַעְתִּי זֶה
וּמִשּׁוֹכֶבֶת חֵיקְךָ שְׁמוֹר פִּתְחֵי פִּיךָ.

Do not reveal someone else's secret. Even what
was not told to you in a secretive manner, you
should conceal within the walls of your heart.
Even if you hear it from another, do not say, "I
have already heard that." Guard the openings of
your mouth from the one who lies in your bosom.

TOSAFOS YOM TOV
Do not tell your wife everything, and do not assume that she will keep
secrets.

42

עֶרֶב וָבֹקֶר וְצָהֳרַיִם שְׁמוֹר הָעִתִּים הַקְּבוּעִים
לִתְפִלָּה, וּפְתַח לִבְּךָ שָׁעָה אַחַת קוֹדֶם תְּפִלָּה.
וֶהֱוֵי זָהִיר שֶׁתִּהְיֶה מֵעֲשָׂרָה הָרִאשׁוֹנִים.
וְאַל תְּדַבֵּר שִׂיחָה בְּטֵלָה בְּבֵית הַכְּנֶסֶת.
וּתְפִלִּין עַל רֹאשְׁךָ וְעַל זַרְעֲךָ אַל יֶחְסְרוּ.

Evening, morning and afternoon, keep the times assigned to prayer. And open your heart for a period of time before prayer. Take care to be one of the first ten [arriving at the synagogue for prayer]. Do not engage in idle talk in the synagogue. And *tefillin* should not be lacking from your head and arm.

❧ *And open your heart for a period of time before prayer.*

Prayer has the ability to make every Jew feel as if he stands and prays before the King. But in order to achieve this, one must first effectively prepare his own heart for prayer.

The order of our prayer, from its start until *Shemoneh Esrei* has been arranged with a goal — to bring one's heart close to Hashem, Blessed is He. That is why *Pesukei D'zimrah* (the series of psalms preceding the *Shema* and its blessings) was arranged as an introduction to prayer. It is meant to prepare the heart and make it capable of prayer. Then comes "And David blessed. . ."(וַיְבָרֶךְ דָּוִיד) and "Then Moses and the Children of Israel sang. . ." (אָז יָשִׁיר), which provide further preparation. These are followed by the blessings which precede the *Shema*: the *Shema* itself, which involves taking upon ourselves the yoke of the Majesty of Heaven and recollection of the Exodus; the blessing which follows the *Shema*, which contains the passages beginning "true and certain. . ." (אֱמֶת וְיַצִּיב) and "the Helper of our forefathers. . ." (עֶזְרַת), leading up to the moment we fulfill the Talmudic injunction to "link redemption to prayer" (*Berachos* 9b) by moving directly into the *Shemoneh Esrei* after giving praise for the redemption from Egypt.

These are all stages preparing the heart for prayer. And with the proper prayer, we have the initial three blessings which deal with the non-material. Only after all this can a person stand before Hashem, Blessed is He, and petition Him; that petition is the essence of prayer — the service of the heart.

The minimal standard of preparation is to concentrate on the fact that *before* beginning *Pesukei D'zimrah*, one should realize that he is now beginning to build towards the *Shemoneh Esrei*. If he wishes his prayer to have any value, he should at least make sure to prepare himself for it properly during *Pesukei D'zimrah*. That is what is meant when we speak of directing the prayer, so that it has its proper form.

The *Rosh* teaches us that in addition to this, we should take a few moments beforehand to ready ourselves for prayer.

(*Or Yechezkel: Reshimos Talmidim*)

43

פַּלֵּס מַעְגַּל רַגְלֶיךָ, לְיַשֵּׁר עַצְמְךָ בְּדֶרֶךְ בֵּינוֹנִי בְּמַאֲכָל וּבְמִשְׁתֶּה, וּבְכָל מִדּוֹתֶיךָ. וְאַל תֵּט יָמִין וּשְׂמֹאל. וּבְדִיבּוּרֶיךָ וּבְהַסְבָּרַת פָּנִים, עִם הָאֱמוּנָה. וּרְדוֹף אַחַר הַשָּׁלוֹם.

"Steer your course to be level" (*Mishlei* 4:26), by regulating yourself on the path of moderation when eating, drinking and in all your traits. Do not veer to the right or to the left. So, too, in your speech and demeanor towards others, be honest, and pursue peace.

ده *"Steer your course to be level"* ... *and in your demeanor towards others, be honest.*

R' Simchah Zissel of Kelm said that the concept of receiving another with a pleasant countenance (see *Avos* 1:15) can only be applied when one honors another — not to save himself embarrassment, nor to flatter him, nor for his external qualities, such as wealth, but because one believes that each man is created in God's image. That is what the *Rosh* alludes to when he speaks about being true in our behavior towards others. (*Orach Yesharim:* R' Eliahu Lopian, *Mekor HaChaim*)

ده The commentators have difficulty understanding why the *Rosh* has introduced the matter of faith (אֱמוּנָה) in this paragraph. The *Tosafos Yom-Tov* understands that the *Rosh* prescribes us to adhere to the truth in all our speech and dealings with others. He takes *emunah* here not in the sense of *belief* and *faith*, but as a synonym for *truth* and *honesty*.

In such a light, the flow of thought in the paragraph is as follows: One is to weigh each step carefully, for only then can he choose the middle road. It is only with such thoughtful judgment that he can cling to the truth in all that he says, and bring about peace and friendship among men.

This can be taken a step further after understanding a teaching of the *Rambam*, who writes (*Hilchos De'os* 2:7): "The general principle is that one should follow the midpoint measure of each character trait, so that all his traits will be aligned at the midpoint. This is what Shlomo meant when he said (*Mishlei* 4:26): 'Steer your course to be level, and let all your ways be firm.' " The *Rambam* explains that this is the highest possible level one may attain, not only in his individual development, but also in his relationship with others.

The *Rosh* points out that such a level cannot be completely attained if one is not fully trustworthy, and does not make an effort to introduce peaceful relations in society. In this light, the phrase "Be faithful" (עם אֱמוּנָה) can be taken in the sense of "belief." For if one does not possess faith, it is difficult to imagine that he will reach the uppermost rung of the ethical ladder. (*Orach Yesharim*)

&§ *And pursue peace.*

To "love peace and pursue it" (*Avos* 1:12) is a very special trait. One should strive with all his power to live by this trait, as the *Rosh* says, "pursue peace" — "seek out peace and pursue it" (*Tehillim* 34:15). The world at large is far from understanding the concept of loving peace. He who possesses this trait is pained by the present lack of peace in the world (may Heaven protect us). For even if he is not personally touched by the actual turmoil, and is not at all to blame for it, he still aspires to and strives for peace. It is a part of his soul.

(*Or Yechezkel: Iggeres* 117, 118)

44

קְבַע עִתִּים לַתּוֹרָה, קוֹדֶם אֲכִילָה,
וּשְׁכִיבָה וְדִבַּרְתָּ בָּם עַל שֻׁלְחָנֶךָ.
וְהִזְהַרְתָּ בָּם אַנְשֵׁי בֵיתְךָ לְהַדְרִיכָם
עַל פִּי הַתּוֹרָה, בְּכָל הַדְּבָרִים הַצְּרִיכִים אַזְהָרָה.
לִשְׁמוֹר פִּיהֶם מִלְהִתְהַלֵּל, [נ"א מלהתחלל]
כִּי תְחִלַּת דִּינוֹ שֶׁל אָדָם קָבַעְתָּ עִתִּים לַתּוֹרָה.

Establish set times for Torah study,
before eating and retiring.
Discuss Torah at your table.
In accordance with them [i.e. the words of
Torah], alert the members of your household to
direct them in accordance with the Torah in all
matters that require caution, so that they guard
their lips from boasting [variant: desecrating
themselves] — for the first issue in a man's
[final] judgment is, "Did you establish set
times for studying Torah?"

ی§ Discuss Torah...

The verse (*Devarim* 6:7) "You shall speak in them" [i.e. in words of Torah] tells us that we are forbidden to engage in idle conversation. There is an additional prohibition alluded to by the prophet: "You weary God with your words" (*Malachi* 2:17), and Shlomo also taught: "All words are wearying" (*Koheles* 1:8).

Rabbeinu Yonah writes that speech is the instrument of intelligence, and is more precious than any treasure. It is through this instrument that man's intelligence and knowledge can be seen. Therefore it is said: "The lips of knowledge are the instrument of a precious thing" (*Mishlei* 20:15). Human intelligence is the aspect of God that was implanted in man, as it is said: "And He blew into his nostrils a breath of life and man became a living being" (*Bereishis* 2:7). *Onkelos* interprets "living being" (נֶפֶשׁ חַיָּה) as a "speaking spirit" (לְרוּחַ מְמַלְלָא), for speech is man's unique distinguishing feature.

The *Rosh* explains how great an effort man must make to control his speech. The basic guideline for achieving that goal is: "Silence is a safeguard to wisdom"(*Avos* 3:17). As the Talmud says (*Chullin* 89a), "man's craft in this world is to make himself as if he cannot speak."

(*Orach Yesharim*: R' Yosef Shlomo Kahaneman, Rav of Ponevezh)

ی§ Guard their lips from boasting...

In the middle of a paragraph devoted to the prescription that one should have set periods for the study of Torah, the *Rosh* includes the admonition not to boast. For a man who allows himself to boast cannot grow in stature in his study. Modesty is one of the forty-eight ways through which we acquire Torah (*Avos* 6:6).   (*Orach Yesharim*)

45

שְׂמַח בְּשָׁמְעֲךָ תּוֹכַחַת, כְּמוֹצֵא שָׁלָל רָב.
וְהוֹכֵחַ לְחָכָם וְיֶאֱהָבֶךָ. כִּי טוֹבָה תּוֹכַחַת מְגוּלָּה
מֵאַהֲבָה מְסוּתָּרֶת וְלַמּוֹכִיחִים יִנְעַם.

Rejoice when you hear reproof, as if you
have found a great treasure. Reprimand the
wise man and he will love you. For open rebuke
is better than hidden love, and it will
be pleasant for those who reprimand.

TOSAFOS YOM TOV
When you hear a reprimand, rejoice as if you have found an important article of booty in war, in which case the joy is that one may take it without paying for it. Reprimand someone who is wise and understanding, and he will love you. For unconcealed rebuke is better than hidden love. And [the knowledge that you appreciate their sincere, loving rebuke will be pleasant to those who reprimand.

৺ *Rejoice when you hear reproof, as if you have found a great treasure...*

The *Rosh* is one of the early giants and one of the pillars of authority throughout the generations. Whatever he writes has the status of a halachic ruling. Thus, we are *required* to rejoice when receiving a reprimand. The *Rosh* uses the phrase "as if you have found a great treasure." He pictures this as a sudden, unexpected success coming on a large scale.

Man is in the midst of a fierce battle with his evil inclination (*yetzer hara*). When a soldier suddenly finds himself surrounded by people desiring to aid him, against his enemy, his joy knows no bounds. The *Rosh* has ruled that we must rejoice in the same way when we are aided by a reprimand.   (*Orach Yesharim*: R' Aharon Kotler, *Mishnas R' Aharon I*, p. 243)

Reprimand stimulates repentance. The *Rambam* writes (*Hilchos Teshuvah* 4:2) that hating to be reprimanded is one of the things that block a person from repentance. A person who detests being reprimanded does not allow an opening for repentance. Man's natural state is that he is sunk in deep sleep. Without reprimand, without someone to roar at him like a lion, he will not awaken from his slumber.

(*Or Yechezkel: Kovetz Inyanim, Elul*, p. 130)

46

תְּחִלַּת מַעֲשֶׂיךָ הַבֵּט הַבֵּט סוֹפָם, וֶהֱוֵי מְחַשֵּׁב הֶפְסֵד
מִצְוָה כְּנֶגֶד שְׂכָרָהּ, וּשְׂכַר עֲבֵרָה כְּנֶגֶד הֶפְסֵידָהּ.
כִּי הֶחָכָם עֵינָיו בְּרֹאשׁוֹ.

At the outset of your actions, look at their
outcome, and calculate the loss caused by doing
a *mitzvah* against its reward, and the gain from a
transgression against its loss. For "the wise man
has his eyes in his head" (*Koheles* 2:14).

ᴇᶳ *At the outset of your actions, look at their outcome.*

I am pleased that you have taken it upon yourself to be a man upon whom one can rely. You should realize, my friend, that you have aimed towards a great goal which encompasses many admirable traits. Yisro counseled Moshe to seek out "men of truth" (*Shemos* 18:21). *Rashi* explains that this means men whose word is trustworthy, for then people will listen to what they have to say. Obviously, this must be a key to many virtues, since it is one of the qualities included in the guidelines for Moshe's choosing judges. Among those virtues is the one to which the *Rosh* refers when he writes: "At the outset of your actions, look at their outcome." We cannot put our trust in those who do not do this, and it follows that people will not listen to what they have to say. Another concept included in being reliable is the great principle mentioned by Rabbeinu Yonah (*Sha'arei Teshuvah III*, Chapter 10), based on the verse (*Mishlei* 21:28) "A man who hears will speak eternally." (*Orach Yesharim*: R' Simchah Zissel of Kelm, *Or RaSaz, Shemos*, p. 133)

~§ *And calculate the loss. . . against its reward. . .*

When a person makes an accounting, he gains two worlds. That is the secret of "you shall cut away the obstinacy of your heart" (*Devarim* 10:16) through which one reaches the height of ethical perfection. This involves reckoning after reckoning, with clarification, thought and careful consideration, and then again another accounting and still one more. This allows man to become the master of his *yetzer hara*. All his bad traits will be annulled, and his desires and drives which are rooted in false judgment will disappear.

Who is the wise man? He who sees the outcome from the beginning (*Avos* 2:13). He has calculated the loss of a *mitzvah* against its gain, the gain of a transgression as against its loss (ibid. 2:1). He is the reverse of the fool who hurries to rush in, whose understanding is never more than superficial. Proper conduct demands: "At the outset of your actions, look at their outcome." One examination after another, accounting after accounting. That is why *Chazal* give such importance to reprimand. Reprimand leads to clarification; it leads to an all-encompassing accounting and examination of every point.

(*Orach Yesharim*: R' Yerucham Levovitz, *Da'as Torah II*, p. 50)

47

הִזָּהֵר שֶׁלֹּא תִסְמוֹךְ בִּלְבָבְךָ וּשְׁמַע עֵצָה וְקַבֵּל
מוּסָר וְתִהְיֶה זָרִיז לַעֲשׂוֹת כָּל מַה שֶּׁמּוּטָל עָלֶיךָ
לַעֲשׂוֹת, וּמִכָּל מִשְׁמָר נְצוֹר לִבֶּךָ.

Take care not to rely on your heart. Listen to
advice and accept guidance. Be diligent
in the performance of whatever you are
obligated to do. Beyond every charge,
safeguard your heart.

~§ *At the outset of your actions. . . Take care not to rely on your heart.*

"At the outset of your actions, look at their outcome (paragraph 46) is followed by "Take care not to rely on your heart" (paragraph 47). It is of prime importance that, at the outset, man contemplate the results of his actions. Even when the act is a *mitzvah*, one should immediately consider the details of the *mitzvah* and the various ways in which he may fulfill it.

The *Rosh* continues by saying that, even if one thoroughly thinks through the steps which he is to take, and weighs each act, he should nevertheless, not rely on his judgment alone. He should seek the advice of others. The *Rosh* makes this suggestion, most likely, because a person's enduring self-interest constantly overrides other considerations. There is a possibility of error, even when his decision seems supported by many proofs, even when his decision is firmly rooted.

Our master and teacher offers a parable to illustrate this point: A large panel stood in the yard of a peasant. On it were many targets. In the center of each bulls'-eye was a bullet hole. The peasant had hit his targets exactly. When asked about his superior sharpshooting, the peasant replied that he had first fired his rifle and then drawn a circle around each bullet hole.

When a person has doubts as to what course of action he should take, he makes a decision on the basis of his own personal nature and self-interests. Only after he has made the decision does he search for support to justify his decision. That is why the *Rosh* warns us not to rely on our hearts alone, but to listen to advice and accept guidance. His final statement, too, follows suit. "Be diligent... Beyond every charge, safeguard your heart." He advises us not to rely on our heart, so that we might preserve the heart's purity and not let our self-interest blind us and befuddle our minds.

(*Orach Yesharim*: R' Ben Zion Brook, *Hegyonei Mussar II*, p. 80)

◆§ *Listen to advice...*

The arrogant man puts his trust in himself because he sees himself in positive terms; he is "something" (יֵשׁ) in his own eyes. He neither listens to advice nor accepts guidance. That is why the *Rosh* says "not to rely on your heart" to any degree, whatsoever. For if you do so, you will neither listen to advice nor accept guidance.

After you have heard the advice and accepted the reproof, be diligent in doing what must be done and do not let your own desires stop you, even though you may think that your motives are good. For such "good ideas" are ploys of the evil inclination. That is what the *Rosh* means in quoting the verse (*Mishlei* 4:23), "Beyond every charge, safeguard your heart" — even though your purpose seems lofty, after listening to your own feelings, you will not properly follow another's advice. *Chazal* had this in mind when they said that one should not postpone the performance of a *mitzvah* (*Mechilta* to *Shemos* 12:17), and that all of the actions of the righteous are done speedily (*Bamidbar Rabbah* 10:17).

(*Or Yechezkel: Reshimos R' Reuven Melamed*)

◄§ *And accept guidance.*

The ability to accept reproof is the key to Torah. It is impossible for one to learn Torah unless he is well aware that people often make mistakes. Even Moshe Rabbeinu could err. When we realize and comprehend the concept of "errors of knowledge" (טְעוּתֵי חָכְמָה), we will then understand why we can only make proper judgments, after taking counsel with others. "Take care not to rely on your heart. Listen to advice and accept reproof." The one who accepts reproof will love it "as if you have found a great treasure" (paragraph 45). For he knows that there is no true reality in relying on oneself. *Chazal* have constantly taught us that he who accepts reproof is called wise.

(*Orach Yesharim:* R' Yerucham Levovitz, *Da'as Torah II* p. 174)

◄§ *Be diligent in the performance of whatever you are obligated to do.*

Chazal have said that it is as difficult to acquire Torah as it is to acquire gold vessels, and as easy to lose it as it is to lose glass vessels (*Chagigah* 15a).

Glass can be used for both hot and cold; it can hold anything. But one must be careful not to use it for something hot just after it has been used for something cold, or the reverse, without making the necessary preparations.

Man should know that he, too, can "be diligent in the performance of whatever you are obligated to do"— he can do anything, but there is a condition: " Beyond every charge safeguard your heart" — do not leap from one thing to another without preparation. With proper preparation, even glass vessels can withstand different temperatures.

(*Orach Yesharim:* R' Avraham Yaffen, *Chayei HaMussar*, p. 111)

48

אַל תָּקוּם מִמִּטָּתְךָ כְּאִישׁ עָצֵל

כִּי אִם בִּזְרִיזוּת כְּדֵי לַעֲבוֹד לְיוֹצְרֶךָ.

Do not rise from your bed like a lazy person, but with alacrity, in order to serve your Creator.

49

אַל תְּאַחֵר לָרוּץ אֶל בֵּית הַתְּפִילָה. וְשָׁמַרְתָּ רַגְלֶיךָ
פֶּן יִהְיוּ מְטוּנָפוֹת אַל תָּשִׁים לִבְּךָ אֲחוֹרַנִּית
בִּשְׁעַת הַתְּפִלָה, וְהִתְכַּוֵּין לְבָרֵךְ לְיוֹצְרֶךָ.

Do not delay to run to the house of prayer.
Protect your feet lest they become filthy.
Do not turn your heart [to look] behind
[you, so to speak,] during prayer, and
concentrate on blessing your Creator.

TOSAFOS YOM TOV
Do not be late, but run quickly on your way to the synagogue. Also, guard
your shoes from all filth and dirt. During the time of prayer, do not allow
thoughts into your mind that will lead you away from the prayer. Be swift
to glorify your Creator, the Holy One, Blessed is He.

◆§ *...Run to the house of prayer.*

Why does the *Rosh* mention proper intention in prayer almost as an
afterthought to the need to *run* to the house of prayer? Furthermore,
why does he speak of proper intent in prayer here? He has already
written: "Have proper intention in your prayer" (paragraph 36).

R' Chaim of Brisk distinguishes between two kinds of proper
intention (כַּוָּנָה) in prayer. There is that which involves concentration on
the words. If a man concentrates on the words throughout the first
blessing only (until מָגֵן אַבְרָהָם, "Shield of Avraham"), he has fulfilled
the minimum requirement. However, there is another kind of proper
intention. One must realize that he is standing before his Creator. Such
thought must be present throughout the prayer, and not only during the
first blessing (see *Chiddushei R' Chaim HaLevi, Hilchos Tefillah* 4:1).

It is possible that in paragraph 36, the *Rosh* was discussing the
requirement to concentrate on the words. Here, in paragraph 49, he is
speaking of the need to realize before Whom we stand. Thus, the topic
of proper intention is not an afterthought to the topic of running to the
synagogue; it is all one topic. His admonition concerns our actions both

before and during prayer. We must continuously be aware of the fact that we are standing before Hashem, Blessed is He. Therefore, before prayer, we are to run to the house of prayer and see that our feet are clean. During prayer, we should not let our attention wander, but constantly remember before Whom we stand, and always concentrate on blessing Him. (*Orach Yesharim*)

50

אַל תְּדַבֵּר בְּלַעֲגֵי שָׂפָה וּבְלָשׁוֹן אַחֶרֶת כָּל עֵת שֶׁהַחַזָּן מִתְפַּלֵּל, וְתַעֲנֶה אָמֵן.

Do not speak [even] in an abbreviated speech or in a different tongue [i.e. in code words] as long as the *chazzan* is praying. And answer: "Amen."

TOSAFOS YOM TOV
Do not speak, even concisely or in half-utterances, the whole time the prayer-leader is praying. And guard yourself to be prompt in answering "Amen" with proper intention.

◆§ *Do not speak [even] in an abbreviated speech or in a different tongue [i.e. in code words] as long as the chazzan is praying.*

The commentators have wondered what this means. Assuming that "a different tongue" means Hebrew, they wonder why the *Rosh* felt that speaking in Hebrew should be any better (or worse) than speaking in some other language during the Reader's (*chazzan's*) repetition of the *Shemoneh Esrei*. Besides, the *Rosh* has already forbidden talking while the prayer-leader is repeating the *Shemoneh Esrei* (paragraph 14). What new prohibition does the paragraph add? The *Tosafos Yom-Tov* translates ". . .in an abbreviated speech or in a different tongue" (בְּלַעֲגֵי שָׂפָה וּבְלָשׁוֹן אַחֶרֶת) as "concisely or in half-utterances." This would be a new aspect which was not previously discussed. It would also explain why, were it not for the *Rosh's* warning, one might have thought that speaking in this manner would be more permissible than ordinary speech. (*Orach Yesharim*)

51

אַל תְּנַשֶּׁה פְּגִיעַת הַמָּוֶת שֶׁתָּבוֹא פִּתְאוֹם,
וְתִזְכּוֹר מַעֲמַד הַדִּין.

Do not forget the stroke of death,
which will come suddenly. And bear in mind
that one will stand in judgment.

⊷ *Do not forget the stroke of death...*

One should not allow his evil inclination and foolishness to per-
suade him that life and death depend on natural causes. He might then
assume that since he observes the necessary precautions according to
the laws of nature, and is healthy, he need not think of death. On
the contrary — he should believe fully and sincerely that life and
death are not a matter of natural cause, but that there is a Heavenly
decree, and it is Heaven that determines everything.

(*Or Yechezkel: Mekor HaChaim*)

⊷ R' Simchah Zissel (the Alter of Kelm) would say: Everyone is aware
of death and knows that death comes to every man. We see this with
our own eyes. The earlier generations no longer exist; they have died
and disappeared from the world. And yet man acts as if he knows
nothing of death; he aspires and strives to amass wealth and possessions
as if he were going to live forever. As the *Zohar* puts it: "Man walks
about this earth and thinks that it is his, and that he will remain upon
it for all generations."

Why is this so? Even after he knows and understands death
intellectually, his heart, that heart of stone, distances itself from the idea
of death. And that is our whole task — to penetrate the heart.

(*Orach Yesharim: Kovetz Inyanim, Elul*, p. 35)

52

אַל תִּתְעַסֵּק בְּמִצְוָה כְּדֵי לְקַבֵּל פְּרָס וְאַל תִּרְחַק
מִן הָעֲבֵרוֹת מִפְּנֵי הָעוֹנֶשׁ, רַק עֲבוֹד מֵאַהֲבָה.

Do not engage in a *mitzvah* to get a reward,
and do not avoid transgressions because of
the punishment, but serve only because of love.

◆§ *Serve only because of love.*

The *Rosh* has already written: "...to magnify the acts of kindness of
your Creator, Who formed you from the time you were in the womb and
Who gives you your food in its proper time. And when you perform His
mitzvos, let your service not be in order to receive a reward" (paragraph
34). There, however, he means to say that you should conclude in your
heart that you do not deserve a reward because of the greatness of your
sins. Yet, one should still consider the great kindnesses he has received.
Here, he is not speaking of any such reckoning. He wishes to point out
that one should serve the Creator out of love, and not think about rewards
at all. (*Orach Yesharim*)

◆§ "Do not be like servants who serve their master in order to receive a
reward, but like servants who serve their master without thought of
reward" (*Avos* 1:3). Reward should not even be a consideration, as the
service itself is the greatest possible pleasure. One need not have a pious
turn of mind to come to this conclusion. One need merely be sensitive.
Not only should one not think of his service in terms of reward, he should
neither think of his own benefit in elevating his spirituality and becoming
more complete. He should feel that it is a joy and a pleasure because he
has been found worthy to serve the Creator.

(*Orach Yesharim: Kovetz Inyanim, Elul*, p. 133)

⚜ Wednesday ⚜

53

אַל תִּתְרַשֵּׁל בְּמִצְוָה אִם בָּאָה לְיָדְךָ
וְתַעֲשֶׂנָה לְשֵׁם שָׁמַיִם בְּלֹא אִיחוּר.

Do not be negligent about [performing]
a *mitzvah* if it comes to hand.
Perform it for the sake of Heaven without delay.

54

אַל תִּתְעַצֵּל בְּבִרְכַּת הַלְּבָנָה שֶׁאִם לֹא זָכוּ יִשְׂרָאֵל
אֶלָּא לְהַקְבִּיל פְּנֵי שְׁכִינָה בְּכָל חוֹדֶשׁ דַּיָּם.

Do not be indolent regarding the Blessing
of the Moon, for if Israel had gained nothing
more than the privilege of receiving the
Divine Presence (*Shechinah*) each month,
that would have been sufficient for them.

TOSAFOS YOM TOV
Do not be negligent or indolent when it comes time to sanctify the moon,
for this *mitzvah* is greatly honored in Heaven. Its significance is that we
should remember, each time, that it is as if one is receiving the Divine
Presence. For the Holy One, Blessed is He, from the time He took us out
of Egypt until the destruction of the Temple, caused His residence to be
with us. He was close to us both in the Tabernacle and in the Temple.
This "closeness" is called the *Shechinah*, Divine Presence. Therefore, in
our day, when one recites the blessing to sanctify the moon, this matter
is renewed: namely, that the Holy One, Blessed is He, brings His

Presence close to us. How, then, could we not be diligent so as not to miss this blessing? For even if Israel had merited to receive nothing else from the Holy One, Blessed is He, except this, that His Presence draws close to us one time a month and we receive the *Shechinah*, this would be a great privilege bestowed upon us by the Holy One, Blessed is He.

55

אַל תַּעֲשֶׂה דָבָר שֶׁיִּלְעִיגוּ הַבְּרִיּוֹת,
שֶׁדַּרְכָּם לְהַעְלִים הַטּוֹבוֹת וּלְגַלּוֹת הָרָעוֹת.

Do not do that which people will ridicule, for it is their nature to ignore the good and expose the bad.

TOSAFOS YOM TOV

Do not do that which people will misunderstand or ridicule. For the nature of the ignorant is to uncover the errors and bad things in others, while the good things are ignored and allowed to pass without comment.

≈§ *Do not do that which people will ridicule.*

In paragraph 77, the *Rosh* seemingly says something contrary, that one should "not lay aside the way of piety, even though people ridicule you" whereas here he says, "Do not do that which people will ridicule."

The distinction may lie in his use of *that* (דָּבָר) here, as against *way* (דֶּרֶךְ) in paragraph 77. Let me give an illustration.

When I was in Lomze, the young married yeshivah men would make a special effort to bring cool riverwater (מַיִם שֶׁלָנוּ) for the baking of *matzos* on *erev Pesach*. They would go two by two, and carry pails on a pole slung across their shoulders. There were some locals who mocked them. This is an example of doing "*that* which people will ridicule," which the *Rosh* decries here. However, if a man should perform such an act specifically to overcome his shyness (which has its root in pride), this *way* would be an example of which the *Rosh* speaks in paragraph 77. If it is a *way*, and he has concluded that through it, he will break himself of bad traits, he should not forsake that *way*.

(*Orach Yesharim*: R' Reuven Melamed in the name of R' Eliahu Lopian)

∾ *For it is their nature to ignore the good and expose the bad.*

The greatest of virtues do not have the power to cover up even the slightest of faults [in people's eyes]. That is what man's self-interest does. All one's virtues do not have significance when people catch sight of some lack — because their self-interest comes into play. Such are the forces at work within us. *Chazal* reveal these forces to us, including those which a person would deny, even to himself.

Even if a deed does not begin properly, but in the end, all comes out well, the beholder tends to overlook the end result and look at the beginning; making an issue of it, mocking and shaming the doer. That is what the *Rosh* means by: "For it is their nature to ignore the good and expose the bad" — they will divide even a single act and choose to dwell on the shell and throw away the nut.
(*Orach Yesharim*: R' Avraham Yaffen, *HaMussar V'HaDa'as II*, p. 15)

∾ *To ignore the good and expose the bad.*

I was moved today by the words of *Chazal* in *Shabbos* 118b: "R' Yosi said, 'I never called my wife, 'wife' or my ox, 'ox.' Rather, I have always called my wife, 'my home,' and my ox 'my field.' " This is not the usual manner of thinking. People tend to ignore the good and expose the bad. They credit themselves with everything, and see nothing of worth in the next person. But R' Yosi attributed all that happened at home to his wife, so much so, that he never called her his wife but his home. He acted similarly in all his affairs. By calling his ox his field, he intimates that everything which transpired in his field depended on the ox. For if he had not viewed everything in such a light, he would not have attributed everything that happened at home to his wife.

How great is the lesson found in R' Yosi's teaching! It shows us how to acquire this virtue. And how wonderful this virtue truly is! To always be able to see the good in another, and the improvement which he adds to our life. But man, may Heaven help us, constantly looks for the defects of others.   (*Or Yechezkel: Iggeres* 220)

∾ Would it be that we would always seek the good in everything! The *Chovos HaLevavos* writes in the sixth chapter of the *Sha'ar Hakniah*: "Remember the lesson of the story about the wise man who, together with another, passed by a carcass. The other man said, 'What a horrible stench!' But the wise man said, 'How white its teeth are!' " The wise see the good side of things. But others are always searching for faults.

It is of this that the *Orchos Chaim* speaks: "Do not do that which men will ridicule. For it is in their nature to ignore the good and expose the bad." It is a terrible trait. Man is constantly viewing the whole world critically.

Obviously, someone with a critical outlook will be removed from loving others and desiring the best for them. This trait also distances one from faith, as he neither sees the Divine nor the goodness of the Holy One in everything.

It is worthwhile to accustom ourselves bit by bit to achieve the opposite trait, to judge everyone in the best light. For example, we could begin by putting into practice *Chazal's* injunction (*Avos* 1:6) to "judge everyone with a presumption of merit." That, too, is contrary to human nature. Of course, achieving this is dependent on improving all of one's traits. (Ibid. 170)

◆§ It is human nature that as soon as one sees some slight fault in another, he totally forgets all of that person's good points. Even if one's friend is an otherwise highly exalted soul, one sees only what is lacking. However, when a man looks at himself, the reverse process takes place. Even if his personality is a completely negative one and he possesses but one positive trait, he sees only that single virtue. Such an approach does not reflect the truth.

So too, it is human nature that even if a person has received many favors from another, if he has once experienced some slight unpleasantness from him, all good is forgotten because of that single unpleasant experience.

Nor is a man's attitude any different towards his Creator, Blessed is He. Though he has received much good from the Creator, let him but once suffer pain and all that good is forgotten, and he now comes forward with complaints. (*Or Yechezkel: Reshimos Talmidim*)

◆§ The *Rosh* has not written שֶׁיְּלַעֲגוּ, "will ridicule," but שֶׁיַּלְעִיגוּ, which literally means "will cause ridicule." Sometimes a deed is good and does not deserve to be ridiculed, but its nature is such that people can make it into a mockery. The *Rosh* wishes to tell us that one should not become involved even in such an action. Why not? The reason given by the *Rosh* is that "it is their nature to ignore the good and expose the bad."

Why didn't the *Rosh* give us a different reason here? After all, by doing the type of deed that can be mocked, a person may develop the negative trait of being overly bold and not taking others into consideration. Perhaps the answer is that the *Rosh* wished to give a reason which would have a greater effect on the reader. For a person fears shame more than he fears the possibility of acquiring a bad trait.

(*Or Yechezkel*: Main Disciples)

56

אַל תַּקְלֶה אָבִיךָ וְאִמֶּךָ, וְאַל תְּצַעֵר אוֹתָם,
וְכַבְּדֵם כְּפִי יְכָלְתְּךָ כָּל יְמֵיהֶם.

Do not hold your father and mother in light
esteem, and do not cause them pain. Honor them
to the best of your ability all their days.

57

אַל יִהְיוּ פָנֶיךָ זְעוּמוֹת נֶגֶד עוֹבְרִים וְשָׁבִים,
וְקַבֵּל אוֹתָם בְּפָנִים מְאִירִים.

Let your face not be angry toward wayfarers.
Receive them with a radiant countenance.

58

אַל תִּשְׁכַּח לְהַעֲנִיק לָהֶם צֵדָה
וְלַעֲשׂוֹת לִוְיָה לָהֶם וּתְנַחֲמֵם בִּדְבָרִים.

Do not forget to give them food, provide them
with an escort, and soothe them with words.

TOSAFOS YOM TOV
For they are far from home and depressed

59

אַל תָּשִׂים עֵינְךָ לְמִי שֶׁעָלָה לְעוֹשֶׁר יוֹתֵר מִמְּךָ,
אֶלָּא לְמִי שֶׁהוּא תַּחְתֶּיךָ.

Do not fix your gaze on one who has
become wealthier than you,
but on the one who is below you.

TOSAFOS YOM TOV

Do not look at people who have become wealthier than you. On the
contrary, contemplate those who are poorer than you. In this way, you
will not be jealous of anyone. You will be satisfied with your wealth, and
will be able to live a God-fearing, Jewish life.

60

אַל תְּבַהֵל לִקְצוֹף מִשּׁוּם דָּבָר. וְהַאֲרֵךְ אַפֶּךָ,
פֶּן תְּאַבֵּד אֶת חָכְמָתֶךָ.

Do not be provoked to anger about anything.
Be slow to anger, lest you lose your wisdom.

61

אַל תּוֹצֵא מִמְּךָ עִקְשׁוּת פֶּה וְנִיבּוּל פֶּה
כִּי עַל כָּל דְּבָרֶיךָ תָּבֹא בְּמִשְׁפָּט.

Do not let crooked speech nor obscene language
come forth from your lips, for you shall face
judgment for all your words.

⤳ Crooked speech... obscene language...

R' Simchah Zissel pointed out that the *Rosh* likened crooked speech to obscene language. Perhaps such crookedness is worse than obscenity. *Chazal* have taught that even if one has had a favorable decree handed down for him in Heaven, for a seventy-year period, the use of obscenity can change it to an evil decree (*Shabbos* 33a). Yet, the seemingly minor fault of crooked speech, which does not even appear in the *Shulchan Aruch*, is equated here with obscene language.

The reason is as follows. It is important that a person have a healthy personality. Crooked speech twists the truth and consequently deforms one's human structure. This is what *Chazal* meant when they said that the reward of Torah study is logical thought (*Berachos* 6b). Man essentially gains straight thinking through learning Torah. This is how *Chazal* interpreted, "I give you uprightness." The *mitzvos* are not an end in themselves; their purpose is to make man upright. That is the supreme gift, and man's task is to make his human structure whole. This is the meaning of the term, "perfection" (תְּמִימוּת). Once one achieves this, he will automatically be "with Hashem," as it is written: "You shall be perfect (*tamim*) with Hashem your God" (*Devarim* 18:13). That is why the *Rosh* has written: "Do not let crooked speech nor obscene language come forth from your lips." The obscene language has its origin in the crookedness.   (*Orach Yesharim*: R' Yerucham Levovitz)

⤳ Crooked speech

The Alter of Kelm said that "crooked speech" does not refer to a sin, but simply to speech that is not straight. Even in purely material matters, crookedness can come into play. For example, in arranging furniture in one's house, deciding where to place the bookcase and so on, if one does so in a lopsided fashion it is not a sin, but he shows that crookedness is a part of him; and if so, there will be crookedness in all that he does. The *Rosh* likens it to obscenity. For one who habitually speaks crookedly will descend lower and lower until eventually he will also fall into the sin of obscene language.

(*Orach Yesharim*: R' Reuven Melamed citing R' Eliahu Lopian)

⤳ For you shall face judgment...

The *Rosh* has put crooked speech and obscene language together, and both bear the same penalty. *Chazal* have indicated the punishment for obscenity: "Much suffering comes; harsh decrees are enacted; youths die... if one speaks an obscenity, even if Heaven has passed a seventy-year favorable decree upon him, it will be changed to evil; and they deepen *Gehinnom* for him. R' Nachman bar Yitzchak says that the same penalty applies to one who hears obscene language and remains silent" (*Shabbos* 33a).

The same punishment ensues for crooked speech. For the essence of truth is uprightness (*yashrus*). That is the basic factor in the success of the soul — "*Hashem is good and upright*" (*Tehillim* 25:8); "*the ways of Hashem are upright*" (*Hoshea* 14:10). All of Torah and *mitzvos* depend on it. Avraham was able to learn Torah on his own because of his uprightness. For whoever is upright must come to have faith having realized that there is a Creator; it is a direct result of uprightness — for an honest person admits that nothing could create itself.

But crookedness is heresy. By speaking crookedly one becomes crooked. That crookedness is the root of all sin. It links a person with obscenity, and the lot of the crooked speaker is similar to the one who fouls his mouth with obscenity.

(*Or Yechezkel: Reshimos R' Reuven Melamed*)

62

אַל תַּחֲזִיק כַּעַסְךָ עִם חֲבֵירְךָ יוֹם אֶחָד,
וְתִכָּנַע לְפָנָיו לְבַקֵּשׁ מִמֶּנּוּ מְחִילָה קוֹדֶם.

Do not maintain your anger against your comrade for [even] a single day. Rather be submissive before him to beg his forgiveness first [before he apologizes to you] .

◆§ *Do not maintain your anger against your comrade for [even] for a single day.*

Do not retire at night while you still have a disagreement with another. Go and placate him until he has forgiven you.

Even if he has wronged you, ask him for reconciliation. Do not say that he wronged you and therefore he must come to placate you. Overcome your evil inclination (*yetzer hara*) and go to him. Do not allow your heart to swell with pride and cause you to be an object of disgust in the eyes of the Creator.

(*Orach Yesharim*: Rabbeinu Yonah, *Sefer HaYirah* 176)

63

אַל תְּדַבֵּר בְּצַוָּאר עָתָק וְאַל תָּעֵיז מֵצַח
שֶׁלֹּא לְקַבֵּל עָלֶיךָ יִרְאַת שָׁמַיִם.

Do not speak with insolence and do not be
brazen faced, by not accepting
the fear of Heaven upon yourself.

64

אַל תָּשִׁיב לִמְחָרְפֶיךָ וְלִמְכַזְּבֶיךָ, [נ"א ולמבזיך]
וְתָשִׂים יָד לַפֶּה וּשְׁתוֹק, פֶּן יֵחַם לִבָבֶךָ.

Do not reply to those who shame you and to those
who call you a liar [variant: humiliate you]; rather,
put your hand on your mouth and be silent,
lest your heart become inflamed.

≈§ *Do not reply to those who shame you...*

Although the *Rosh* has already written: "And should others curse or
vilify him, he should not answer them at all, but should be among those
who are insulted [but do not insult others]" (paragraph 22), he has added
here: "Put your hand on your mouth and be silent, lest your heart
become inflamed."

The apparent repetition can be explained in terms of the *Gemara* in
Shabbos 88b: "Those who are shamed and do not shame, who hear their
shame and do not answer, who act out of love and rejoice in their
suffering, of them it is written: 'And those who love Him are like the
rising sun in its strength' " (*Shoftim* 5:31). *Rashi* explains that they act
out of love of Hashem, and rejoice in the suffering of the shame that has
come upon them.

Not only do they listen to their shame and do not reply (which is the teaching of paragraph 22), but they also rejoice in the suffering, that is, their hearts do not become inflamed with anger at all. This is what the *Rosh* has added here. (*Orach Yesharim*)

⋘ *And be silent...*

Silence is a fence for wisdom (*Avos* 3:17). A fence defines a route, a path to attain wisdom. Man should restrain the desires of his heart and not allow them to lead him wildly like a stormy sea. If one has come to the point where he can be silent in the face of his heart's desires and thoughts, if he can hem them in and not allow them free vent before giving them the attentive ear of wisdom, he is called a wise man. King Shlomo, may peace be upon him, reached this point. *Chazal* have said that he was praised for never having exceeded any boundary.

(*Or Yechezkel: Reshimos Talmidim*)

⋘ If one is envious of another, the best advice is to "put his hand on his mouth and be silent." He should not give any opening to sin. For if he begins talking, he will, like it or not, enter into a quarrel. Envy will find room to bear fruit. The end result reveals the true nature of the beginning, as it is said: "Cain spoke to his brother Hevel... and Cain arose against his brother Hevel and slew him" (*Bereishis* 4:8).

(*Orach Yesharim*: R' Yerucham Levovitz, *Da'as Torah I*, p. 28)

65

אַל תִּתְעַבֵּר עַל רִיב לֹא לָךְ,

כִּי לְסוֹף הֵם יַשְׁלִימוּ בֵּינֵיהֶם וְאַתָּה תִּשָּׁאֵר בְּכַעַס.

Do not take sides in a quarrel that is not yours,
for in the end they will make peace between
themselves and you will be left with anger.

⋘ *For in the end they will make peace... and you will be left with anger.*

They will certainly make peace between themselves; for everyone must mend his ways either in this world or the next. Therefore they will make peace with one another, since some justification can certainly be found for each party to the quarrel. Possibly, one angered the other and he could not control himself. But you will be left with your anger. For you will have no excuse for it. Your anger can only be attributed to defective character, and your punishment will be greater than theirs.

(*Or Yechezkel*: Main Disciples)

66

אַל תִּתְגָּאֶה עַל הַבְּרִיּוֹת,
וְתִהְיֶה שְׁפַל רוּחַ וְכֶעָפָר שֶׁהַכֹּל דָּשִׁין בּוֹ.

**Do not be arrogant towards people;
be humble and like the dust
upon which everyone treads.**

67

אַל תְּהִי בָּז לְכָל אָדָם וּלְכָל דָּבָר, שֶׁאֵין לְךָ אָדָם
שֶׁאֵין לוֹ שָׁעָה וְאֵין לְךָ דָּבָר שֶׁאֵין לוֹ מָקוֹם.

**Do not despise anyone or anything,
for there is no man who does not have his time,
and nothing that does not have its place.**

◆§ *For there is no man who does not have his time...*

"They will call you by your name and put you in your own place and give you of yours." (*Yoma* 38a). This means that the totality of each man can be found and recognized within his name — that lot which is his alone, his and no other's, in this world. "And put you in your own place" — one man cannot lower another by a whit, even if he makes all the effort in the world. For on the day of his creation, when he receives his name, each man receives all the honor that is his due. This is what the Mishnah means when it says: "For there is not a man who does not have his time nor a thing that does not have its place" (*Avos*

4:3). It follows then, that each person can be certain of acquiring his fit place. *(Or Yechezkel: Reshimos Talmidim)*

◆§ *And nothing that does not have its place.*

Man must approach his service of Hashem from antithetical extremes. On the one hand, he must behave as though no one else exists except him, as *Chazal* have expressed it: "The world was created for my single soul" (see *Sanhedrin* 37a); that is, for his root and essence. If he does not serve God from such a perspective, his service will not be strengthened but will become weak and disintegrate.

On the other hand, he must be aware that the Creator possesses a Creation which encompasses far more than him alone, and each facet of this great Creation has its place. Although these two viewpoints are antithetical, the soul can embrace them both.

"For there is no man who does not have his time" Why is this reason necessary? Are we not forbidden to shame another and speak malicious gossip (*lashon hara*)? The point, here, is that our internal attitudes, our heart, must be in tune with our deeds. For example, when speaking of charity, the Torah says: "Let your heart not feel bad when you give to him" (*Devarim* 15:10). It is not enough to give; your heart must also feel good about your behavior towards the recipient.

Similarly, one may refrain from malicious talk and the like, yet not appreciate the worth of the other person. And the Torah demands an internal attitude and not just an external act. One must not shame anyone in his heart, but must feel that the other person has worth; then he will certainly not shame him in word. Furthermore, it is highly unlikely that he will be able to avoid harmful talk about a person if he scorns him in his heart. For if his mind but wanders from the need to muzzle his mouth, the harmful talk hidden in his heart will rise and come out into the open.

(In paragraph 104 the *Rosh* speaks about not deceiving a non-Jew, for there is no non-Jew who does not have his time. Perhaps, he is referring to an evildoer or an idolater, of whom it is permitted to speak maliciously, and whom one may shame. Nevertheless, he is to take care not to do so, because the other could harm him.)

No creation should be treated lightly. For everything exists through the Will of Hashem, Blessed is He. For example, we attach little importance to a bird and certainly less to crawling things or to the inanimate, such as smoke. Yet King David, may peace be upon him, says: "Praise God from the earth, the leviathans and all the depths, fire, hail, snow, smoke. . ." (*Tehillim* 148:7-8). This shows us that there is nothing in Creation that is negligible. Everything praises its Creator. *Tomer Devorah* translates *Tehillim* 104:24 as: "How important are Your creations, Hashem." Whoever contemplates this will see its truth.

(*Or Yechezkel*)

68

צֶדֶק צֶדֶק תִּרְדּוֹף, כִּי רוֹדֵף צְדָקָה וָחֶסֶד יִמְצָא חַיִּים צְדָקָה וְכָבוֹד. וְאַל יֶחְסַר מִמַּחֲצִית הַשֶּׁקֶל בְּכָל שָׁנָה בְּפַעַם אֶחָד, וּבְכָל חֹדֶשׁ וּבְכָל שָׁבוּעַ כְּפִי מִסַּת יָדְךָ. וּבְכָל יוֹם לֹא תֶחְסַר מַתָּנָה מוּעֶטֶת לְכָל הַפָּחוֹת קוֹדֶם תְּפִלָּה. וְאִם הִגִּיעַ לְמַעֲשֵׂר תִּתֵּן. וִיהִי טֶרֶף בְּבֵיתֶךָ. בְּכָל אֲשֶׁר תִּמְצָא יָדֶיךָ לִגְמוֹל, הֵן לַחַיִּים הֵן לַמֵּתִים הֵן לָעֲנִיִּים הֵן לָעֲשִׁירִים.

Always pursue charity, for he who pursues charity
and kindness will find life, righteousness, and
honor. Do not fail to give a half-shekel once each
year — and each month and each week, whatever
you can afford. Every day do not fail to give some
small gift, at least before prayer. If you have income
to tithe, give it. See to it that there are provisions in
your home at all times, so that you may benefit the
living and the dead, the poor and the rich.

◦§ *Pursue charity...*

The *Rosh's* source seems to be *Bava Basra* 9a: "Rav Asi says: No one should avoid giving a third of a *shekel* a year, as it is said, 'And we placed upon ourselves commandments to give a third of a *shekel* a year to the service of the House of our God' (*Nechemiah* 10:33)."

The *Gemara* bases itself on the law introduced by Nechemiah. Now, there is mention of a half-*shekel* in the Torah; yet that refers to participation of the entire community of Israel in the expenses of the sacrifices. Nechemiah's prescription was, like his others, meant to arouse Israel and make them aware that they neglected the laws of the Torah. He introduced new ordinances. For example, he forbade the conduct of business on *Shabbos*. And in the same vein, he imposed the annual third of the *shekel* for charity. The *Gemara* there continues: "Rav Asi says that charity is equal to all the *mitzvos*, as it is said, "And we placed upon ourselves commandments (*mitzvos*)..." Nechemiah's third of a *shekel* formed the basis of the ruling by the *Rambam* and the *Shulchan Aruch* that everyone is required to give a third of a *shekel* annually, and one has not fulfilled the *mitzvah* of charity if he gives less.

What then is the source of the half-*shekel* mentioned by the *Rosh?* Is he speaking of charity and not of participation in the expenses of the sacrifices? If so, from where did he derive the prescription for a half-*shekel?* Nechemiah's prescription for charity speaks of a third of a *shekel*, not a half.

Perhaps after Nechemiah's time the value of the coinage rose. What had previously been a half-*shekel* now, during Nechemiah's time, became a third of a *shekel*. Nechemiah's ordinance was essentially that they give a half of the old *shekel*; now, this had become a third of a *shekel*. The half-*shekel* of the *Rosh* reflects the original value of the coin.

(*Orach Yesharim*: R' Yosef Shlomo Kahaneman, Rav of Ponevezh)

◆§ *Do not fail to give some small gift, at least before prayer.*

We find reference to such a practice: "R' Elazar would give a *perutah* (a small coin) to a poor man, and then pray. He would explain: It says (*Tehillim* 17:15), 'I will see Your Face through righteousness.' The word "righteousness," צֶדֶק, is understood as referring to charity, צְדָקָה." (*Bava Basra* 10a).

On the surface, we can understand the association of prayer and charity. In prayer we direct our pleas and requests to the Creator like the poor man who stands and begs at the door. When we give charity to the poor, we involve ourselves in the whole matter of giving and receiving, and therefore our prayers are received by the Creator, and He gives us our needs, in a parallel way.

But there is a more profound explanation which might be suggested. The *Gemara* there asks: "What does the verse mean: 'Charity shall uplift a people (גּוֹי), but the kindness of nations is a sin (חַטָּאת)' (*Mishlei* 14:34)?"

"R' Elazar answered and said: 'Charity shall uplift a people.' This refers to Israel, for it is written, 'Who is like Your nation, a unique people (גּוֹי) on the earth?' (*Divrei HaYamim I* 17:21) 'But the kindness of nations is a sin' — all the charity and kindness of idolatrous nations are a sin (חֵטְא), for they do such things only to become greater" (*Bava Basra* 10b).

◆§ Charity uplifts the Jew; it arouses his soul and through it he is uplifted, whether or not he actually feels this. Even if he has become accustomed to giving charity, his soul is uplifted with each giving, as the *Gemara* says: "When a person gives a *perutah* to a poor man, he is rewarded and comes face to face with the Divine Presence" (ibid.). He is uplifted and *becomes* close to the Divine Presence.

Man was created in the image of God, and he need only bring into practice the injunction: "Just as He is compassionate, you should be compassionate" (*Shabbos* 133b). Compassion and the desire to benefit another have been engraved into his heart, because he was created in God's image.

My father-in-law, R' Leib Wilkomirer, once made a wondrous comment on a *midrash* in *Eichah Rabbah* discussing the verse: "The hands of compassionate women cooked their children; they were food (לְבָרוֹת) for them" (*Eichah* 4:10): "R' Huna said in the name of R' Yosi: The Holy One said, 'They did not allow Me to stretch forth My hand against My world. . .' " The whole of Creation stood in danger of being utterly destroyed. The Creation did not fit the form the Creator had in mind, and He wished to destroy it. What held back the decree? What inner true essence remained in existence and prevented the devastation of the world? It was the compassion engraved in the heart of every Jew. That compassion found expression at the time of the Destruction, when things were so terrible that compassionate women cooked their children.

Can we picture a situation when man is completely torn from the normal course of life, and the necessity of survival forces him to cook and eat beloved little ones? And yet in such terrible times, when the nature of man has become so degraded, compassion burns in the Jewish soul and the hands of compassionate Jewish women, in their dire straits, mindfully bring their neighbors in mourning the consolation meal (סְעוּדַת הַבְרָה)! (That is how the *midrash* interprets the word לְבָרוֹת in our verse: not "food," but "consolation meal.")

This incident sheds light on the nature of the Jew, on what is hidden in his heart, and on how he can improve and develop himself with acts of *mitzvos*, as it is written: "Charity shall uplift a people" — unlike other nations which lack that inner core. All their acts of charity are a result of self-interest, the drive of pride, the desire for honor or conquest. It is these interests which push them to give charity. Such charity cannot uplift them. Israel is uplifted by its charity, and they are found worthy to receive the Divine Presence.

The merit of receiving the Divine Presence belongs only to one whose essential being is capable of it, who is close to and connected with it.

That is specifically the Jew, in whom the 'traits of God' are engraved, and it is from those engraved traits that his good deeds flow. Therefore, he is found worthy to see the Divine Presence.

The *Rosh* offers us advice on improving our prayer, the sole purpose of which is to uplift man. When a person gives charity before prayer, he reaches a lofty state. Prayer will then be a continuation of that state, so that he can be uplifted and exalted to see the Divine Presence.   (Ibid.)

69

רְצֵה בַּאֲשֶׁר יִרְצֶה יוֹצְרֶךָ, שְׂמַח בְּחֶלְקְךָ
אִם מְעַט וְאִם הַרְבֵּה. וְהִתְחַנֵּן לְפָנָיו תָּמִיד לְהַטּוֹת
לְבָבְךָ לְעֵדוֹתָיו. וּבִשְׁאָר דְּרָכֶיךָ הַשְׁלֵךְ עַל ה'
יְהָבְךָ וְאַל יִקְשֶׁה בְּעֵינֶיךָ לְהוֹצִיא לִכְבוֹד הַשַּׁבָּת
וְיוֹם טוֹב בְּכָל הַצָּרִיךְ. וְהִשְׁתַּדֵּל לְכַבְּדָם, וּלְקַבְּלָם
מִבְּעוֹד יוֹם. וּלְהִתְעַנֵּג בָּהֶם בַּאֲכִילָה וּשְׁתִיָּה
וְחֶצְיוֹ לְבֵית הַמִּדְרָשׁ. וְכַבְּדֵהוּ בִּכְנִיסָתוֹ וּבִיצִיאָתוֹ,
לַעֲרוֹךְ שֻׁלְחָן בְּמוֹצָאֵי שַׁבָּת.

Desire what your Creator desires. Rejoice with your lot, whether small or great, and entreat Him constantly to turn your heart to His testimonies. In all your other ways cast your burden on Hashem. Do not consider it difficult to spend [money] for any necessities of the Sabbath and festivals. Make an effort to honor them and accept them [i.e. those days] upon yourself while it is still day. Enjoy them with food and drink, and spend half the time in the house of study. Honor [Shabbos] when it enters, and when it departs by setting a table in the evening, after Shabbos is over.

Agree to and desire to fulfill everything that your Creator, the Lord, Blessed is He, demands and wants of you. Be content and satisfied with what you have, and be just as happy with a little as with a lot. Constantly plead in prayer to the Holy One, Blessed is He, that He will open your heart to His *mitzvos*. And regarding your needs and livelihood, cast your burden on Hashem, and do not let your financial needs worry you. On the contrary, remember that when you cast your burden on Hashem, He will abundantly grant you everything you need, at the right time. Take care to honor *Shabbos* and *Yom Tov* with good food, sweet drink, and nice clothing. Accept *Shabbos* and *Yom Tov* upon yourself while it is yet day. Devote half of each *Shabbos* and *Yom Tov* in study and prayer in the synagogue. And honor *Shabbos* not only when it enters, but when it departs. Even after you have prayed the Evening Prayer when *Shabbos* departs, set your table for a meal.

◆§ *Desire what your Creator desires.*

Be content and satisfied with your state of affairs, both material and spiritual. For it comes from your Creator, and a son is always content with what he receives from his father.

Rejoice in your portion, both in quantity and in quality. For He is your Creator and knows what your needs are and how to be of benefit to you. As *Chazal* have said: "All the works of Creation were created in their particular state, willingly" (*Rosh Hashanah* 11a). Every creation recognized that its particular state was good both objectively and for itself. This does not mean that one should consider his lot meager but accept it anyway. Rather, one should understand that he has no concept at all of what is innately good for him. If his lot is small, it must be that this is good for him as seen from the perspective of eternity.

(*Or Yechezkel: Reshimos R' Reuven Melamed*)

◆§ The fact is that man does not, indeed, know for what to wish. The *Rosh* does not teach us, as most imagine, to desire that which God wishes, even though the results are not those which we want. That assumes, that we know what it is for which we should wish — namely, Torah and *mitzvos*. And if Hashem does not do as we wish, we should nevertheless not change those desires.

This is not so. We should realize that we do not know for what to wish; we do not know if any desires, even good ones, are actually good. The only solution is: "Desire what your Creator desires" That should be your desire. For what is man? Does he know "that which has already been decreed" (*Koheles* 2:12)? How, then, can he know what to want?

Wednesday: 69 / 167

When I thought about this, I achieved full tranquility and I do not suffer from anything which occurs. At first I wished for something. Now that it did not happen, I assume that I do not know for what to wish, and that we should only wish for that which Hashem, Blessed is He, desires; and I remain eternally at ease and await the final result.

(Orach Yesharim: R' Yerucham Levovitz, Da'as Chochmah U'Mussar III, p. 254)

◦§ "What is the difference between Bil'am, who said, 'I cannot trangress the word of Hashem' (*Bamidbar* 22:18), and our forefathers?" the Alter of Kelm asked.

Bil'am said that he could not act against the Will of God, but he did not negate his own wishes. And he thought of ways and means to have the Holy One agree to that which he desired. In the end, God did agree and allowed him to go with the ministers of Balak as he had wished.

A man is led along the path he wishes to follow. And as the *Ramban* notes (commentary to *Vayikra* 19:1), one can act repulsively within the permitted framework of Torah law.

Our forefathers, however, changed their will to His Will. They had no independent will, but sought only to do their Creator's Will. The *Rosh* makes this point: "Desire what your Creator desires" The righteous have always wished to know the Holy One's Will and examined their deeds meticulously lest even some trifling element of self-interest enter into them. They wished that all their acts be pure and for the sake of Heaven.

(Orach Yesharim: R' Yaakov Neiman, Darkei Mussar, p. 77)

◦§ Man's whole task is to truly desire, to acquire Torah and to incorporate within himself the good traits which the Torah instills. Only then can he be certain of achieving that which he truly desires: "Make His Will your will so that He will make your will His Will" (*Avos* 2:4).

(Or Yechezkel: Iggeres 446)

◦§ *Rejoice with your lot, whether small or great...*

We believe that we live by His Will; that only by clinging to His Will can we ensure eternal existence; that by fulfilling His Will we will gain the World to Come. That is why the *Rosh* has written: "Desire what your Creator desires — that is, want to do what He wants us to do. That is the basic principle where will is concerned, to want only His Will. I fulfill all the *mitzvos* because it is His Will. I do nothing except by His Will, like the son who desires to fulfill his father's will and whose only wish is just to be near him, because he is his father, and for no other reason. The son has no idea as to whether what he does is good for him or not, and his only concern is to be close to his father and meet with him constantly. Your whole task is to do His Will. Therefore: "rejoice with your lot...and entreat Him constantly." That, too, is His Will, that you entreat Him to increase your lot in the levels of the spirit. But in practice, you should be happy with your lot, even if it is small.

(Or Yechezkel: Reshimos Talmidim)

◆§ Man's major task is to cut away the evil within himself. There is no excuse in any situation as to why he cannot now, in his present state, purify his traits. Any such excuse is not true. Basically what is demanded is that he remove his evil in the state in which he finds himself, as much as he can, bit by bit. When the *Rosh* says "Desire what your Creator desires" he is not only expressing a command, but explaining that this is your reality. Therefore, desire what your Creator desires — in the state in which He has placed you to serve Him, "whether small or great." It makes no difference. You must rid yourself of the evil in the situation in which you find yourself. That is the essence of what is demanded of you. One is not required at all to understand why he has been relegated to that state in which he finds himself; for He, Blessed is He, is your Creator. And no creation can grasp the intentions of the Creator. Just as an animal cannot complain of his state, or an angel his, so, too, the state in which each one finds himself is the one which is ultimately for him. There is no room for complaint.

(Ibid.)

◆§ "Desire what your Creator desires. Rejoice with your lot, whether small or great." This is what man should do. In whatever state he finds himself, there he will find success. In that state he will have his trials, whether for good or evil. Each one has been created with his portion of Torah and fear of Heaven. Fortunate is he who toils and seeks to attain the full measure of his portion. Some acquire this world in one decisive hour. One should strive with all his might to be satisfied with his lot and acquire some tranquility. This will heal him, both in body and in soul.

(Or Yechezkel: Iggeres 106)

◆§ *Turn your heart to His testimonies.*
We can only come close to knowing Hashem's Will by engaging in and learning Torah for its own sake (לִשְׁמָהּ). Such study brings man to love Hashem, and this leads him "to make His Will your will" (*Avos* 2:4). One should aspire "to turn your heart to His testimonies." That is man's purpose.

(Orach Yesharim: R' Yosef Shlomo Kahaneman, Rav of Ponevezh)

70

אַל תִּישַׁן כְּעָצֵל שֵׁינָה רַבָּה, וְתַרְגִּיל אֶת עַצְמְךָ
לְהָקִיץ בְּהָנֵץ הַחַמָּה, וּלְקוֹל הַצִּפּוֹר קוּם מִמִּטָּתֶךָ.

Do not sleep a long sleep like a sluggard,
but accustom yourself to wake at sunrise.
Rise from your bed upon the song of the bird.

71

אַל תִּתְפַּלֵּל בְּלֹא נְקִיּוּת כַּפַּיִם וּבְלֹא טָהֳרָה,
כִּי תְּפִלָּתְךָ לֹא תְּהֵא נִשְׁמַעַת.

Do not pray without clean hands and without
purity, for your prayer will not be heard.

72

אַל תִּתְפַּלֵּל כִּי אִם בְּכַוָּנַת הַלֵּב וּבְנַחַת,
כְּדֵי שֶׁיִּשְׁמַע הָאוֹזֶן.

Do not pray except with the proper intention in
your heart and with calm, so that your ear will
hear that which you utter.

TOSAFOS YOM TOV
Do not swallow the words, but say each word individually and distinctly.

⇥§ *Pray. . . with the proper intention. . .*

The *Rosh* has already discussed the topic of proper intention (כַּוָּנָה) in prayer several times. If we follow the *Tosafos Yom-Tov's* division of the *Orchos Chaim*, we find this topic in the first day (paragraph 20), the second day (paragraph 36), the third day (paragraph 38), and the fourth day (paragraph 72). This is because prayer encompasses all the paths of life. It is meant to draw the soul to God through service of the heart. Therefore, the *Rosh* has made repeated mention of proper intention during prayer, since prayer without such proper intention is like a body without a soul. And prayer is food for the soul.

(*Orach Yesharim*: R' Yosef Shlomo Kahaneman, Rav of Ponevezh)

73

אַל תִּשְׁכַּח צוּר יְלָדְךָ וּמְחוֹלְלֶךָ וּבְכָל דְּרָכֶיךָ דָעֵהוּ וּתְבִיאֵהוּ [נ"א ותשווהו] לְנֶגְדְּךָ תָּמִיד.

Do not forget the Rock Who gave you birth and formed you. In all your ways, know Him and place Him constantly before you.

⊸ *Do not forget the Rock Who gave you birth...*
The *Rosh* has joined, "In all your ways, know Him" (*Mishlei* 3:6), to "Do not forget." By not forgetting "the Rock Who gave you birth," you will come to "know Him in all your ways." For your heart itself is good; there is a sacred flame hidden within it. It is just that the force of forgetfulness overcomes it, as it is written: "You forget the Rock Who gave you birth" (*Devarim* 32:18). When forgetfulness is removed, awareness increases, and one can reach the level of: "Know the God of your father" (*Divrei HaYamim I* 28:9).

(*Orach Yesharim: Nesiv Chaim*)

⊸ The *Rosh* has this paragraph follow the two paragraphs on prayer.
Perhaps he has done this because prayer demands that we both understand what we are saying and that we be aware of Him, Whom we address. Thus, immediately after speaking about prayer, he warns us not to forget "the Rock Who gave you birth."   (*Orach Yesharim*)

⊸ You should try to do only that which is His Will and nothing else.
You cannot find the right path on your own. You should place Hashem before you constantly, and He will straighten your paths.

(*Or Yechezkel: Reshimos Talmidim*)

❄️ Thursday ❄️

74

אַל תַּרְבֶּה לִשְׂמוֹחַ. וּזְכוֹר, כִּי ״רוּחַ חַיֶּיךָ״.
אַתָּה נוֹצָר מֵעָפָר, וְאַחֲרִיתְךָ רִמָּה.

**Do not be overly happy. Remember that your life
is [mere] wind. You were created from dust
and your end will be rot.**

❧ *Do not be overly happy.*

[From a letter to a disciple and friend who was about to celebrate his son's marriage:] I intend to share in your honored joyous occasion and wish you *mazal tov*... May it bring about joy and happiness like the joy of Mar the son of Ravina when his son married. When he saw that the Sages were in a rather jocular mood, he brought a goblet worth four hundred *zuz*, and smashed it before them. They became sad. A similar story is recorded about Rav Ashi (*Berachos* 30b-31a).

The stories puzzled me. Are the wise saddened by the loss of money? The damage was already done. Their sadness would not make the cup whole again. Besides, why should they be so sad? The goblets were broken intentionally.

The *Rosh* gives us an answer. He tells us not to be overly happy. But should we be even slightly happy? "What is the use of joy?" (*Koheles* 2:2). Have the Sages not said: "The Holy One was not happy with His world, for it is said, 'Let God be happy with His works' (*Tehillim* 104:31), but He was not happy. And you wish to be happy?" (*Tanchuma, Acharei Mos* 2). Why, then, has the *Rosh* spoken out only against *excess* joy?

The answer is that the *Rosh* is referring to joy where it is a *mitzvah* to have joy. Even then, only its proper measure, nothing more, is permitted.

Chazal taught that it is as difficult to acquire Torah as it is to find gold, but it can be lost as easily as a vessel of glass (*Chagigah* 15a). By breaking the goblet, Mar the son of Ravina indicated to the Sages that an excess of joy causes one to forget the fear of Heaven, and one's Torah may easily be forgotten. When the Sages and Rav Ashi caught the hint given by Mar the son of Ravina, that just a little excess, even when the joyous occasion is a *mitzvah*, and even in a company such as theirs, can cause Torah to be forgotten, they became sad.

What then shall we say about a joyous occasion which is not a *mitzvah*; and about an occasion arranged by others than Mar the son of Ravina or Rav Ashi? Moreover, what is there to say when knowledge of fear of Heaven is somewhat lacking — and all the more if it is greatly lacking? How dangerous this extra expression of joy, as far as forgetting Torah is concerned, was even for those who labor and learn like the disciples of Rav Ashi and Mar the son of Ravina! Small wonder that they became sad. They were frightened of losing their greatest possession, their vast knowledge. They could not be certain of retaining it for the rest of their lives.

One need only remember the High Priest Yochanan who served as *Kohen Gadol* for eighty years but in the end succumbed to the heresy of the Sadducees and joined them. Were we to live as long as Methuselah, we would still be amazed. Imagine a *Kohen Gadol* who served for eighty consecutive years and nevertheless became a Sadducee!

The Sages who attended these weddings thought of how Rav Ashi and Mar the son of Ravina cast a worried eye at them for but a moment's joy. How could they be vigilant throughout the length of their lives so as not to indulge in excessive joy? It is not difficult to understand how far a man who has no fear of Heaven is from Torah; and how he may distance himself even more through improper displays of excessive joy. This should strongly reinforce the idea that *mussar* must be studied; it decisively refutes those who oppose its study.

(*Orach Yesharim*: R' Simchah Zissel of Kelm)

75

אַל תֹּאמַר עַל שׁוּם מִצְוָה אֲשֶׁר אוֹתָהּ לְמָחָר,
שֶׁמָּא לֹא תִפָּנֶה לַעֲשׂוֹת.

Do not say of any *mitzvah*, "I will do it tomorrow." For perhaps you will not be free to do it.

76

אַל תִּפָּרֵד מֵהֶגְיַית [נ"א מהגיון] חָכְמָה וּמוּסָר,
וְתִתְאַבֵּק בַּעֲפַר רַגְלֵי חֲכָמִים וְהִתְחַכֵּם.

Do not separate yourself from thinking about
wisdom and moral instruction (*mussar*). Sit in
the dust of the Sages' feet, and become wise.

ⅇ§ *Do not separate yourself...*

An animal suffers if it cannot breathe in air for even a moment; it
will be close to death. A man should feel great suffering, in a similar
manner, if he cannot breathe in wisdom and knowledge, even for only
a moment. They are the true sources of life for the soul, because the soul
is an intelligent entity. The *Rosh* has indicated this in saying: "Do not
separate yourself from thinking about wisdom and moral instruction."

(*Orach Yesharim*: R' Avraham Yaffen, *Yesodei HaDa'as*, p. 38)

ⅇ§ *And become wise.*

It was very often stated in the *Beis HaTalmud* of Kelm that in order
for man to listen to and understand *mussar*, he must first sensitize his
feelings. Without that, he might listen and learn for an entire lifetime
and not know at all what *mussar* is or what it demands of him. For
mussar involves the most delicate sensitivity, and it is possible that even
after one knows the material, he lacks the sensitivity needed to digest it.

(*Or Yechezkel: Kovetz Inyanim*, *Elul*, p. 26)

77

אַל תַּנִּיחַ דֶּרֶךְ חֲסִידוּת אַף עַל פִּי שֶׁמַּלְעִיגִין עָלֶיךָ,
וְאַל תֵּיבוֹשׁ לִדְבַר מִצְוָה.

Do not lay aside the way of piety,
even though people ridicule you,
and do not feel ashamed regarding a *mitzvah*.

◆§ Even though people ridicule you . . .

The *Mesilas Yesharim* (Chapter 20) writes: "However, there are certain additional acts of piety (חֲסִידוּת) which will cause common people to laugh, when they see people acting this way in front of them. They will mock and scorn him. It is better if the pious man refrains from doing it, rather than do it." This would seem to contradict what the *Rosh* says here in paragraph 77.

We should understand matters in this fashion: Should a man wish to do something that he sees as good, but it is not part of his essential behavior, he should refrain from doing it. Thus, he will avoid causing others to fall into sin by mocking his actions. However, if it is part of his essential behavior, and he has come to the conclusion that by so doing, he will break himself of bad traits, he should not refrain because of those who will mock him. As the *Tanna* says (*Avos* 5:23): "Be bold like a leopard."   (*Orach Yesharim*: R' Simchah Zissel of Kelm, *Ahavas Meisharim*, p. 141)

◆§ If one acts piously because this is a good path for him, i.e. he has come to the conclusion that, in light of his particular make-up, such behavior will help him in controlling his evil inclination (*yetzer hara*), this means that such behavior is not mere piety, but rather, a very basic principle. He should not hesitate to act, despite the fact that he will be mocked. Those who mock such behavior are the evil sinners who do not act like decent human beings. "Pour it down the wicked man's throat and he will die." One should not set aside his pious behavior because of them, for they are mocking the essence of the *mitzvos*.

However, when the *Mesilas Yesharim* (Chapter 20) speaks of avoiding an excess of piety in front of the common people, he is speaking of simple souls who might mistake one's piety for arrogance. Then it is fitting to set aside one's pious behavior
                    (*Or Yechezkel*: *Reshimos R' Reuven Melamed*)

◆§ And do not feel ashamed regarding a mitzvah.

The *Tosafos Yom-Tov* has interpreted this as follows: If you are doing something pious [as opposed to a basic *mitzvah*], do not break off in the middle of doing it because men are mocking you; and do not feel shame in fulfilling any *mitzvah*.

Previously (in paragraph 55) he interpreted: Do not do anything about which men might be mistaken or mock. There he seems to speak about matters which are optional (*reshus*), not a *mitzvah*, or an act of piety.

Thus we have three levels: a) That which is optional. He should not do this if people will mock it and he should stop immediately, even if he has already started to act. b) He should not begin an act of piety if it will cause mockery, as the *Mesilas Yesharim* writes. But if he has begun, he should not stop in the middle of things. c) If it is a *mitzvah*, he should begin even if he knows it will be mocked.

78

אַל תִּקְפֹּץ יָדֶיךָ מִלִּיתֵן תָּמִיד אֶל הָעֲנִיִּים וְלָאֶבְיוֹנִים, וּמִבְּשָׂרְךָ אַל תִּתְעַלֵּם.

Do not close your hand from giving constantly to the poor and the destitute, and do not ignore your flesh and blood [relatives].

79

אַל תְּאַחֵר לָרוּץ וּלְמַהֵר וּלְהָכִין לִפְנֵיהֶם שֻׁלְחָן וָלֶחֶם, כִּי שֶׁמָּא הֵם רְעֵבִים.

Do not delay to run and to hurry to set a table and food before them, for perhaps they are famished.

80

אַל תִּתְעַצֵּל לְהָבִיא מַעֲשֵׂר אֶל בֵּית הָאוֹצָר, כִּי מַתָּן בַּסֵּתֶר יִכְפֶּה אָף.

Do not be indolent in bringing tithes to the treasury, for secretly given [charity] suppresses [Hashem's] wrath.

⋖§ For secretly given [charity]

In Kelm, they used to say that the concept of giving in secret applied even to the giver of tithes and charity himself. The fact that he has given should be hidden even from himself, as it were, and thus he will fulfill the principle of "walking modestly with your God" (*Michah* 6:8). He should not feel that he has done something glorious and say, "Rejoice, my innards, over me."

The only way to avoid this sense of pride is by action that is done so quickly that there is no possibility of the baser aspects of one's character clinging to his acts and thoughts. That is why the *Rosh* has put these two together: the injunction, "Do not be indolent in bringing tithes to the treasury," and the concept of giving in secret.

(*Orach Yesharim: Orchos Chaim*, ed. R' Schechter)

81

אַל תַּבִּיט לְמִי שֶׁהוּא קָטָן מִמְּךְ
בַּעֲבוֹדָה וּבְיִרְאָה, כִּי אִם לְגָדוֹל מִמְּךָ.

Do not look at one who is inferior to you in service and fear [of the Creator], but [look] to one who is superior to you.

⋖§ . . . .But [look] to one who is superior to you.

The *Rosh* chooses the word תַּבִּיט, which means looking carefully and closely. When you look carefully at people, do not examine only those who stand below you. Look at those who are above you, and learn from them how to become greater, and rise higher and higher.

The Talmud says: "I have learned much from my teachers. . .and from my pupils most of all" (*Taanis* 7a). That is said with respect to learning Torah. But when the issue is serving and fearing Hashem, these are acquired only by hard and diligent work. It takes much toil to learn the path of knowledge and understanding of this service and fear, even from one who stands lower than yourself. For man's whole purpose is to elevate himself in fearing and serving Heaven by learning from those who stand higher than he.

The *Rosh* teaches us an important new principle and fundamental concept. Man by nature aspires and searches; he always desires twice that which he possesses. He is never satisfied with what he has. And this paragraph teaches us that man should direct his natural drives only to the service of God and the fear of Heaven. For they will inspire him to grow. That is the force of the verse: "Man is born to toil" (*Iyov* 5:7); that is the way of life, to elevate oneself and become wise.

(*Orach Yesharim*: R' Yosef Shlomo Kahaneman, Rav of Ponevezh)

Ș It is common knowledge that a small child makes much greater progress in his character development and education than a grown man. An adult, on the other hand, stops developing. Why is this? It is because the child always looks towards those who are bigger than him and aspires to be like them. That is why he makes rapid progress and takes giant steps. But when he becomes an adult he ceases making such rapid advances. He thinks he no longer has anyone from whom he might learn. The *Rosh* therefore admonishes us: "Do not look at one who is inferior to you in service and fear [of the Creator]" If you do, you will stagnate and cease to grow. "...but [look] to one who is superior to you." Then you will elevate yourself and become desirous of attaining even higher levels. (Ibid.)

82

אַל תָּרִים יָדֶיךָ עַל חֲבֵירְךָ, וְאַף אִם הוּא
מְקַלֵּל אֶת אָבִיךָ וְאֶת אִמְּךָ בְּפָנֶיךָ.

Do not lift your hand against your comrade, even if he curses your father and mother to your face.

Ș *Do not lift your hand...*

The *Rosh* does not say: "Do not lift your hand to strike your friend." Obviously, one who would do that would be called wicked.

The *Rosh*, however, refers to a situation in which a man has a disagreement with your father. In the debate, you may become angry; you may express your opinion or lift your hand as if to brush aside the other man's view, since he is not showing the courtesy and respect that your father deserves. By using this expression or gesture of dismissal, you might cause embarrassment to the other man. The *Rosh* admonishes you, that although you should defend the honor of your father, you should nevertheless not react if this will result in a sin against your fellow man.

(*Orach Yesharim*: R' Nosson Tzvi Finkel, the Alter of Slobodka)

◦§ Do not lift your hand — that is a humiliating act and causes shame.

When one strikes the jaw of a Jew, it is as if he strikes the jaw of the Divine Presence. For Israel is, as it were, the face of the Holy One, as it is said: "You who cling to Hashem, your God" (*Devarim* 4:4).

Chazal have also taught us that man has the likeness of the Holy One's countenance because of his soul, which is a Divine part of man which comes from above; man's soul resembles the Divine Presence — for man was created in His likeness and image.

The respect and honor due to parents is compared to the respect and honor due to God (*Kiddushin* 30b), and I might think, therefore, that one should protest the shaming of one's father, even by striking the offender. Nevertheless, the *Rosh* tells us that even if a man hears his father being cursed, he should not react by using his hand; for "Whoever raises his hand against another Jew, even if he does not hit him, is called wicked" (*Sanhedrin* 58b).

(*Orach Yesharim*: R' Yosef Shlomo Kahaneman, Rav of Ponevezh)

83

אַל תּוֹצִיא דִבָּה וּלְשׁוֹן הָרָע עַל שׁוּם בְּרִיָה. וְלֹא לֵצוּת וּרְכִילוּת.

Do not speak slander or malicious gossip of anyone, nor be a participant in quarrel-mongering or talebearing.

◦§ *Or talebearing.*

One should take care not to allow himself to even be suspected of wrongdoing, as *Chazal* have phrased it: "Keep perverse talk far away from yourself."

The reason is not merely to prevent others from thinking that you are not following God's Will. There is a further reason, based on a psychological truth. If a person has no care or fear that others will suspect him of evil actions and intentions, this shows that he is not far removed from these sins. For if he were, indeed, completely removed from them, how could he not at least fear the possibility of suspicion falling upon him? If, in truth, he is distant from such matters and hates them, how could he not be repelled by the idea that people would think such thoughts of him (even though he knows that his intentions are proper)? However, by not fearing suspicion, he shows that these faults are not so terribly disgusting in his view. He shows that although he does not act sinfully now, at another time he may do so.   (*Or Yechezkel*: Main Disciples)

84

אַל תְּהִי נִבְהָל לְהָשִׁיב בְּעַזּוּת
לְמִי שֶׁאָמַר דְּבָרִים אֲשֶׁר לֹא טוֹבִים.

Do not hurry to respond brazenly,
[even] to one who has said that which is not good.

85

אַל תַּשְׁמִיעַ בַּחוּץ קוֹלֶךָ, וְאַל תִּהְיֶה צוֹוֵחַ כַּבְּהֵמָה.
וּדְבָרֶיךָ יִהְיוּ בְּנַחַת.

Do not make your voice heard outside.
Do not screech like an animal.
Let your words be [spoken] calmly.

TOSAFOS YOM TOV
Do not shout at home so that your voice will be heard in the street.

⋘ *Do not make your voice heard outside.*

The wise man should not yell and scream while speaking, like the beasts and animals. And he should not raise his voice in an exceptional manner. But his speech should be gentle when he speaks to everyone. And when he speaks gently, he should not stand at such a distance that makes him appear to be arrogant.

(Orach Yesharim: Rambam, Hilchos De'os 5:7)

86

אַל תַּלְבִּין פְּנֵי חֲבֵרְךָ בָּרַבִּים, כִּי הָעוֹשֶׂה כֵּן אֵין לוֹ חֵלֶק לְעוֹלָם הַבָּא.

Do not shame another in public, for one who does so has no portion in the World to Come.

◄§ Do not shame another in public.

Rabbeinu Yonah asks: "Why did *Chazal* not decree that the murderer loses his portion in the World to Come? The reason is that the man who shames another is not aware of the enormity of his sin. His soul is not bitter because of what he has done as is the murderer's. He is, therefore, far removed from being repentant (*Sha'arei Teshuvah, Sha'ar 3,* par. 141).

The murderer knows how great his sin is and it is likely that he will have some regret about committing murder. But one who shames another does not recognize how badly he has acted, and thus is far from repentance.

Lack of awareness puts him into a position in which he loses his portion in the World to Come. We should learn, therefore, that whoever is not aware of the sinfulness of his actions and their consequences, and whose soul is not bitter because of what he has done, is most certainly far removed from repentance; he will be sentenced to be destroyed, Heaven forbid.

That is the intent of what *Chazal* have said: "The sin of the later ones (the wicked in the period of the destruction of the Second Temple) was not revealed; therefore the end of their exile was not revealed" (*Yoma* 9b). The lack of "revelation," the lack of awareness of their sin, made the sin more severe. Because of this lack of awareness, the second *Beis Hamikdash* was destroyed and no indication was given as to how long it would lie in ruins.

(Or Yechezkel: Emunah, p. 44; Reshimos Talmidim)

For one who does so has no portion in the World to Come.

He has no portion in the World to Come because he is not fit to be a part of the society of the World to Come; he does not belong there. This loss of a portion in the next world is not only a matter of punishment; it is a description of the reality of things. His essence does not agree with the essence of the next world. For the World to Come is totally good, and he is totally evil.　　　　(Or Yechezkel: Main Disciples)

87

אַל תַּרְאֶה יְכוֹלֶת נֶגֶד שׁוּם אָדָם אִם יָדְךָ גָּבְרָה,
כִּי לֹא תֵדַע אִם תַּחֲלוֹשׁ.

Do not show your power before any man, though your arm is strong, for you do not know when you will be the weaker.

88

אַל תִּרְדּוֹף אַחַר הַכָּבוֹד, וְלֹא תַעֲלֶה
בְּמַעֲלָה שֶׁאֵינָה רְאוּיָה לָךְ.

Do not pursue honor, and do not ascend to a height that is not fit for you.

Do not pursue honor...

The reason for this paragraph is as follows: "Do not let people honor you, lest someone rebel and humble you." Man should run to acquire the virtues and flee from the vices, for the good that he receives in this world, without taking into account the reward and punishment of Heaven. For vices make a man the butt of laughter and mockery. They pursue him and rob him of the joy of this world. Virtues, however, grant man peace, tranquility, repose, and safety in this world.

(Or Yechezkel: Reshimos R' Reuven Melamed)

∽§ Honor

Man aspires to receive honor. The sense of honor, however, has been given to man so that he may fulfill the verse: "And his heart became elevated in the ways of Hashem" (*Divrei HaYamim II* 17:6). That is the end for which Creation was intended — the honor of Heaven.

Through faith and the study of Torah, man sanctifies the Name of Heaven by rising to the level of: "Just as He is, so should you be," (מַה הוּא אַף אַתָּה) (*Shabbos* 133b). This brings one to become "a part of the Divine on High." *Chazal* say that honor flees from one who pursues it. This happens because he uses the power granted to him, the desire for honor, in an improper fashion — to acquire personal honor.

This explains the statement of the *Mishnah* that "envy, desire, and honor remove a man from the world" (*Avos* 4:28). These traits are the foundation of man. It is his duty to break himself of these bad traits until he reaches the lofty level of: "And You found his heart loyal before You" (*Nechemiah* 9:8). R' Yisrael Salanter said that one must guard against envy, desire, and honor until the last moment of life, because they are the foundation of man.

In our prayers (at the close of the *Shemoneh Esrei*) we say: "Guard my tongue from evil, and my lips from speaking deceit, and let my soul remain silent to those who curse me." The three requests are with reference to envy, desire, and honor. The medicine which can heal these primal drives is mentioned in the same prayer — "Open my heart with Your Torah." What, then, should one pursue? The prayer continues: "Let my soul pursue Your *mitzvos*." And for that pursuit, the prerequisite is: "Let my soul be as dust to all." One asks that he not pursue honor.

That is what the Gaon of Vilna refers to when he writes (in the *Even Sheleimah*) that the all-embracing framework of bad traits is anger, desire, and pride.

The *Rosh* tells us: "Do not pursue honor, and do not ascend to a height that is not fit for you." Honor will come, in the end, as it is written: "The wise will inherit honor" (*Mishlei* 3:35), for this is the foundation of man and Creation. But one should not search for honor or pursue it. One's quest should be only for the ultimate goal and the truth: namely, the Honor of Hashem. As it is said (*Yeshayahu* 43:7): "All who are called by My name, I created, fashioned, and made for My Honor."

(*Orach Yesharim*: R' Yosef Shlomo Kahaneman, Rav of Ponevezh)

89

אַל יְכַבְּדוּךְ בְּנֵי אָדָם פֶּן יְבַעֵט וְיַשְׁפִּילָךְ.
Do not let people honor you,
lest someone rebel and humble you.

TOSAFOS YOM TOV
Do not force people to honor you, for it is likely that one of them will tire of you, and is liable to humble you.

Lest someone rebel and humble you.
If people honor a man, it is most likely that they do so from the hope to gain something from him. If he does not fulfill these wishes, they will rebel against him and humble him.

(Orach Yesharim: Derech Chaim)

If you are given honor and others see that you are respected, this may awaken their bad traits and they will envy you. That envy will bring them to rebel against you and humble you.

(Or Yechezkel: Reshimos R' Reuven Melamed)

90

אַל תֶּרֶף יָדְךָ מִלְבַקֵּשׁ רֵעִים וְאוֹהֲבִים.
וְאַל יִמְעַט לְפָנֶיךָ שׂוֹנֵא אֶחָד.
Do not slacken your hand from seeking
friends and those who love you.
And do not underestimate even a single enemy.

Do not slacken your hand from seeking friends...
He who does not toil to acquire the love of men, will of necessity fall into a *Gehinnom* of the hatred of men. For man's nature tends toward that direction. *(Orach Yesharim: R' Simchah Zissel of Kelm,*
Chochmah U'Mussar I, p. 191)

⋘ A man is required to seek friends constantly, without pause. Even if he has but a single enemy, he should not see this as inconsequential. Even a single enemy can cause much unpleasantness.

The *Rosh* speaks of one who is inimical to you because he is a wicked man, whom you have reproved for his evil deeds. For if this lone enemy were justified in his hatred, why should the *Rosh* feel required to make his statement? The Torah itself explicitly tells us that we are forbidden to hate another in our heart (*Vayikra* 19:17). The *Rosh* tells us that you should not make such criticisms even to the wicked man as that will make him your enemy. Even a lone enemy should not be taken lightly. Everyone should constantly try to see that he does not have even one enemy.

(Or Yechezkel: Reshimos R' Reuven Melamed)

⋘ *And do not underestimate even a single enemy.*

This goes beyond the plain meaning, namely, that an enemy can harm you by his actions.

When a person causes suffering to another, he takes something away from the portion that the other person should have received in this world. The portion which was removed will make demands that it be enjoyed, and the one who caused the removal will be punished.

If your enemy has justice on his side, it is obvious that you should beg his forgiveness and ask him to relinquish his hatred. But even if you are right, you should try to rid him of his hatred.

This should teach us to avoid causing unpleasantness to another even when we are right. For by causing discomfort, we take something away from the portion that Heaven has granted him in this world; we will be punished for that. How much care this requires! Without the labor of *mussar* it cannot be understood.

(Or Yechezkel: Reshimos R' Reuven Melamed)

⋘ This is puzzling. Why should a single enemy be considered as important as a multitude of friends? But the answer is: What one gains by having a hundred friends can be lost by having a single enemy!

(Orach Yesharim: R' Abba Grossbard)

⋘ It is good for a person to have many close friends. For if a Heavenly decree is passed against him (Heaven forbid), they would be pained by his suffering if he were to be punished. And if they do not deserve that pain, he will be saved by virtue of their merit.

I have heard that the Alter of Kelm quoted the *Rosh*: "Do not slacken your hand from seeking friends and those who love you. And do not underestimate even a single enemy." He explained it as we have — that his friends might save him from trouble. The verse "A God of faith and there is no injustice . . ." (*Devarim* 32:4) is explained in this way: Hashem does not give punishment if the suffering of the sinner would cause undeserved pain to others.

We should take it as good advice at all times, but most especially just before Rosh Hashanah, to all who join together in bonds of friendship — so that we might at least be partners, to feel happy in a friend's happiness or to truly feel pain when (Heaven forbid) he is pained. How great the merit of each one will increase towards the Day of Judgment, if his friend shall be acquitted because of him!

(*Orach Yesharim*: R' Eliahu Lopian, *Lev Eliahu I*, p. 70)

અ§ The *Rosh* makes the point that even a single enemy is a matter of concern. For each man is a world in himself, containing the whole of Creation within him. Man is created in God's image, and in hating that image, it is as if one hates the Holy One. This is expressed in the *Pesikta Zutra* to *Beha'aloscha*: "Whoever hates a man is as if he hates Hashem, Who created the world."

(*Orach Yesharim*: R' Yosef Shlomo Kahaneman, Rav of Ponevezh)

અ§ Constantly seek friends. One should not say, "It is impossible that the whole world will be my friends." On the contrary, that should always be his goal. And when the *Rosh* speaks of a single enemy, he does not mean an enemy who has a just complaint. The commandment, "Love your fellow man" (*Vayikra* 19:18), would of course apply to such an enemy. The *Rosh* is speaking of a situation where justice is on our side, but the other person does not act with piety and has his complaints against us. We should not consider it is a small matter nor brush it off lightly, since in the final analysis, his complaints are a "mark" against us.

There should be no complaints against us, not only from speaking creatures, but even from the mineral, vegetable, and animal kingdoms. The *Chovos Halevavos* says that these last three can raise claims against man for his negative behavior towards them. Thus, *Chazal* have said (*Rosh Hashanah* 11a) that all the works of Creation were created willingly in their particular form; they were asked if they wished to be created into their particular state. "The heavens are Hashem's heavens, but He has given the earth to mankind" (*Tehillim* 115:16). The earth has been given to man without any reservations. He is master upon earth both in his decisions and in his actions.

Now, man is a social being, and if society decides that he is not fit to be received and counted as a member in it, he will, indeed, be isolated. "So that he be loved above and a delight below" — everyone should find him delightful; everyone should seek his company, and should wish to be with him. When this does not occur, he has not fulfilled his obligation within Creation.   (Or Yechezkel: Reshimos Talmidim)

◦§ Let us examine our ways. We will find that we are flawed by sins that are not obvious. Who can bear witness that he has never indulged in causeless hatred? We do not really know what causeless hatred is. Whoever is not steeped in love of others can be placed together with the haters. Whoever is not constantly thinking and trying to do acts of kindness to others can be said to hate without cause. The rule is: As long as one does not devote labor and toil to uprooting these faults, they must, of necessity, be hidden within him.

(Or Yechezkel: Emunah, p. 147)

91

אַל תִּגְנֶה מֶקַח חֲבֵירְךָ, וְאַל תַּחֲלִישׁ דַּעְתּוֹ
כִּי זֶה מִנְהָג לַחֲסִירֵי דַעַת.

Do not deprecate another's purchase
and do not cause him uncertainty,
for that is the way of those who lack sense.

92

אַל תֹּאמַר בְּצִדְקָתִי [נ"א בצדקתי העשרתי]
וְתִירָא שֶׁלֹּא תְקַבֵּל שְׂכָרְךָ בָּעוֹלָם הַזֶּה.

[When Hashem grants you benefits] do not say,
"It is because of my righteousness
[variant: because of my righteousness,
have I become wealthy]." Be fearful that you
should not receive your reward in this world.

◦§ Because of my righteousness...
The subject here includes a righteous, pious man who is satisfied with his small portion, even though he is poor. His sense of satisfaction makes

the little he has seem like great wealth in his eyes. He feels good in the state in which he finds himself. The *Rosh* admonishes even one such as he: "Do not say, 'Because of my righteousness. . .' " Even in such a state of piety, a man might say that the little he has — which is great in his own eyes — comes to him through his righteousness. This shows how deep Heavenly justice is: Even one who stands on such an elevated plane is told to fear, lest he not receive his reward in the next world.

(*Or Yechezkel: Reshimos Talmidim*)

ـ§ *Be afraid that you may receive your reward in this world.*

In Kelm they taught that whoever says, "I was made wealthy because of my righteousness," receives his reward in this world.

There is no possibility of reward for a *mitzvah* in this world. For an hour in the next world gives more pleasure than one's entire life in this world (*Avos* 4:22). Thus, all the combined pleasures of this world are not enough to pay the reward for a single *mitzvah*.

Generally, the righteous receive their reward in the next world. Only those who do not have patience to wait for their reward in the World to Come, and have doubts about God's reliability, ask for their reward on the spot. They receive their reward in this world. There are two reasons for this: a) Each one has the freedom to choose either a material reward in this world or an eternal reward in the next. b) Because the reward is given immediately, in this world, God is shown to be trustworthy. For if they question God's reliability and ask to receive their reward now, He gives them their reward in a very weak currency. It is preferable that the currency of their reward be debased than that His credibility be questioned.　　　(*Orach Yesharim: Orchos Chaim*, ed. R' Shechter)

93

אַל תַּטֶּה אֶת חֲבֵירְךָ מִדֶּרֶךְ טוֹבָה אֶל דֶּרֶךְ רָעָה,
כְּגוֹן מֵסִית וּמַדִּיחַ וְכַיּוֹצֵא בָּזֶה.

Do not lead your comrade from
a path of goodness to a path of evil,
such as the one who entices and drives
a person [toward idolatry], and the like.

⋙ *Do not lead your comrade. . .*

The Torah has taken a severe line with one who entices others to idolatry. But, it is not limited to this. The same attitude also exists towards anyone who turns another to an evil path. The *Rosh* explicitly writes: "Do not lead your comrade from a path of goodness to a path of evil, such as the one who entices and drives a person [toward idolatry], and the like." Enticement to idolatry is a basic concept which embraces any leading astray to evil. For with such an act, the quality of Heavenly kindness turns most severely to that of indictment.

(Orach Yesharim: Mishnas R' Aharon Kotler: Ma'amarim I, p. 245)

⋙ Why has the *Rosh* used enticement to idolatry, which is among the most major sins, as an example? Perhaps, in this way, he demonstrates the harmful potential of imperfect character traits, and reveals the forces hidden in man's heart. Everyone can stumble into committing some aspect of enticement to idolatry when his self-interest is involved. He could very well waver a bit from the correct path. Even though this is not truly an actual enticement to idolatry, it is certainly its offshoot. When the *Rosh* writes "such as the one who entices. . .," he is not just referring to actual enticement to idolatry but to its offshoots and consequences as well. *(Or Yechezkel: Mekor HaChaim)*

⋙ *And the like.*

The Alter of Kelm would sigh when he read this paragraph and would say: "Who knows what is included in the last phrase written by the *Rosh*: '. . .and the like?'" Who can be certain that he is not among those who lead the public to sin? The *Gemara* in *Rosh Hashanah* (17a) tells us, "The heretics. . . and those who led the public to sin. . . descend to *Gehinnom* and are sentenced there for generations upon generations."

(Or Yechezkel: Reshimos R' Reuven Melamed)

94

אַל תּאכַל אֲכִילָה גַּסָּה עַד שֶׁתִּמַלֵּא כְּרֵיסְךָ,
כִּי הַרְבֵּה חֳלָאִים בָּאִים עַל רוֹב אֲכִילָה.

**Do not gorge yourself with food, to the point
that you fill your stomach,
for many illnesses result from overeating.**

~§ *Do not gorge yourself with food. . .*

The *Rambam* has written that keeping the body healthy is one of the
ways in which one serves the Creator. For how can he serve the Creator
if he is ill? And the *Rambam* has included a full chapter on diet in his
Hilchos De'os. Additionally, overeating retards man's spiritual growth.

When the *Rosh* writes: "many illnesses stem from overeating," he
means to include mental illness (Heaven protect us). Eating is meant to
help a person reach a position where his personality is upright. Likewise,
in all one's deeds and in all his practices, he should act only for the
service of Hashem; and He will straighten your paths.

(*Orach Yesharim:* R' Yosef Shlomo Kahaneman, Rav of Ponevezh)

~§ Before eating, it is fitting to indicate how much you intend to eat.

And you should eat even the designated portion with pauses and not
all at once. The Alter of Kelm said that even if one ate all that was for
him, if he paused in the midst of his meal or before he finished, that, too,
might be viewed as self-affliction and breaking one's desire. Certainly,
too, when you eat the little which the *Rosh* prescribes, though it is true
that you are not overeating, you should not eat it greedily but peacefully
and in tranquility. (*Or Yechezkel: Reshimos Talmidim*)

95

אַל תְּהִי בְּסוֹבְאֵי יַיִן בְּזוֹלְלֵי בָשָׂר,

פֶּן תִּשְׁכַּח אֶת בּוֹרְאֲךָ וְתֶחֱלִיא. [נ"א ותחטא]

Do not be one of those who swill wine and gorge
themselves on meat, lest you forget your Creator,
and become ill [variant: and sin].

~§ *Gorge themselves on meat. . .*

The *Chofetz Chaim* would say: If I had eaten meat every day, would
I have been able to write the *Mishnah Berurah?*

(*Orach Yesharim: Chayei HaMussar II,* p. 161)

~§ There are those who stupidly imagine that they can follow the
dictates of their will and nature's tendencies and not affect their lot in
the World to Come; that their portion remains whole and intact. R'

Yerucham said that our teachers in Kelm would express their amazement at this idea by means of a penetrating parable about people's paradoxical behavior in the bringing up of children: "The father and mother put the youngster on a horse and dance before him saying, 'My child, may you become a great scholar!' But the fact is that if a child associates with a horse, then he becomes like the horse."

If a man bends to his desires and his natural wishes, then his acts are the acts of an animal. He is astride an animal, and he still thinks he is whole and untouched and that his place in the next world is reserved for him.

(*Or Yechezkel: Reshimos Talmidim*)

⋖§ *Lest you forget your Creator . . .*

Every man is obligated to constantly maintain an awareness of the ultimate goal of life. The events of this world distract man from his objective. What the *Rosh* has written is known: "Lest you forget your Creator and sin." For if you forget, you will certainly sin.

(*Orach Yesharim: R' Yerucham Levovitz,*
Da'as Chochmah U'Mussar III, p. 76)

96

אַל תַּטִּיל אֵימָה יְתֵירָה בְּתוֹךְ בֵּיתֶךָ
כִּי הַרְבֵּה קִלְקוּלִים בָּאִים עַל רוֹב מוֹרָא.

Do not cast excessive fear on your household, for
much harm comes from great fear.

97

אַל תִּתְיַיחֵד עִם שׁוּם אִשָּׁה
חוּץ מֵאִשְׁתְּךָ וְאִמְּךָ וּבִתֶּךָ, וַאֲפִילוּ עִם שְׁתֵּי נָשִׁים.

Do not be secluded with any woman
other than your wife, mother, or daughter;
not even with two women.

98

אַל תְּשַׁבֵּחַ אִשָּׁה בְּיָפְיָה.
וּבְטוּב מַעֲשֶׂיהָ, יְאַשְׁרוּהָ הַשּׁוֹמְעִים.

Do not praise a woman for her beauty,
nor for her good deeds, lest those
who hear also praise her.

TOSAFOS YOM TOV
Do not praise a women for her beauty or for her good deeds for those
who hear will begin praising as well.

◆§ *Do not praise a woman for her beauty...*

This is usually understood to mean: Do not praise her beauty, but you should praise her for her good deeds. But the Alter of Kelm read: "Do not praise a woman for her beauty or for her good deeds, lest those who hear also praise her." This variant forbids one to praise her good deeds as well. The same variant is adopted by *Marganisa Tava* (paragraph 25), printed at the end of *Ahavas Chessed*: "Do not praise a woman for her beauty or for her good deeds." The *Tosafos Yom-Tov*, in his translation, follows a similar line, but instead of *lest* those who hear praise her, he implies that they *certainly* will praise her.

It seems likely that there is a scribal error here, and the correct reading is: "... lest those who hear desire her."

(*Orach Yesharim*: R' Reuven Melamed citing R' Eliahu Lopian)

◆§ One should take care not to speak to one's fellow in praise of one's wife. The *Rosh* has written: "Do not praise a woman for her beauty, lest those who hear will begin praising her as well." In his *Sefer HaYirah*, Rabbeinu Yonah has written: "Do not praise a woman for her beauty to your friend, lest he come to covet her because of you."

(*Orach Yesharim*: *Hilchos Derech Eretz*, p. 14)

99

עַל תִּתֵּן תִּפְאֶרֶת לְעַצְמְךָ וְאַל תְּיַקֵּר גּוּפְךָ בְּעֵינֶיךָ,
וְתַקְטִין אֶת עַצְמְךָ.

**Do not give yourself [airs of] grandeur and do not
hold yourself in high esteem; make yourself small.**

100

אַל תְּבַהֵל מַעֲשֶׂיךָ.

Do not be hasty in your actions.

⋖§ The basic cause of the destruction of a man's soul is confusion of
mind, which continues without a single pause throughout his
lifetime. If he would put a halt to this confusion even once, and allow his
mind to properly portray the fate which awaits him, he would, beyond
a doubt, alter his behavior. If he does not alter his behavior, that
indicates that he has not put a halt to the confusion even once. The
matter is most terrifying. (*Orach Yesharim*:
R' Simchah Zissel of Kelm, *Chochmah U'Mussar II*, p. 212)

⋖§ "Do not be hasty in your actions." This means that a person should
take care not to do anything in a rush, even though his mind tells
him that it is proper to hurry; even if he will suffer a loss if he does not
act quickly. Let him hold to this general rule and do nothing in haste.
Nothing good will result from that which is undertaken rashly. If one
wants to realize a good outcome, one must act only after careful
deliberation.

Why is this so? Firstly, because His mind cannot embrace all the
details involved when he proceeds hastily. It is conceivable that after
examining matters he will discover some fact which indicates that he
should avoid this action. Secondly, because when one does something
quickly, he cannot search his inner heart and contemplate what his heart

tells him about the matter. His mind may perceive nothing wrong, indicating that all is well and it is seemingly good to act. But perhaps his heart knows more than his intelligence; perhaps it has a different feeling and does not agree with his mind.

(*Orach Yesharim*: R' Moshe Rosenstein, *Ahavas Meisharim*, p. 167)

◁§ Is it possible to admonish an individual and ask him why he does not possess calm? [We may admonish] only a person who is engrossed in the Torah. He believes in Hashem and knows what his duty is in this world, and that he must gather provisions for the journey that comes after this life. But he still lacks the virtue of tranquility which would allow him to analyze his position.

The man of the world has no chance of possessing tranquility. He lives in the constant flow of the world. And the true definition of tranquility is that all of man's strength is focused on perceiving and improving his spiritual level.   (*Or Yechezkel: Reshimos Talmidim*)

◁§ Tranquility is an offshoot of faith. Whoever believes in Hashem and His Oneness and believes that all is directed from above will have a calm soul. For his soul is supported by, and trusts in, the Creator in all that he does.

The man who lacks faith, however, and assumes that matters depend on his own power and on his own efforts, will always act with haste and turbulence. He imagines that if he chases after his heart's desire, he will catch it. He is disturbed by others; they seem to prevent him from attaining his goals.

The more a man tends toward being tranquil, the more he is prepared to achieve eternal good.

Tranquility is an end in itself, aside from being a means to achieve other virtues. It is a world in itself — a world of pleasure, wholeness, and eternal life. Rashness and haste are its opposite. Without tranquility, we lack the foundation to build man. The Alter of Kelm would often say that when one acts in a confused and hasty manner, he rustles the "graveyard leaves." For when one is in a rush, his heart turns aside as if he is dead.   (*Or Yechezkel: Reshimos R' Reuven Melamed*)

◁§ When one is preoccupied and in a rush while eating and drinking, he does not enjoy the taste of his food. In a like manner, a rushed individual will not taste the foods of his spirit — Torah and *mitzvos*. He will not enjoy the taste of his good deeds. He will not be able to distinguish between a good act and a bad one. To him, everything is flat and bland.

But the calm person will be aware and may contemplate the difference between a good act and a bad act. He can contemplate and perceive the mixture of good and evil in his actions and distinguish between light and dark, between truth and falsehood. (Ibid.)

◦§ If a house is furnished with all the necessary implements, a tranquil individual can make order by placing each tool in its proper place. When he needs a particular one, he takes it and uses it. But the hasty man does not set the tools in order and cannot find one when he wishes to use it.

Man's personality is like that house. He might possess all the virtues, but he does not enjoy their use if he is rash and his virtues are not placed in an orderly fashion. He cannot find the particular virtue which is appropriate for any given moment, and therefore cannot use it either to benefit himself or others. (Ibid.)

◦§ In the *Beis HaTalmud* of Kelm they would recite the *Orchos Chaim* of the *Rosh* daily at the end of the morning prayers. This was instituted by our master and teacher, the Alter of Kelm, Rabbeinu Simchah Zissel, of blessed memory. The congregation read it paragraph by paragraph while the prayer leader recited it aloud with a specific melody. But when this paragraph: "Do not be hasty in your actions" was read, they drew out the melody longer than for any other paragraph. For the keystone of all the other virtues, in the *Beis HaTalmud*, was tranquility of soul and clear and calm reflection. Rashness would destroy all the good traits.

In the *Beis HaTalmud* we were also taught to understand the verse: "Unstable as water, you will no longer be first" (*Bereishis* 49:4), which Yaakov applies to Reuven, as follows: It was not that Reuven lost his title of firstborn and merely became the equal of his brothers. For he is called the firstborn of Yaakov immediately after his "sin" (*Bereishis* 35:23). But he was a firstborn with a blemish. That blemish disqualified him from the priesthood and the monarchy. Those require the greatest degree of careful deliberation. A rash person cannot issue commands or be a judge.

There was an oft-repeated statement in Kelm with reference to this paragraph of the *Rosh*: This is the entire man — as we say in our prayers (*U'va L'Tzion*): "May we not give birth to rash confusion."

(*Orach Yesharim: Orchos Chaim*, ed. R'Shechter)

101

אַל תַּרְבֶּה לְדַבֵּר בִּדְבָרִים הַמּוֹעִילִים,
וּבְלֹא נֶזֶק, כִּי אִם בְּקוֹצֶר לָשׁוֹן.

Do not speak too much [even] about matters that
are useful and not harmful, but speak briefly.

102

אַל תֶּרֶף יָדְךָ לִקְנוֹת לְךָ חָבֵר נֶאֱמָן
וּשְׁמוֹר אוֹתוֹ וְאַל תְּאַבְּדֵהוּ כִּי טוֹב.

Do not slacken your hand
from acquiring a loyal friend.
Guard him and do not lose him, for it is good.

TOSAFOS YOM TOV
Do not slacken your hand from acquiring a loyal friend even if you must
purchase the friendship.

⤐ *Do not slacken your hand from acquiring a loyal friend.*

The *Rosh* has spoken several times on the issue of having good and
proper friends: He warns against keeping the company of idlers
(paragraph 11); he speaks of being a good companion of those who fear
Hashem (paragraph 33); sitting in the dust at the feet of Sages
(paragraph 76); of acquiring a loyal friend (paragraph 102); and the
topic is touched upon again in paragraphs 125 and 132.

Man has the power to influence his fellow man. In this he reflects
Hashem in Whose image he has been created. Of Hashem it is said: "I
am Hashem, your God, Who teaches you for your good" (*Yeshayahu*
48:17). The reason for man's being endowed with the power of
influencing others is only for the sake of Torah study. This is what lies

behind the expression, "Either companions (*chavrusa*) or death" (*Ta'anis* 23a). It is only in the company of friends that one can improve and grow. The source for this is: "Because you were a companion to Achaziahu, Hashem disrupted your works" (*Divrei HaYamim II* 20:37).

(*Orach Yesharim*: R' Yosef Shlomo Kahaneman, Rav of Ponevezh)

◆§ *Guard him and do not lose him, for it is good.*

"What is the proper way to which a man should cling? R' Eliezer said, 'a good eye'; R' Yehoshua said, 'a good friend' " (*Avos* 2:13). This seems difficult to understand.

True, "a good eye" can be understood as a general principle for proper behavior in life. He who possesses a good eye seeks only good for his friends, and will certainly rejoice if others have good fortune.

Having a good friend, however, seems to be only a specific detail; namely, that one should rejoice in a good friend or good neighbor. But this does not seem to be a general, all-encompassing way of life. Yet, this too can be seen in more general terms. For one cannot live his whole life on good terms with a friend if one does not first improve himself and become habituated, over an extended time, to observing good ethical standards. Similarly, when we speak of a good companion or neighbor, we must invest much time, great care, and prolonged effort to improve ourselves morally; and this is certainly an all-encompassing way of life.

(*Or Yechezkel: Reshimos Talmidim*)

❧ Friday ❧
103

אַל תְּפַתֶּה אֶת חֲבֵירְךָ בִּשְׂפְתֵי חֲלָקוֹת וּבַחֲנִיפוּת,
וְאַל תְּדַבֵּר בְּלֵב וָלֵב.

Do not entice another with a smooth tongue and flattery, and do not speak with a contradictory heart.

❧ *Do not entice another with a smooth tongue and flattery . . .*

Although the *Rosh* has warned us at the beginning of this work (paragraph 2) to remove oneself as far as possible from flattery, he repeats this admonition again here. For although he tells us in paragraph 102 to acquire a loyal friend, he now warns us not to employ flattery in so doing. In the beginning of the work he tells us to avoid acquiring the *vice* of flattery. Here he speaks of not using flattery in any fashion whatsoever. (*Orach Yesharim*)

104

אַל תַּכְעִיס [נ"א תּוֹנֶה] לְשׁוּם נָכְרִי כִּי אֵין עַכּוּ"ם
שֶׁאֵין לוֹ שָׁעָה וְעָבְרְתָם שְׁמוּרָה נֶצַח.

Do not anger [variant: cheat] any non-Jew, for there is no non-Jew who does not have his time [when he can retaliate], and their anger is harbored permanently.

105

אַל תִּתְחַבֵּר לְאָדָם רָע וְחוֹטֵא וְכַעֲסָן וּכְסִיל פֶּן תָּבִיא כְּלִימוֹת עָלֶיךָ.

**Do not be friendly with an evil man, a sinner,
an angry man, or a fool,
lest you bring humiliation upon yourself.**

◆§ Do not be friendly with an evil man...

It is known that the *Rosh* wrote the *Orchos Chaim* for his own use.
He did not say that one should not be friendly with a man who is
completely wicked. That is neither mentioned, nor does it require
admonition. He is speaking of evil forces and potentials, far below the
level of the completely evil individual. Yet, a person with such potential
is also called wicked. It is possible that a man can be classified as wicked
even when he does not sin. For "evil" [as used by the *Rosh*] refers to an
evil characteristic, a trait. And a "sinner" means: one who has the
character of a sinner. So, too, the "angry man" refers to a man who
contains the force of anger within himself, even though he has not
actually expressed it. (When his anger becomes actual, he has become
the previously mentioned "sinner." For the angry man, as is well
known, is a sinner; many sins stem from anger.) The "fool" is the man
who has desires (תַּאֲוָה) and is dominated by his will (רָצוֹן). From this we
learn that there are limitless gradations between one sin and the next,
and we should not classify everyone, as we are accustomed to do, under
the blanket heading "the wicked."

(Or Yechezkel: Reshimos Talmidim)

106

אַל תַּעֲלֶה בְּדַעְתְּךָ לְנַצֵּחַ אֶת הֶחָכָם
כִּי לֹא תַרְבֶּה עַל חָכְמָתְךָ חָכְמָה.

Do not contemplate triumph over a wise man
[to make yourself seem wiser than he],
for doing so will not increase your own wisdom.

TOSAFOS YOM TOV
Do not even think of attempting to outdo a Torah scholar, imagining that
in this way you will be considered a greater scholar; for you know that in
this way you will not rise [in wisdom], and will not improve your wisdom.

107

אַל תְּהִי קַפְּדָן לְדָבָר מוּעָט נֶגֶד שׁוּם אָדָם
פֶּן תְּלַקֵּט שׂוֹנְאִים עַל חִנָּם.

Do not become angry at any sort of person
over a minor issue lest you
accumulate enemies needlessly.

◆§ *Do not become angry. . . over a minor issue. . .*

Are we, then, allowed to become angry over a large issue? Of course
not. But the *Rosh* is setting forth an educational program here. Since it is
difficult not to become angry over a major issue which arouses anger, he
advises us to first accustom ourselves not to become angry over minor
matters; that is easier to accomplish. Then, we will find that we are able
to progress from the simple to the more difficult, and will eventually

reach the level where we do not get angry even when faced with a major issue. (*Or Yechezkel: Reshimos Talmidim*)

∾ He who labors to be counted among the worthy, will realize that there is no reason to be angry at another. Since he makes demands on himself to improve, and is aware how much his morals need correction (Heaven save us), how can he be angry at another?

(*Or Yechezkel: Iggeres 444*)

108

אַל תְּהִי לָהוּט לָדַעַת הַסְּתָרִים שֶׁבֵּין אָדָם לַחֲבֵרוֹ
וְדָבָר הַמְכוּסֶה מִמְּךָ.

Do not be overanxious to know secrets
between one man and another,
nor that which is hidden from you.

109

אַל תַּעַשׂ בַּסֵּתֶר מַה שֶׁתִּתְבַּיֵּישׁ בְּגָלוּי
וְאַל תֹּאמַר מִי רוֹאֵנִי.

Do not do privately that which you would be
ashamed to do publicly,
and do not say, "Who sees me?"

∾ *Do not do privately that which you would be ashamed to do publicly...*
When Rabban Yochanan ben Zakkai was on his deathbed, he told his disciples: "May it be the Will of Hashem that the fear of Heaven be upon you just like the fear of flesh and blood." His disciples said, "Just that?" He said, "If only it would be that! Know that when a man sins he says, 'I hope nobody will see me'" (*Berachos* 28b).

This shows us the great gap between the master and his disciples. What they viewed as obvious — "Just that?" — their master viewed as: "If only it would be!" From this we can glimpse the great profundity of fear of Heaven.

(Or Yechezkel: Reshimos HaTalmidim)

110

אַל תַּחְשׁוֹב עָוֹן לְמִי שֶׁיָּבוֹא לְהִתְנַצֵּל לְפָנֶיךָ אִם אֱמֶת וְאִם שֶׁקֶר.

Do not impugn a person who comes before you to apologize whether it is the truth or a lie.

◄§ The *gaon*, R' Yitzchak Blazer, would say that when a man comes before another to appease him for an injustice which he has done and to ask forgiveness, his friend, following the general pattern of human nature, will say: "Why do you make such an issue out of the matter? You didn't really do anything."

On the surface this seems admirable. But the truth is quite different. Belittling injustice stems from the injured party's unwillingness to listen to any excuse. He really desires that the man who caused him the injustice remain without an excuse, and continue to be despicable and corrupt in his eyes.

The *Rosh* has touched on this point and said: "Do not consider it a sin if a man comes before you to excuse himself, whether he is being truthful or false." If he comes "in truth," you certainly have an obligation to pay attention to all that he says, and see the truth, and come to the realization that he has not caused you injury at all.

But, when he comes "in falsehood" — and you, indeed, know the truth; how does one behave when you see he is approaching you with total falsehood, and he wishes to fool you into thinking that he is a proper fellow? Even in this instance you are, nevertheless, obligated to ignore what you know and to hear him out from beginning to end. You must give him the impression that he has, truly, fooled you and that you think he is in the right. If you do not do so, it is very likely that you, the injured party, are committing a greater injustice than the original offender.

(*Orach Yesharim*: R' Yerucham Levovitz, *Da'as Torah I*, p. 259)

◦§ When someone excuses himself, even when it is done falsely, he shows some hint of shame and repentance, or a desire for peace. This throws further light on paragraph 67: "Do not despise anyone" — even when there is only a trace of good.

(*Orach Yesharim*: *Orchos Chaim*, ed. R' Shechter)

111

אַל תִּסְמוֹךְ לְיַד מַתְּנַת בָּשָׂר וָדָם
וְתַעֲבוֹד לְבַקֵּשׁ מְזוֹנוֹתֶיךָ.

Do not rely on the gifts of human beings, but
work to seek your sustenance.

112

אַל יְהִי מָמוֹן שֶׁלְּךָ חָבִיב עָלֶיךָ יוֹתֵר מִגּוּפְךָ,
כְּמוֹ לַעֲבוֹר עַל הַמֶּכֶס וְלָלֶכֶת יְחִידִי.

Let not your money be dearer to you than your
body, for example by violating customs
regulations or traveling alone.

◦§ *Let not your money be dearer to you than your body...*

Chazal speak of a man whose money is dearer to him than his own body (*Berachos* 61b), and they are not critical in the extreme of such behavior. But this is only with regard to charity and kindness, by which one fulfills the *mitzvah*, "you shall love your fellow Jew like yourself" (*Vayikra* 19:18). For example, when one feels that his money is dearer to him than his physical self, he may assume that the next person feels the same way. Thus, if one's friend is in bad economic straits, one feels greater anguish than at the thought of losing one's own life. And, feeling sympathetic pain, he will gladly give the other what he needs. [Chazal will not be overly critical of an attitude which gives priority to money if it leads to such behavior.]

However, placing money before one's self is reprehensible in other situations, and all the more so if it means endangering one's life. One should not rely upon miracles. (Orach Yesharim: Nesiv Chaim)

113

אַל תִּתֵּן בִּלְבָבְךָ קִנְאָה
שֶׁזוּ הִיא חוֹלָה רָעָה שֶׁאֵין לָהּ רְפוּאָה.

Do not put envy into your heart;
for it is a serious illness that has no cure.

⋖ Do not put envy into your heart...

R' Daniel of Kelm explained what envy is. If a man were to be born with wings, he would be considered blemished. If a person were to receive that which he envies in another, he would bear a blemish. For if he truly needed that which he envies in the other, the Holy One would have given it to him. If he does not possess it, he undoubtedly does not need it, and would be similar to the person with wings. It would be superfluous; and anything superfluous is a blemish.

R' Daniel's point makes clear why the Rosh calls envy, and envy alone, "a serious illness that has no cure." (Orach Yesharim)

⋖ The first sin in the world was that of envy. The snake envied Adam.

The second sin was Cain's envy of Hevel. Yosef's brothers envied Yosef; Korach envied Moshe.

The Holy One, Who is timeless and boundless, created man to be eternal, timeless, and boundless, too. Therefore a person feels pain when he sees that someone has something which he lacks. For this means that he is limited, and he senses that he was meant to be unlimited.

Thus, the root of envy, which is implanted in man, — not to be satisfied with what he has, but to envy that which his neighbor has —

was placed there so that he may rise higher and higher; it comes from a holy source. Man's sin is to take this force and use it for impure purposes. That is why Cain is told: "If you improve, you will be forgiven" (*Bereishis* 4:7). Man was essentially created to fight, and break, the trait of envy.

❧ *For it is a serious illness that has no cure.*

It is a serious illness, because the afflicted individual is unaware of his sickness. Envy is internal and is rooted in man by nature. That is why it has no cure. When it entwines itself in one's heart, it turns to hatred. And the *Orchos Tzaddikim* has written: "There always exists the hope of curing hatred because once the matter [in dispute] is repaired, the hatred will remove itself. So it is in all cases, except when hatred stems from envy."

But this, too, can be cured, if one implants the foundations of faith in one's heart. This means an awareness that he cannot, and need not, understand everything. As the *Mesilas Yesharim* (Chapter 11) writes: "If they would only know and understand that no one can touch that which is prepared for another, even by a hairsbreadth; if they would realize that all comes from Hashem's plan and His marvelous Wisdom which is unknowable, they would have no reason at all to be pained by the good fortune of others." (*Or Yechezkel: Reshimos Talmidim*)

❧ Just as the body can suffer disease and sickness, so, too, can the soul.

The disease and sickness of the soul are its bad traits and sins. When the wicked one turns back and repents of his evil ways, Hashem will heal the sickness of the sinning soul.

(*Orach Yesharim*: Rabbeinu Yonah, *Sha'arei Teshuvah* 4:40)

114

אַל תְּהִי רָגִיל לֹא בִשְׁבוּעָה וְלֹא בִנְדָרִים
כִּי בַּעֲוֹן נְדָרִים בָּנִים מֵתִים.[1]

Do not be accustomed to take oaths or make vows, for children perish because of [their parents'] transgressions regarding vows.

---

1. In the Tosafos Yom Tov Edition there is no paragraph 114. We added it based on manuscripts.

115

אַל תַּרְגִּיל לִישָׁבַע עַל גּוּפְךָ וַאֲפִילוּ עַל דְּבַר אֱמֶת.

Do not accustom yourself to swear by your body
[i.e. by accepting bodily harm] if you violate the
oath], even on matters that are true.

116

אַל תְּאַחֵר לַעֲשׂוֹת תְּשׁוּבָה שְׁלֵמָה,
וּלְבַקֵּשׁ רְפוּאָה לְחוֹלִי נַפְשֶׁךָ.

Do not delay to repent fully
and to seek a cure for your soul's sickness.

117

אַל תַּעֲמוֹל לָרוּחַ, וְאַל תִּשְׁמַע דְּבָרִים בְּטֵלִים.

Do not labor for [that which blows away with]
the wind [i.e. for matters of no value],
and do not listen to idle words.

◆§ *Do not labor for [that which blows away with] the wind...*

By listening to inconsequential trivialities, man loses all those spiritual
items which he has gained through hard labor. Torah and meaningless
matters cannot co-exist in a man's heart. It is to this which the *Rosh*
refers when he says: "Do not labor for [that which blows away with] the
wind." (*Orach Yesharim: Mekor HaChaim*)

118

אַל תְּכַנֶּה שֵׁם רָע [נ"א לחברך] כִּי הַמְכַנֶּה שֵׁם
[נ"א רע] לַחֲבֵרוֹ אֵין לוֹ חֵלֶק לָעוֹלָם הַבָּא.

Do not call another by a derisive nickname
[variant: **for your comrade**], for one who calls
another by a [variant adds: **a bad**] nickname
has no portion in the World to Come.

119

אַל תִּבְטַח בְּעָשְׁרְךָ כִּי הַבּוֹטֵחַ בְּעָשְׁרוֹ
מְלַקֵּט שׂוֹנְאִים, וְיִכָּשֵׁל תַּחַת שׂוֹנְאָיו.

Do not rely on your wealth, for one who relies
on his wealth accumulates enemies,
and will stumble beneath his enemies.

  Do not rely on your wealth.

Although he has written forcefully on the subject of trust in
paragraph 29, here the *Rosh* adds a rational argument explaining why
having trust in Hashem is a virtue.   (*Orach Yesharim*)

120

אַל תְּהִי סַרְבָּן אֶל אַנְשֵׁי עִירְךָ,
לְבַטֵּל רְצוֹנְךָ מִפְּנֵי רְצוֹן אֲחֵרִים.

Do not be stubborn towards your townsmen;
submit your will to the will of others.

ও Do not be stubborn towards your townsmen.

The *Tosafos Yom-Tov* writes: "*Also* (גַּם) do not be stubborn towards your neighbors nor towards the leaders of your city." He seems to interpret this as a continuation of the previous paragraph, for they both have the same reason: that you not gather enemies in vain and fall beneath them.

(*Orach Yesharim*)

121

אַל תַּרְגִּיל עַצְמְךָ לֶאֱכוֹל חוּץ מִבֵּיתְךָ,
עִם קִיבּוּץ הַרְבֵּה שֶׁלֹּא לִסְעוּדַת מִצְוָה.

**Do not accustom yourself to eat
outside of your home, in a large gathering,
when it is not a meal for a mitzvah.**

122

אַל תְּשַׁבֵּר [נ״א תשכר] גּוּפְךָ לְהִשְׁתַּכֵּר מִיַּיִן,
פֶּן תִּהְיֶה מְגוּנֶּה וּתְנַבֵּל אֶת פִּיךָ וְתִתְחָרֵט.

**Do not break your body [variant: intoxicate
your body] by becoming drunk from wine,
lest you be disgusting, speak foully, and regret it.**

123

אַל תִּכְעַס בְּאִשְׁתְּךָ, וְאִם רְחַקְתָּ אוֹתָהּ בִּשְׂמֹאל
קָרֵב אוֹתָהּ בְּיָמִין בְּלֹא אִיחוּר.

**Do not be angry at your wife. If you have pushed
her away with your left hand, bring her
close with your right hand without delay.**

124

אַל תְּבַזֶּה אֶת אִשְׁתְּךָ וְכַבֵּד אוֹתָהּ,
וּתְסִירֶנָּה מִן הַחֵטְא.

**Do not degrade your wife.
Honor her and thereby remove her from sin.**

TOSAFOS YOM TOV
Do not offend your wife in any way. On the contrary, honor her, and you
will thereby prevent her from sinning.

125

אַל תְּהִי רָגִיל לֵישֵׁב עִם הַלֵּצִים פְּחִיתֵי הַנֶּפֶשׁ
פֶּן יַחֲטִיאוּךָ.

**Do not accustom yourself to sit among the
scorners and lowlifes, lest they cause you to sin.**

126

אַל תִּתְעַצֵּל לְבַקֵּשׁ חָכְמָה,
וּלְיַסֵּר אֶת חֲבֵירְךָ בְּסֵתֶר וְדֶרֶךְ כָּבוֹד.

**Do not be indolent in seeking wisdom, nor in
rebuking another privately and respectfully.**

⊸ *Do not be indolent in seeking wisdom...*

The quest for knowledge and truth is in itself the key to achieving
them, as it is said, "Seek His dwelling place and you shall come there"

(*Devarim* 12:5). The Torah should logically have said: "You shall come there and seek the Divine Presence." But the Torah wishes to tell us that if you seek out the Divine Presence, you shall arrive there; otherwise, you shall not.   (*Orach Yesharim*: R' Yerucham Levovitz)

◦§ *Nor in rebuking another...*

On the surface, what connection is there between seeking wisdom and rebuking one's friend? Whoever knows how to acquire wisdom knows how to rebuke another in a way in which that person will properly accept it.   (*Orach Yesharim*: R' Abba Grossbard)

◦§ Man, who is lazy, finds it difficult to seek wisdom and to direct others, privately and in a respectful fashion. Both tasks are of similar importance [from this point of view]. Thus, the *Rosh* admonishes us not to be indolent.   (*Orach Yesharim*: An anonymous scholar)

127

אַל תְּדַבֵּר בְּלֹא עִתּוֹ וּבְדָבָר שֶׁאֵין בּוֹ תּוֹעֶלֶת,
וּשְׁמוֹר פִּתְחֵי פִּיךָ

Do not speak at an inappropriate time, or on a useless matter. And safeguard the openings of your mouth.

> **TOSAFOS YOM TOV**
> Be judicious in choosing when to speak.

◦§ *Do not speak... on a useless matter.*

What has the *Rosh* added to what he has written above (paragraph 101): "[Even] about matters that are useful and not harmful, [do not speak at length,] but speak briefly?"

Indeed, the *Mekor HaChaim* explains that "on a useless matter" indicates that which will not be heeded — i.e. one should not rebuke another if he knows that his rebuke will not be accepted. Perhaps, then, the answer is that in paragraph 101 the *Rosh* was referring to speech about worldly matters; but here, in paragraph 127, he teaches that one should not even speak on matters of Heavenly concern, such as rebuke, when no purpose is served.   (*Orach Yesharim*)

128

אַל תְּדַבֵּר עִם מְהוֹלָל וּמְשֻׁגָּע
שֶׁלֹּא יְקַבֵּל דְּבָרֶיךָ וְיִבְזֶה אוֹתָם.

Do not speak with someone who is mad or
mentally incompetent, for he will not accept
your words, but will hold them in contempt.

129

אַל תְּהִי כְּפוּי טוֹבָה,
וְכַבֵּד כָּל מִי שֶׁפָּתַח לְךָ פֶּתַח לְבַקֵּשׁ דֵּי סִיפּוּקֶךָ.

Do not be an ingrate. Honor anyone who has
opened a door to help you seek your needs.

ﻼ Honor anyone who has opened a door to help you...

If someone opens a "door" for us, our soul is obligated to him. This
might simply mean that he took us into his house, even though he gave
us nothing. For he opened the door to take us in by his own free choice.
He did so because of the virtue of his soul. And there is an especially
lofty quality in this act, because it was not instinctive, unlike the
instinctive good done by a father or mother, which is motivated by
natural impulse.   (*Or Yechezkel: Reshimos R' Reuven Melamed*)

130

אַל תּוֹצִיא מִפִּיךָ דְּבַר שֶׁקֶר וְכָזָב,
וְנֶאֱמָן לְכָל אָדָם וַאֲפִילוּ לְנָכְרִי.

Do not utter a false or unreliable word.
Prove trustworthy to every man, even a non-Jew.

⇥ Do not utter a false or unreliable word.

When you acknowledge that someone has done good for you, and you express your thanks, do not do so in a lifeless manner. If you do, this is a falsehood and a lie. This is an extension of paragraph 129.

(*Orchos Chaim*, ed. R' Shechter)

131

אַל תִּתְעַצֵּל לְהַקְדִּים שָׁלוֹם לְכָל אָדָם,
וַאֲפִילוּ לְנָכְרִי מִפְּנֵי דַרְכֵי שָׁלוֹם.

Do not be indolent in being the first to extend a greeting to everyone, even if he is a non-Jew, in order to preserve the ways of peace.

⇥ Do not be indolent in being the first to extend a greeting to everyone...

The *Rosh* gives us a novel thought: It is not only pride that prevents us from greeting others even before they greet us. It is conceivable that there is another factor: simple laziness. (*Or Yechezkel*: Main Disciples)

132

אַל תַּרְגִּיל עַצְמְךָ לַעֲמוֹד, כִּי אִם אֵצֶל חָכָם,
וּשְׁמַע וְהַאֲזִין דְּבָרָיו.

Do not accustom yourself to stand anywhere but near a wise man. Listen and pay attention to his words.

⇥ Do not accustom yourself to stand anywhere but near a wise man.

One should accustom oneself to be constantly in the company of a wise man, and to "listen and pay attention to his words" as the *Orchos Chaim* prescribes. One should always imagine that he is standing beside very wise men and wonder if his wisdom and understanding will be sufficient for them. For, when his days are over, he will always be in their presence. What will he speak about to them if he is a man of little intellect? (*Orach Yesharim*: R' Simchah Zissel of Kelm)

৵§ *Near a wise man.*

The Alter of Kelm said: "If you have no wise man, see to it that you yourself become wise, so that you may constantly stay near wisdom."
(*Orach Yesharim*: R' Reuven Melamed citing R' Eliahu Lopian)

৵§ How great is the body's potential light! Yet, how can that be? Its material is murky and pitch dark. But it is joined to the light of the soul, and the soul lights up even the gloomiest of places, such as the body. The *Rosh* says: "Do not accustom yourself to stand anywhere but near a wise man." You should put the body under the influence of the soul and the intellect. If it is not subordinate and attached to the intellect, the body can have no light. Whoever divorces himself from his intellect is like a dead tree. (*Orach Yesharim*: R' Yerucham Levovitz, *Da'as Chochmah U'Mussar III*, p. 241)

৵§ *Listen and pay attention to his words.*

"Bring up the child in His way. When he grows old, too, he will not stray from it" (*Mishlei* 22:6). It was said in Kelm, that R' Simchah Zissel had an unusual interpretation of this verse. It is not that a man will not stray, even in old age, from that which he has learned in youth. But, rather, that he will not stray from the process of education, even in old age. One should continuously be like a youth even in extreme old age, and continue to learn and be taught.

Fortunate is he who has attained this! That is the unique description of Shmuel, who is equated to Moshe and Aharon — "And the youth was a youth" (*Shmuel I* 1:24). It is this quality which makes Israel exalted among the nations. They are called "children of Hashem" (*Devarim* 14:1) — children in the sense of pupils; and thus *Chazal* interpret the verse: "And you shall teach your children" (*Devarim* 6:7) — "Your children," means your students.
(*Orchos Chaim*, ed. R' Schechter)

סליק הנהגה אשר תיקן הרב רבנו אשר זצ"ל

This concludes the code of conduct arranged by the Rosh z"l

אוֹרַח חַיִּים לְמַעְלָה לְמַשְׂכִּיל
לְמַעַן סוּר מִשְׁאוֹל מָטָה

This is the way of life
to ascend for the wise man,
in order that he turn away
from the abyss below.

⊰ The Sabbath ⊱

1

שֶׁיַּפְרִישׁ מַעֲשֵׂר מִכָּל רֶיוַח שֶׁיָּבִיא ה׳ יִתְעַלֶּה לְיָדוֹ.

One should set aside a tenth of all profit that
Hashem, Exalted be He, brings to his hand, [and
spend the tenth for charity and other *mitzvos*].

2

שֶׁיִּתֵּן מִיָּד לִצְדָקָה אֲשֶׁר תַּשִּׂיג יָדוֹ,
וְלִבְסוֹף כָּל חֹדֶשׁ וּלְסוֹף כָּל שָׁנָה זָהָב וָחֵצִי.

One should give what he can to charity
immediately; and at the end of each month
and each year, one-and-a-half gold coins.

3

שֶׁיִּתְפַּלֵּל עֶרֶב וָבוֹקֶר בְּכָל יוֹם עִם הַצִּבּוּר.

One should pray with the community
every day, evening and morning.

4

שֶׁיָּנִיחַ תְּפִילִין בְּכָל יוֹם.

One should put on *tefillin* each day.

5

שֶׁיִּקְבַּע מְזוּזָה בְּכָל שַׁעֲרֵי בֵּיתוֹ הַמְחוּיָּבִים בִּמְזוּזָה.

One should place a *mezuzah* on all
the gateways of his home that require a *mezuzah*.

6

שֶׁיִּקְבַּע עִתִּים לַתּוֹרָה.

One should establish fixed times for Torah study.

7

שֶׁיִּהְיֶה נֶאֱמָן בְּמַשָּׂאוֹ וּבְמַתָּנוֹ וּבְדִבּוּרוֹ.

One should be trustworthy
in his business dealings and in his speech.

8

שֶׁיְּכַבֵּד לוֹמְדֵי תּוֹרָה בְּכָל יְכָלְתּוֹ.

One should honor those who study Torah
as much as he can.

9

אֶת עֲמִיתוֹ וְלֹא יִשָּׂא עָלָיו חֵטְא.

One should reprove his fellow, but not bear a sin
on his account [by embarrassing him].

10

שֶׁיָּדִין אֶת חֲבֵירוֹ לְכַף זְכוּת.

One should judge his fellow
with a presumption of merit.

11

שֶׁיִּמְחוֹל בְּכָל לַיְלָה קוֹדֶם שֶׁיָּלִין
לְכָל מִי שֶׁחָטָא לוֹ בִּדְבָרִים.

Every night before retiring, one should forgive
everyone who has sinned against him in word.

12

שֶׁיִּשְׁתַּדֵּל לְהַכְנִיס שָׁלוֹם
בֵּין אִישׁ לְאִשְׁתּוֹ וּבֵין אָדָם לַחֲבֵירוֹ.

One should try to bring peace between a man and
his wife, and between a man and his fellow man.

13

שֶׁיַּזְהִיר אֶת בְּנֵי בֵּיתוֹ עַל הַתְּפִילָה
וְעַל נְטִילַת יָדַיִם וְעַל בִּרְכַּת הַנֶּהֱנִין.

One should alert the members of his household
about prayer, washing of the hands, and the blessings over enjoyment (food, drink and aromas).

14

שֶׁיִּפְרַע הַתָּמִיד בְּכָל שִׁשִּׁי.

One should make up for the
Continual Offering (*Tamid*) each Friday.

TOSAFOS YOM TOV
He should give charity each Friday and thereby fulfill his charity
requirement, if he has not done so in the middle of the week

15

שֶׁיִּלְמוֹד הַפָּרָשָׁה בְּכָל שָׁבוּעַ
שְׁנַיִם מִקְרָא וְאֶחָד תַּרְגּוּם, וּפֵירַשׁ"י ז"ל.

One should study the weekly Torah portion each
week, twice in the Hebrew, once in the Aramaic
translation, and with the commentary of *Rashi, z"l.*

16

שֶׁיִּקְרָא אִגֶּרֶת הַתְּשׁוּבָה שֶׁחִבֵּר רַבֵּינוּ יוֹנָה ז"ל
בַּשָּׁבוּעַ שֶׁיָּחוּל רֹאשׁ הַשָּׁנָה לִהְיוֹת בְּתוֹכָהּ.

One should read the "Letter on Teshuvah"
by Rabbeinu Yonah, during the week
in which Rosh Hashanah falls.

17

שֶׁיִּקְבַּע סְעוּדָה שְׁלִישִׁית בְּכָל שַׁבָּת אַחַר מִנְחָה.

One should have a third meal
every Shabbos after the *Minchah* prayer.

18

שֶׁיְּכַבֵּד אֶת הַשַּׁבָּת כְּבִרְכַּת ה' אֱלֹקָיו אֲשֶׁר נָתַן לוֹ.

One should honor Shabbos, according to the means
with which Hashem his God has blessed him.

19

שֶׁיַּעֲרוֹךְ שֻׁלְחָן בְּכָל מוֹצָאֵי שַׁבָּת
וְיֹאכַל אֲפִילוּ דָּבָר מוּעָט.

One should set his table every *Motzaei Shabbos*
(the evening after Shabbos has departed) and eat,
even if only a small amount.

20

שֶׁיְּסַיֵּיע לַחֲבֵירוֹ בְּכָל מַה שֶׁיִּצְטָרֵךְ בְּגוּפוֹ וּבִדְבָרָיו.

One should help his fellow man
in every way he may require,
whether physically or by speaking with him.

21

שֶׁיִּתְוַדֶּה בְּכָל לַיְלָה קוֹדֶם שֶׁיִּישָׁן מִלְבַד הַלֵּילוֹת
שֶׁהֵן אֲסוּרוֹת בְּהֶסְפֵּד וּבְתַעֲנִית וְיִתְאַבֵּל עַל
עֲווֹנוֹתָיו וְעַל אוֹרֶךְ גָּלוּתֵנוּ וְעַל חוּרְבַּן בֵּית
מִקְדָּשֵׁנוּ וְתִפְאַרְתֵּנוּ שֶׁיִּבָּנֶה בִּמְהֵרָה בְּיָמֵנוּ.

One should confess his sins each night before
going to sleep, except for the nights when it is
forbidden to eulogize or to fast, and one should
grieve over his sins, the length of our exile, and
the destruction of our sacred and glorious
Temple, may it be built quickly in our days.

22

שֶׁיַּעֲשֶׂה יוֹם אֶחָד תַּעֲנִית בְּכָל חֹדֶשׁ
בְּיוֹם שֶׁקּוֹרִין בַּתּוֹרָה וְאִם לֹא יָכוֹל לְהִתְעַנּוֹת
שֶׁיִּתֵּן שְׁנֵי פְּשִׁיטִין לִצְדָקָה.

One should fast one day each month, on a day
when the Torah is read; and if he cannot fast,
he should give two coins to charity.

23

שֶׁיְּקַיֵּם בְּהַצְנֵעַ לְכַלְכֵּל מַעֲשָׂיו הַטּוֹבִים כִּי הוּא
עֲבוֹדַת ה׳ יִתְבָּרַךְ הַנִּבְחֶרֶת וְהָרְצוּיָה לְפָנָיו.

One should act modestly [away from
the public eye], in perfecting his good deeds,
for that is the service of Hashem that is
most desirable and acceptable before Him.

סְלִיק סַלִּיק סַלִּיק

Completion

This volume is part of
THE ARTSCROLL SERIES®
an ongoing project of
translations, commentaries and expositions
on Scripture, Mishnah, Talmud, Halachah,
liturgy, history, the classic Rabbinic writings,
biographies and thought.

For a brochure of current publications
visit your local Hebrew bookseller
or contact the publisher:

Mesorah Publications, ltd
4401 Second Avenue
Brooklyn, New York 11232
(718) 921-9000
www.artscroll.com